THE BIBLICAL
DOCTRINE OF MAN

by

John Laidlaw

Foreword by
Dr. Cyril J. Barber

Printed by Klock & Klock in the U.S.A.
1983 Reprint

Originally published by
T & T Clark
Edinburgh, 1895

ISBN: 0-86524-157-0

Printed by Klock & Klock in the U.S.A.
1983 Reprint

FOREWORD

One of the most crucial questions of our age concerns the nature of man. Three thousand years ago, the psalmist turned his eyes heavenward and, with a mixture of perplexity and awe, asked, "What is man . . .?"

The sciences of philosophy and anthropology, historiography and psychology have probed the nature of man from every conceivable point of view. Procedures have been developed for the systematizing of the data. The explanations, however, have failed to adequately lay bare the essence of human nature.

Plato, the Athenian philosopher (428-347 B.C.), in considering man's form said, "Man is an animal, biped and featherless". For this astute definition, he was applauded by his students. Diogenes, however, went and plucked a fowl and, on bringing it into the lecture room, released it, saying, "Here is Plato's man." As far fetched as this story may sound to our sophisticated 20th century ears, let us remember that in recent years Desmond Morris has defined man as "the naked ape." This only serves to show us that, at least as far as the biological sciences are concerned, there has been little advance in our knowledge of man for two and a half millenia.

One of the most popular contemporary approaches to the nature of man is Communism. Communism has a view of man which causes the individual to loose his identity within a shapeless collectivism. As a system, Communism manipulates the mind of its adherants so that they willingly believe the propaganda given them and exert themselves to achieve the predetermined ends of their leaders. When these ends have been served, the individuals are discarded--as "expenditures"--without dignity, for their sole value was in the service of the system.

In contrast to Communism, our democratic society and economic system has fostered this approach to life characterized by materialism. Competition for the possession of things, coupled with the promise of an enriched life through the acquisition of wealth, has ensnared millions of people. Materialism teaches that man's worth lies in his productivity. Unfortunately, when he can no longer work, he looses his sense of worth.

A third approach to the study of man is humanism. Humanism is an attitude or way of life centered on human interests and values. It builds upon a philosophy that asserts that the dignity and worth of man, and his capacity for self-realization through reason, enables him to be self-sustaining and self-sufficient. In its very root form, humanism rejects supernaturalism, is non-theistic, disregards all belief in the hereafter and, in effect, deifies man collectively and individually. Through knowledge of self, man can become the determiner of his own future and responsible for his own well-being. At the basis of humanism, therefore, lies the cult of self. When faced with ultimate realities, however, humanists find that their approach to life leaves them impotent.

While Communism gives its adherents a sense of belongingness, it deprives them of any feeling of dignity or lasting significance. While materialism provides its devotees with a feeling of personal accomplishment, it fosters a "dog-eat-dog" environment which effectively robs a person of any inner sense of acceptance and lasting competence. And while humanism stresses self-determination and accomplishment, it alienates people from each other and is unable to give them any enduring feeling of worth.

Plainly, a better solution to the question, *"What is Man?"* is needed. The most satisfactory solution to the issue of the nature of man is to be found in the Bible. In Genesis we read that man was made in the image of God (Genesis 1:26-27). But what does this mean? After the varying views of theologians from Augustine to the present have been analyzed, the best answer seems to be that, in making man, God gave him some of His attributes. These attributes have been marred through the Fall. Through the new birth, however, and the renewing of each believer's mind, there exists the possibility of becoming conformed to the image of Christ.

Only Christianity has an adequate explanation of the *imago Dei*, and only as the Bible's teaching is understood and applied will believers be able to enjoy the sense of belongingness, worth and competence which Adam and Eve possessed before the Fall.

One of the best explanations of the Bible's teaching on the nature of man was produced by John Laidlaw (1832-1906) in his Cunningham Lectures delivered at the New College, Edinburgh.

John Laidlaw was a Scot. His parents were peasants and belonged to the Cameronian or Reformed Presbyterian Church which was known for its intense zeal and staunch adherence to the doctrines of the Reformation. When John was only twelve years of age, the Disruption of the Church of Scotland took place and, from this time onwards, he was associated with the Free Church movement.

After attaining competency in Latin and Greek, mathematics and philosophy, John Laidlaw was graduated from the University of Edinburgh in 1854. The manner of his graduation was most unusual. He had submitted a dissertation to the faculty before completing all of the requirements for the course of study leading to the Master of Arts degree. The *Senatus* of the University esteemed his work so highly that, to mark their recognition of his prowess, they interposed the bestowing of the degree on him *honoris causa*.

Following graduation from the University of Edinburgh, John Laidlaw enrolled in the Hall of the Reformed Presbyterian Church to study for the ministry. At this time, he also became a member of Free St. George's Church, whose minister was Dr. Robert Candlish. This association made a deep impression on him.

During his years as a divinity student, John Laidlaw also had the privilege of studying under Dr. John Duncan and Principal William Cunningham. His biographer writes that in Dr. Duncan "ran a vein of pure religion and theological genius" and in Dr. Cunningham, Laidlaw found "an immensely powerful nature, and erudite as well as formidable controvertialist, and an unriviled exponent of masculine and authentic Calvinism, whose mark was clearly discernable upon the Free Church ministry of that period."

John Laidlaw was fluent in more than one European language and, upon graduation, spent the summer of 1858 in Germany where he travelled extensively. Upon his return to Scotland, he was appointed the assistant of Dr. A. B. Davidson of Free Lady Glenorchy's Church in Edinburgh. Dr. Davidson was not in good health and a considerable share of the preaching fell on John Laidlaw.

Four years later, Laidlaw accepted the call to the Free West Church in Perth, and here he developed into one of the finest expositors in Scotland. In spite of the pressures of his pastoral duties, he continued to read widely and remain abreast of current trends in theology. His health suffered in the climate of Perth and although he endured bravely, he was never really well. For this reason, when a unanimous call came to him to become the colleague of Dr. Robert Candlish, John Laidlaw considered it seriously. It was a surprise to many that he declined this offer, choosing instead to remain at Perth where he felt his work was not yet accomplished.

In 1869, John Laidlaw married the sister of his college friend, John Hamilton. For their honeymoon, the Laidlaws journeyed through Switzerland and then returned to Perth where they remained for three more years. In 1872, John accepted a call to succeed Dr. A. B. Davidson in the Free West Church, Aberdeen, where he remained for many years.

It was while living in Aberdeen, that John Laidlaw received the invitation to deliver the Cunningham Lectures on "The Bible Doctrine of Man" at the New College, Edinburgh. Of these lectures, his biographer says, "[There was] apparent [in these messages] his rare doctrinal aptitude, and his fine pictorial gift and the originality and vigor of his applications of truth to modern problems and sins. No preacher ever knew the human heart better, or more skillfully sounded its depths. In his master hand, the heart became revealed--a world of wonder, sorrow, and tears--with all its virtues, frailties, and deceits laid bare; and [there was] infinite pity and tenderness in his appeal. While he disclosed the fault, and blamed the error of the sinful soul, he never delivered a harsh message, or gave way to cynicism, rancor, or ill-will."

Whereas John Laidlaw had received from the University of Edinburgh the distinct honor of an *honoris causa* Master of Arts degree, the New College now conferred upon him their coveted doctorate in divinity (1880). This act ironically paved the way for him to succeed the Professor MacGregor as chairman of the Department of Systematic Theology.

Leaving the congregation in Aberdeen, where he had served for 23 years, was a very difficult task. Dr. Laidlaw naturally shrank from stepping out of the pulpit to be seated in a professorial chair. It was with great reluctance, therefore, that he resigned his pastorate and moved back to Edinburgh.

As a professor, Dr. Laidlaw was fortunate in being at liberty to concentrate his mind on a single, well defined area of study. He taught Christian dogmatics and covered the material in a manner that awakened the minds of his students to the value of theology and apologetics in the work of the church.

The system of Christian doctrine which Professor Laidlaw set before his classes was permeated by an ardent sympathy with the theology of the Reformation. He was thoroughly conservative in his beliefs, but by no means narrow or obscurantist in his thinking. He was uncompromising in his adherance to the tenets of Scripture, yet also exhibited a keeness in his desire to understand and unravel contemporary movements in theology.

One noteworthy feature of Professor Laidlaw as a systematic theologian was that he cared profoundly for his subject. He always left the impression on his students that he thought nobly of Christian theology as an intellectual discipline. In handling the vast array of biblical and philosophical material, he did so with the objectivity of a scientist and the devotion of a true follower of Jesus Christ. He realized full well that theology is the child, not the parent, of saving faith; and that while the history of the developement of various doctrines provides a fascinating arena for scholarly inquiry, theology should summarize the teaching of Scripture on the topic under consideration.

We are indeed fortunate that Dr. Laidlaw's Cunningham Lectures were published, for they preserve for us something of his content, style and competence as a theologian.

We are also happy that, in our day, they have been made available again, for now we may all read them for our enlightenment and spiritual edification.

Cyril J. Barber
Author, *The Minister's Library*

PREFACE TO REVISED EDITION

In issuing the "Seventh Series of the Cunningham Lectures" in this revised form, I renew my acknowledgment of the kind assistance rendered by my friends —Professor S. D. F. Salmond, D.D., of Free College, Aberdeen, and Rev. W. Cruickshank, M.A., Inverurie, in the preparation of the original edition. To several friends in my own College I am indebted for help with the proof-sheets now. The present is an entire recast of the book, and many pages have been rewritten. While retaining the substance and almost every detail of the work as first published, and maintaining without exception the positions then taken up, I have found it desirable to discard the cumbrous form, customary in such publications, of printing so many Lectures as orally delivered, together with a mass of Notes and Citations as Appendix. The continuity of the work, even to the eye, has been provided for, by retaining the title-pages and ground-texts of the Six Lectures in the former edition, as the Six Divisions of the present. The whole, however, is further divided into sixteen Chapters, for greater distinctness of topical treatment. The appended material of the former issue has now been adopted into the text, so far as practicable, while that which still retains the form of Appendix is distributed as Notes on the several Chapters to which it is immediately relevant. Some small portion of the original Appendix is left out as no longer necessary.

The aim is to present in one view the Bible Theology and Philosophy of Man and his Nature. What is claimed for this endeavour, in the specific department of Biblical Psychology, is to have called attention to the distinction which the Bible attributes to "spirit," as the highest element in man's constitution, and on the possession of which is grounded its unique doctrine of man's likeness to his Maker. It also claims to be a consistent exposition of the relations of "soul" and "spirit" in man. Rejecting as unscriptural and unsupported by reason the notion which founds upon the Bible use of these terms a Tripartite Theory of man's nature, cause is yet shown why the neglect of that usage, as a meaningless parallelism, must yield to accurate exegesis and historic fact. These two discussions specially exemplify that which it is the object of the whole treatise to maintain, namely, that a study of the psychological ideas of Scripture throws valuable sidelights on its doctrinal teaching.

The " Literature " now prefixed to each section is not, of course, meant as a complete Bibliography. It is confined almost entirely to naming the books which have been consulted for this work.

JOHN LAIDLAW.

NEW COLLEGE, EDINBURGH,
    May 1895.

CONTENTS

DIVISION I

INTRODUCTORY—THE BIBLE ACCOUNT OF MAN'S ORIGIN

DIVISION II

MAN'S NATURE—THE BIBLE PSYCHOLOGY

DIVISION III

THE DIVINE IMAGE AND MAN'S PRIMITIVE STATE

DIVISION IV

MAN FALLEN—HIS NATURE UNDER SIN AND DEATH

DIVISION V

PSYCHOLOGY OF THE NEW LIFE

DIVISION VI

MAN'S NATURE AND A FUTURE STATE

I

INTRODUCTORY—THE BIBLE ACCOUNT OF MAN'S ORIGIN

Τὰ μὲν οὖν περὶ ψυχῆς . . . τὸ μὲν ἀληθές, ὡς εἴρηται, Θεοῦ ξυμφήσαντος τότ ἂν οὕτω μόνως διισχυριζοίμεθα.—PLATO, *Timæus*, 72 D.

"The truth concerning the soul can only be established by the word of God."—JOWETT.

"Quomodo possit cognitio de substantia animae rationalis ex philosophia peti et haberi? Quinimo ab eadem inspiratione divina hauriatur, a qua substantia animae primo emanavit."—BACON, *De Augmentis Scientiarum*, lib. iv. cap. iii. § 3.

Psalm viii. 4–9 (R.V.).—" What is man, that Thou art mindful of him ? And the son of man, that Thou visitest him ? For Thou hast made him but little lower than God, and crownest him with glory and honour. Thou madest him to have dominion over the works of Thy hands ; Thou hast put all things under his feet : all sheep and oxen, yea, and the beasts of the field ; the fowl of the air, and the fish of the sea, whatsoever passeth through the paths of the seas. O LORD, our Lord, how excellent is Thy name in all the earth ! "

CHAPTER I

IT will be at once understood that our subject is not Anthropology in the sense in which that forms a *topic* in the theological systems, but the Anthropology of the Bible in the stricter sense; that is to say, we seek some answer to the question, What views of man's nature and constitution are taught in Scripture, or are to be held as necessarily implied in its teaching?

Any study which may be classed under the head of Biblical Psychology has in most minds initial prejudices to overcome. The chief of these arises out of the extravagant claim which has sometimes been made on its behalf. To frame a complete and independent system or philosophy of man from the sacred writings is an impossible task. The attempt cannot commend itself to the judicious interpreter of Scripture. It is certain to foster one-sided views in theology, or to become a mere reflex of some prevailing philosophical school. It is an opposite extreme to say that Scripture affords us no knowledge of the soul's natural being,—that the texts on which a so-called biblical psychology has been founded, do not teach what the nature of man is, but only declare

3

his relation or bearing towards God.[1] No doubt the
relation of man to God is that aspect in which the Bible
chiefly regards him. But for that reason its whole
structure rests on most important assumptions as to
what man was and is. Even should we adhere rigidly
to the view [2] that the Bible is to be construed as giving
us religious and spiritual, but no merely natural knowledge, far less any scientific information, we should still
be compelled to admit that this religious and spiritual
teaching involves presuppositions regarding man and his
nature which are of immense interest for anthropology
and psychology. These presuppositions cannot be
separated from the substance of the record. Let it be
ever so strenuously maintained that the religion of the
Bible is the Bible, this religion includes such relations of
man to God, to the unseen, to the everlasting, as manifestly to imply a very definite theory of his essential
nature and constitution. Let it be further remembered
that the Bible is, upon its own representation, the history
of God's dealings with man in a special course of religious
and spiritual communication ; that therefore this record
of revelation contains an account of man's origin, of his
original nature, of the changes which have befallen it,
and of the changes which by divine grace have been and
are still to be wrought upon it. Such an account is

---

[1] See v. Hofmann, *Der Schriftbeweis*, i. p. 284.

[2] Recently expressed thus : "That inspiration was not a general but a
functional endowment, and consequently limited to subjects in which
religion is directly involved ; and that in those which stand outside it,
the writers of the different books in the Bible were left to the free use of
their ordinary faculties," etc.—Row's *Bampton Lecture*, 1877, p. 43.
That a writer should be more free to use his faculties when uninspired
implies a mistaken view of inspiration.

surely a contribution to the knowledge of man, and to the history of the race. Is there not reason to expect that, in the progress of such a revelation, light should be shed on man's nature and constitution, and that such information, apart from its saving and spiritual purpose, should be of moment for the student of psychology?

Far more, however, than any other department of nature touched upon in the Bible, the nature of man falls within the field of theology. Hence it becomes us to inquire, in the interest of Scripture doctrine, in what sense the Bible notion of man is authoritative, uniform, and available for such treatment as we propose. How far Bible doctrine has in it a true knowledge of man, formed for itself " in its own light out of the revelations of the Spirit," [1] how far the view of man's constitution which pervades the Bible enters into the subject-matter of the revelation, are questions turning upon the relation between the natural and the supernatural element in Scripture, or perhaps upon the more general relation of natural to revealed truth. It is quite what we should expect, that in rationalistic schools of theology the treatment of this biblical topic appears as " the psychology of the Hebrews," and that their "science" can have nothing to do with any biblical psychology which professes to be more than a view of the notions of the Hebrew people. Such questions, however, become most pregnant for those who are interested in maintaining the really divine character of the Bible revelation. For it is exactly here that the authoritative character of the Bible assumptions

---

[1] Beck, *Umriss der biblischen Seelenlehre*, Vorwort, p. vi. 3te Aufl. 1871.

in regard to natural fact seems to form an essential
element in its claim to be from God. It is in such
regions as this that the maxim, " The religion of the
Bible is the Bible," will not unlock all difficulties. We
cannot easily, if at all, draw the line, in what Scripture
says of man, between that which is religious and that
which is non-religious. If we should say that the Bible
notion of man as a natural being must submit to the same
criticism as that which is contained in other ancient
literature, what are we to say of the information which
the Bible gives us about man's creation, the fall, the new
birth, the resurrection? Have these no bearing upon
our idea of man as a natural being? Have not these
entered into the very marrow of the philosophy of man
in all nations that know the Bible? That man was
made by God, and in His image; that the present
anomalies in man's nature are explained by a great moral
catastrophe which has affected his will; that nevertheless his spirit stands in such relation to the divine as to
be capable of renovation and possession by the Spirit of
God: that soul and body alike are essential to the
totality of man, and are both brought within the scope
of redemption,—these are positions which undoubtedly
belong to the essence of the Bible revelation, and which
have also greatly influenced the philosophical conception
of human nature.

The view which would relegate all the elements of
natural knowledge contained in Scripture to the region
of the merely popular notions prevalent in the age and
mind of the writers, no doubt makes short work with
biblical psychology. But such a view involves the

widest issues with regard to the word of God. In the highest of all interests it has to be resisted at every point, and met with another and more adequate theory, namely, one which will neither on the one hand give up the statements of the Bible regarding natural facts as subject to all the errors of their age, nor claim for them on the other the anomalous character of supernatural science.

Let us, for the sake of analogy, glance at a kindred topic, namely, the Scripture account of the Origin of the World. The position to be maintained here by the believer in revelation is one which refuses the dilemma that the representations contained in the first chapter of Genesis must be either scientifically correct or altogether worthless. Their supremely religious character, fundamental as they are to the whole revelatiou, in teaching the being, unity, spirituality of God and His relation to the creatures, places them in a totally different region from that of science. They must soar above and stand apart from the special discoveries and provisional statements of any stage of scientific attainment. To forget this has been the great mistake of those who have sought to harmonise science and Scripture, though the blame of the mistake has often been misplaced. The complaint of science is that theology has resisted her progress. Might not the accusation be shifted, if not retorted ? Is it not theology that has been unfortunately encumbered with physical science, or with the philosophemes which stood for science at some particular period ? Interpreters of Scripture have allowed the prevailing theories of their own day so to colour their statements of Bible doctrine, that natural discoverers of the next age have

raised the cry, "The Bible with its theology stops the
way!"—the fact being that i' was not the Bible at all,
nor even theology, which opposed itself to their discoveries, but only the ghosts of defunct philosophical or
scientific opinion, clothing themselves in the garments of
religious thought.

For instance it is frequently asserted that the account
of Creation, given in the chapter named above, has
always been read by theologians either literally, or as
in some way scientific, whereas nearly the reverse of this
is true.   It is a comparatively modern idea to view the
passage as a vision or foretelling of scientific truths.
The most ancient Christian interpreters, even, did not
take the six days literally.   Some of them thought the
world was created in an instant of time, and that the
six days were expressed as a mode of indicating gradation
and order in creation, and as laying a foundation for
the observance of the seventh-day rest.[1]   Others, like
Augustine, expressly deny that they were ordinary days.[2]
We are now in a position to do more justice than these
ancient interpreters could to the magnificent general ideas
of Creation, of its unity, order, progress, and scope, contained in this divine cosmogony; but the true foundation
of a right exegesis is to regard it mainly, as they did,
from the religious point of view, as an expression of
belief in God, in a Creator, and in a plan of Creation,
ideas which all belong properly to an inspired system
of spiritual truth.   It is not necessary to refer to the

[1] For a catena of opinion on the whole topic, see ⌐ry on *Genesis*,
pp. 29–42.
[2] *De Civitate Dei*, xi. 6, 7.

countless and shifting modes of reading into this chapter the discoveries and often merely the conjectures of science which have prevailed within the last fifty or sixty years. That which has become most favourably known in this country is the theory of Kurz, so luminously and poetically expounded by Hugh Miller. It is based upon the conjecture that "the knowledge of pre-Adamite history, like the knowledge of future ages, may have been communicated to Moses, or perhaps to the first man, in prophetic vision ; that so, perhaps, vast geological periods were exhibited to the eye of the inspired writer, each appearing to pass before him on so many successive days." The result aimed at was to establish a correspondence between the discoveries of modern science, as to the different geological eras, and the various steps in this sublime passage of Scripture. No one who cares for the subject can fail to be acquainted with the gorgeous prose poem on this theme which the stone-mason of Cromarty evolved out of his scientific knowledge, acted on by a brilliant and devout imagination. A wise and weighty dictum of his own, however, is well worth considering in connection with it : "Were the theologians ever to remember that the Scriptures could not possibly have been given to us as revelations of scientific truth, seeing that a single scientific truth they never yet revealed, and the geologist that it must be in vain to seek in science those truths which lead to salvation, seeing that in science these truths were never yet found, there would be little danger even of difference among them, and none of collision."[1] This is exactly

[1] *The Testimony of the Rocks*, p. 265.

the principle which it is necessary for us to carry through
all our treatment of Scripture. And it is particularly
applicable to this narrative, for it is just here that there
is a strong temptation to make the Bible appear scientific.
That the main purpose of the chapter is religious cannot
be doubted. It is meant to teach the unity of God—
a protest against the gods many of the nations; the
distinction between God and the world—a protest against
pantheism; the fact of the divine origin of the world—
a protest against atheism, as involved in the notion of
the eternity of matter; above all, to show God's relation
to man and the relation of man to the world, that the
God of revelation and the God of creation are one, and
that the God of grace—the God who sealed His mercy
to Israel with the special institution of the Sabbath—is
the same who made the world in six days and rested on
the seventh.

That along with these spiritual ideas concerning God
and man there are also given in this chapter certain
principles of creation, some great lines of physical and
cosmical truth, must not, of course, be overlooked. No
one can be satisfied to believe that the writer who
conveys here such grand thoughts about the world and
its becoming as those of the original uprise of all things,
—the chaos of earth's primitive state—the birth of light
before the formation of the sun—the orderly succession
of existences, inorganic, vegetable, animal, human,—was
left in framing these thoughts to the false and inadequate
ideas of nature prevalent in his own time. It is clearly
quite otherwise. These grand principles of natural truth
coincide so thoroughly with the findings of science that

we are compelled to say, This is inspiration. It is the unity of truth. It is the harmony of the divine Mind. The light of the same Spirit who framed the world lies on this first page of the great World-Book. This divine light upon God and creation and man's place there is true to the world of fact and nature, and will never, therefore, contradict, but always harmonise with whatever of scientific truth man shall scientifically discover for himself. But it is not science ; and we must protest against this creation-narrative being interpreted as an illuminated transcript of scientific discovery in all its details before the time. The incompetence of such a style of exegesis becomes more apparent the more we think of it. Scientific discovery and scientific guess or hypothesis, going hand in hand, are always moving,— the guesses shifting rapidly, like a framework or scaffolding ; the discovery creeping slowly on, like a noble building rising solidly tier by tier. But how could a prophecy of such discovery be given beforehand, or how could a view of the world's becoming in its scientific shape be given to those who had no science, or even to those who, like us, have an unfinished and imperfect one ? It is all but certain that cosmic and anthropological theories which at present prevail will change, and those speculative readings of geology and evolution into Genesis which have found such favour will be left dry and baseless. No ! the real spirit of this world-picture is very different. It is a view of the Creation which is to serve for all ages of human history, to fit into every single age's need. Each being an age in which scientific research is only at one of its stages, this sublime view of the divine work of world-making, in order to serve its proper purpose, must deal with great spiritual and cosmical principles, and with these alone.

The leading idea of the Bible *Cosmogony*, then, is not scientific, it is religious; yet as a cosmogony it gives principles of the becoming of things which, in their superiority to the corresponding ethnic conceptions, in their substantial agreement with science, contribute important proof of the divine character of the book in which they are found. Coincidence, in such an account, with the findings of science in any one age, would have been as useless as correspondence to the ever-varying results of it throughout the ages would have been impossible. But such a view of the world's becoming as satisfies religion, while it consists with the principles that science is discovering for itself, is a true and proper revelation on the subject.

On this analogy, would we define the character to be attached to the *Anthropology* of the Bible. In answer to the question whether the Scripture view of man as a natural being is not the view of the times in which the Scriptures were written, we reply that it is, in so far as man's notions of himself can furnish adequate and correct foundation for revealed doctrine. For everywhere in Scripture we find evidence of this marvellous quality, that its presuppositions on natural subjects, and especially on the *Origines* of the world and of man, though never given in the scientific form, and not intended to teach science, justify themselves in the face of scientific discoveries as these are successively made. The writers of Holy Scripture, by whatever method of poetic or prophetic elevation, move in the domain of natural facts and principles with a supernatural tact, which at once distinguishes them from all other ancient writers on such subjects, and places the Scriptures themselves above the reach of scientific objections.

On the other hand, some zealous upholders of biblical psychology speak of it as something directly descended from heaven, bearing no relation to the natural psychology of the times. But it is evident there must have been such an adaptation, by the biblical writers, of psychological terms in previous use as to be understood by those to whom their words first came. We cannot afford here, or anywhere else, to forget that in the Scripture the Holy Ghost speaks with a human tongue, and therefore, in speaking of man, must have employed such ideas and expressions regarding his nature and constitution as convey a true and intelligible view of what these are. Such expressions and ideas are undoubtedly those of the age in which the writings arose, but they are at the same time so simple and universal as to find easy access to the mind of mankind everywhere and at all times. And this simplicity speaks to another trait, namely, their uniformity. The tendency of much recent scholarship is to disintegrate the Scriptures, and accordingly objections have been taken to the reception of a biblical notion of man, on the ground that on all topics of natural knowledge the standpoint of each Scripture writer must be considered independent.[1] There is nothing more ground-

---

[1] *E.g.* by Dr. Hermann Schultz in his early tractate, *Die Voraussetzungen der christlichen Lehre von der Unsterblichkeit*, Göttingen, 1861, p. 72. But in the latest edition of his *Old Testament Theology* he does ample justice to the uniformity and simplicity of the Old Testament psychology. See vol. ii p. 242 (Clark, Edin., 1892).

less. The unity of Scripture is precisely one of those facts not explained by Rationalism, but clear in a moment when we regard Scripture as the record of a continuous and consistent historical revelation. And the scope of that revelation being the redemption of man, there is nothing which is more essentially bound up with it, than that idea of man and his nature which pervades the record. It would, indeed, be very difficult to deny the uniformity of psychological view in the Old Testament, were it only on the ground that at the early period to which these writings belong, the refinements of school philosophy, which introduce diversity even where they bring ripeness, had not begun to operate. It cannot be denied that fresh elements from without enter into the psychology of the New Testament, and especially into that of St. Paul; yet little doubt can remain on the mind of any unprejudiced reader of Scripture, that a notion of man pervades both the Old and the New Testament, popularly expressed indeed, but uniform and consistent, though growing in its fulness with the growth of the biblical revelation itself.

Let us understand, then, what we may expect to attain in any study of biblical psychology. Dr. Delitzsch defines the scope of such study very fairly and modestly when he says its aim is "to bring out the views of Scripture regarding the nature, the life, and the life-destinies of the soul, as these are determined in the history of its salvation."[1] We cannot agree with the same writer when he claims for it the rank of "an

[1] *Biblische Psychologie*, p. 13.

independent science," even within "the organism of theology."[1] It is really bound up with the theology which we call biblical. Far less can we allow that these Bible representations of man constitute an independent philosophy of human nature. To use them for such a purpose is to fall into an error like that of reading the Bible account of creation as a prophetic view of geological science. The friendly discussion between Delitzsch and Hofmann of Erlangen, as to the possibility of a Bible psychology, turns mainly on the form which such a study must assume. Notwithstanding the extreme position noticed above, Hofmann does not deny the existence in Scripture of disclosures deliberately anthropologic and psychologic. In his masterly treatise on *The Scripture Proof of Christian Doctrine*, he does not shrink from the discussion of texts involving the fundamental questions of our theme. He has no doubt that the presupposi-tions of Scripture on the subject can be grouped together, that is to say, that they are consistent. He warns us only that we are not to expect of them a scientific whole. Nor should we forget that they come into view just as they are used for the expression of facts which, though touching on the psychological region, do really belong to another, namely, the theological. On the other hand, Delitzsch, though premising that no system of psychology propounded in formal language is to be looked for in the Bible, any more than of dogmatics or ethics, zealously contends that a system can be found and constructed. Under the name of Bible psychology he understands a scientific representation of the doctrine of Scripture on

[1] *Biblische Psychologie*, p. 15.

the psychical constitution of man as he was created, and on the ways in which this constitution has been affected by sin and by redemption. It seems as if Hofmann had overlooked the importance and the purpose of that consistent idea of man's constitution which underlies the Scripture teaching; while Delitzsch slightly misstates its purpose rather than exaggerates its importance.[1] That purpose is not to teach the science of man, but it has a vital use in subservience to theology, nevertheless. To trace that use, in an induction of Scripture utterances, is the proper scope and form of any study deserving the name of biblical psychology.

A single word further of its necessity. The chief argument for attempting a consistent and connected view of man's nature, drawn from the Bible itself, is easily stated. There never has been a theology which did not imply and implicitly base itself upon some philosophy of man. The influence of philosophy upon theology is proverbial. It is notorious how soon Christian doctrine, as discussed in the early Church, became coloured by Platonic speculations; how long the Aristotelic doctrine of the soul held sway in mediæval and even in Reformation theology; how Leibnitz and Descartes became the lords of a system of Protestant orthodoxy. " No philosophy," says Dr. Charles Hodge, " has the right to control or modify the exposition of the doctrines of the Bible, except the philosophy of the Bible itself, that is, the principles which are therein asserted or assumed." [2]   Yet

---

[1] The main paragraphs from each of these writers are subjoined to this chapter. Those of Delitzsch are specially pertinent to the question of the possibility of our study, and form a satisfactory vindication of it.

[2] *Systematic Theology*, iii. 661.

with what *naïveté* do most of our theologians, not excluding the author now quoted, assume that the Bible stands
exactly on the Cartesian postulates as to man, the world,
and the soul! Beck very justly points out the vice of
scientific theology in deriving those most essential conceptions of life, upon which Christianity has to build its
unique doctrines of sin and redemption, not from the
circle of thought which belongs to Christianity itself, but
from some one totally different,—a mode which logically
leads to results entirely opposed to Bible anthropology.[1]
We can only rid ourselves of this vice by carefully
observing those ideas of life and the soul which the
Scriptures themselves assume in all their theological
statements. To ascertain the "science of life," if it
may be so called, which prevailed with the writers of
Scripture, to put together such simple psychology
as underlies their writings, cannot be an unnecessary
task. Theology is not truly biblical so long as it is
controlled by non - biblical philosophy; and such
control is inexcusable when it is seen that a view of
human nature available for the purpose of the theologian is native to the source from which theology
itself is drawn.

Our aim, then, in the following pages is to give
prominence to the psychological principles of Scripture,
—to those views of man and his nature which pervade
the sacred writings. It does not appear, however, that
the psychology of the Bible, or what may be called its
philosophy of man, can be successfully treated as an
abstract system. These natural views of man's constitu-

---

[1] See *Umriss der biblischen Seelenlehre*, p. iv.

2

tion are given to us in the record of a special revelation
which declares the divine dealings with man in order to
his redemption. They should be treated, therefore, in
close connection with the history and development of
those dealings. Accordingly, after stating the Bible
account of Man's Origin, and some general principles of
Bible Psychology, the remaining chapters are devoted
to the exhibition of these psychological principles in the
order of the great theological topics concerning man.
They are first illustrated by the Scripture statements
regarding man's Original Image and Primitive State;
then, by those which describe his Condition under Sin;
next, they are viewed in connection with Regeneration;
and last of all, in their bearing upon Future Life and
Resurrection. No exhaustive treatment of these revealed
doctrines is intended. Each of them is dealt with here
only in those aspects which depend for their correct
apprehension upon a true view of the Scripture
psychology.

The Bible notion of man ought to repay our study.
On the lowest ground it is of interest as a contribution
to the history of opinion regarding man and the soul.
Further, it is indispensable as a key to the theology of
the Bible, for into all those large portions of its teaching
which concern man and his destiny, some view of his
natural constitution must enter. Finally, with believers
in revelation it is axiomatic that revelation should throw
light on that nature which is the field of the divine
operations recorded in it. If Plato could sigh for divine
assistance as the only way by which the knowledge
of the soul could be established, how carefully should

the Christian psychologist give heed to the intimations of Scripture![1]

NOTE ON CHAPTER I

HOFMANN AND DELITZSCH ON BIBLICAL PSYCHOLOGY

Delitzsch, in the second edition of his *System der Biblischen Psychologie*, has quoted and replied to Hofmann's attack on the so-called science which the former so much favours. All that is here given, therefore, will be found substantially in Clark's translation of Delitzsch's *Biblical Psychology*, but in preparing the extracts I have made constant reference to the original of both authors.

Hofmann's words are: "A Biblical Anthropology and Psychology have, it is true, been got together, but without finding any justification in Scripture, of which Harless rightly says that we must not expect from it natural description and natural knowledge, because these were not intended to be given there.[2] That putative science is based merely upon such Scripture texts as do not teach what the nature of man is, but, on the hypothesis that it is understood what kind of creature is meant when man is spoken of, declare his relation or deportment towards God. It is replied that the Scripture does nevertheless give, almost in its first sections, disclosures which are deliberately anthropologic and psychologic, seeing it narrates the process of man's creation. It is further alleged that it must be worth while to bring together its anthropological and psychological presuppositions, since they cannot be so trivial as to be matter of course, nor so inconsequent and unconnected as to be capable of no scientific arrangement. But as regards the disclosures, they only serve the purpose

---

[1] See motto prefixed to this section. Jowett's rendering is taken from his *Introduction to the Timæus* (3rd Edition of his *Plato*, 1892). In his translation of the Dialogue itself, he now paraphrases the words so as to empty them of almost any meaning.

[2] So in the preface to the 4th Edition of his *Christliche Ethik* ; but the remark seems to be withdrawn in the latest edition.

of rightly defining the relation of man to God and to the
world at large, without the knowledge of which relation
there can undoubtedly be no anthropology and psychology
corresponding to the reality. As to the presuppositions,
it is subject to no doubt that one may group them
together, without, however, being justified in the expectation that they will form a scientific whole. For they only
come to light in so far as they are employed for the
expression of facts, which, while they touch on the
anthropologic and psychologic region, themselves belong
to another. A Biblical Psychology is just as little a
psychological system as a Biblical Cosmology is a cosmo-
logical system. And if one finds it feasible to call it
theological instead of biblical, it will also be allowable to
say that there is a Theological Psychology only in the
same sense in which one can speak of a Theological
Cosmogony." [1]

To this Delitzsch replies, that he is very far from
denying that all Scripture Psychology is bound up with
the revelation of redemption. What he maintains is, that
in pursuance of its great design of declaring salvation for
man, the Bible has to say so much on man's spiritual and
psychical constitution, that it must proceed upon a
psychology distinct from that of mere natural knowledge.
He retorts upon Harless and Hofmann, that both use
largely in their respective treatises exactly those utterances of Scripture which refer to the most fundamental
questions in psychology. Hofmann especially, while
asserting that Scripture teaches nothing on the subject,
is constantly attempting to answer from Scripture such
psychological questions as—How is man's soul related to
his spirit? How is the spirit in man related to the Spirit
of God? Is man's constitution trichotomic or dichotomic?
How is man as a nature distinguished from man as a
person?

"Whether, then," he goes on, "we call this teaching or
not, Scripture gives us on all these questions at least the
disclosures necessary for a fundamental knowledge of
salvation. These disclosures must be exegetically set

---

[1] *Der Schriftbeweis*, i. 284, 285, 2te Aufl., 1857.

forth, and because they are of a psychological nature, must be psychologically digested; must be adjusted according to their connection *inter se*, as well as with the living whole formed by the historical and personal facts of redemption.

"And here at once is a system, to wit, a system of Biblical Psychology, as it is fundamental to the system both of the facts of salvation and of the revelation of salvation; and such a system of Biblical Psychology is so necessary a basis for every biblical summary of doctrine, that it may be rightly said of the doctrinal summary which Hofmann's *Schriftbeweis* seeks to verify by Scripture, that from the beginning to the end, from the doctrine of the creation to the doctrine of the last things, a special psychologic system, or (if this expression be objected to) a special complex of psychological primary conceptions, lies at the basis of it. What Scripture says to us of cosmology might certainly appear insufficient to originate a system of biblical cosmology; but it says infinitely more to us about the spirit and soul of man than about Orion and the Pleiades. And I would not assert that Scripture offers to us no natural knowledge of the soul; I believe it rather to the honour of God's word to be compelled to maintain the contrary. For example, that the constitution of man is dualistic, *i.e.* that spirit and body are fundamentally of distinct origin and nature, that is surely a natural knowledge—a tenet with which, in spite of all the objections of rigid scientific investigation, we live and die. And although such utterances as Scripture gives us to ponder—*e.g.* in Gen. ii. 7 and 1 Cor. xv. 45—may deserve no other name than 'finger-pointings,' yet an investigation in Biblical Psychology which takes the way indicated by these finger-signs will be justified. . . . We desire to bring out exegetically the views of Scripture regarding the nature, the life, and the life-destinies of the soul as these are determined in the history of its salvation. And we also desire, according to the unavoidable exigence imposed upon our thinking when engaged in the region of Scripture, to bring these views into systematic connection. . . .

"The task which I propose to myself is practicable; for under the name of Biblical Psychology I understand a scientific presentation of the doctrine of Scripture on the physical constitution of man as it was created, and the ways in which this constitution has been affected by sin and redemption. There is such a doctrine of Scripture. It is true that on psychological subjects, just as little as on dogmatical or ethical, does Scripture contain any system of dogmas propounded in the language of the schools. If it taught in such a way, we should have no need at all to construct from it Psychology, and as little Dogmatic or Ethic. But still it does teach. . . . There belongs essentially to Holy Scripture a quite definite psychology which is equally fundamental to all the sacred writers, and which essentially differs from that multiform system lying outside the circle of revelation. The task of Biblical Psychology, therefore, can be executed as a unity. We have no need first to force the material of the Bible teaching into oneness; it is one of itself.

"The Biblical Psychology so built up is an independent science which coincides with no other, and is rendered superfluous by no other in the entire organism of theology. It is most nearly related to the so-called Biblical Theology, or rather to Dogmatics. For what is usually designated by the former expression—an extremely unfortunate one —more properly falls in partly with the history of redemption, partly with the history of revelation. Biblical, or, as one may also call it, Theological Psychology (to distinguish it from the scientific-empirical and philosophic-rational) pervades the entire material of Dogmatics, inasmuch as it discusses all those phases of man's psychical constitution that are conditioned by the facts and relations —so full of significance in the history of salvation—which form the content of Dogmatic Theology. At all the points of contact, however, it maintains its own special character. Of what is common to it with Dogmatics it only takes cognisance in so far as that common factor throws light or shadow upon the human soul, draws the soul into co-operation or sympathy, and tends to disclose its secrets. Much which is only incidentally dealt with in Dogmatics is a principal subject for the subsidiary science of Psychology : as, for example, the relation of the soul to the blood, a point of some importance for the doctrine of propitiation, or the question whether the soul is propagated *per traducem*, which is of moment for the doctrine of original sin. On the other hand, the scriptural doctrines of the Trinity, of good and evil angels, of the divine-human personality of Christ, which in Dogmatics are main themes, come to be treated by Psychology only in so far as they are connected with the divine image in man, with the good or evil influence of the spirit-world upon him, and with the restoration of true human nature. The new relation of God to humanity in Christ, which is the centre of our entire theology, is also the centre of Psychology, as of Dogmatics. The business of Dogmatic is to analyse and systematise the believing consciousness of this new relationship—a consciousness which relies upon and rests in the Scripture. The business of Psychology, on the other hand, is with the human soul, and through the soul with that human constitution which is the object and subject of this new relationship.

"From this conception of our science, which we are still convinced will stand the crucible of criticism, we turn to the method of its realisation."—Delitzsch, *Biblische Psychologie*, pp. 12–16, 2te Aufl. 1861.

CHAPTER II

THE BIBLE ACCOUNT OF MAN'S ORIGIN

[LITERATURE.—Quarry *On Genesis* (Lond., 1866); Macdonald, *Creation and the Fall* (Edin., 1856); Ewald's papers, " Die Schöpfungsgeschichte nach Gen. i. 1–ii. 3," at p. 77 of his *Erstes Jahrbuch der bibl. Wissenschaft* (1848); " Die Spätere, Gen. ii. 4–25," p. 132 of his *Zweites Jahrbuch* (1849); a " Third," at p. 108 of his *Jahrbuch* for 1850. Numerous references in Hofmann's *Schriftbeweis*, 2te Aufl. (Nördlingen, 1857). Two papers by the late Professor James Macgregor, " The Place of Man Theologically Regarded," " The Christian Doctrine of Creation," in *British and Foreign Evangelical Review* (Jan. 1875, Oct. 1878). Sir J. W. Dawson touches the question of the Genesis-narratives in his three books, *Story of the Earth and Man* (Lond., Hodder & Stoughton, 1874), *Origin of the World according to Revelation and Science* (Lond., 1877), *Meeting-place of Geology and History* (Lond., 1894). F. Lenormant, *Les Origines*, translated under the title, *The Beginnings of History* (Lond., 1882).]

OUR primary question is that of the Origin of Man. What does the Bible say of man's coming into existence at the first? The bearing of this upon all that follows is plain ; for the lines of origin, nature, and destiny run very close together. Our material here must be drawn mainly from the opening pages of the Old Testament, although with constant reference to the use made, all through the Scriptures, of this primal and fundamental statement.

In describing the double account of the origination of man given in the first and second chapters of Genesis, we accept the fact that there are two distinct creation-narratives or paragraphs contained in these two chapters respectively.[1] We take nothing to do with theories that posit an Elohist writer for the one and a Jahvist for the other. Leaving the documentary hypothesis to time and criticism, we begin with this fairly accepted result, namely, that the human author of Genesis found to his hand certain fragments of ancient tradition, either re-cited from memory or preserved in writing, which he embodied in this inspired book. A very similar piecing of documents or narratives is generally admitted in the New Testament at the beginning of the Third Gospel. But surely a history does not cease to be the veritable product of its author because it contains documentary or extracted material. Nor does inspiration, as we understand it, refuse to consist with the recital or inser-tion of older communications enshrined in the religious belief of those to whom were committed the sacred oracles. Accepting, then, the two sections at the open-ing of the book of Genesis as at least two distinct com-positions, in each of which a special phraseology has been maintained, and naming them, for convenience sake, the first and second narratives, we nevertheless do not admit that they contain different accounts of the Creation. Such an assumption is clearly beside the mark. In the first narrative we have the succession in creation of the

---

[1] The first contained in i. 1–ii. 3 ; the second in ii. 4–25.

various elements, and then of the several orders of animated beings. In the second what we have is not a different account of the creation, for the plain reason that it takes no account of the creation at large. It makes no mention of the heavenly bodies, of land and water, of reptiles and fishes, all these having been described in the former narrative. Indeed, the introductory word of the second narrative, if we mark its use all through the book of Genesis, tells the tale quite distinctly, and should have prevented any misconception, for it means invariably not the birth or begetting of those named, but the history of their family.[1] So here, "the generations of the heavens and of the earth" means not their creation at the first, but an account of certain transactions within the heavens and the earth; in short, the dealings of God with mankind. For this second narrative is plainly, as Ewald calls it, the history proper of the creation of mankind.[2]

---

[1] Gen. ii. 4, אֵלֶּה תּוֹלְדוֹת : "These are the generations, *i.e.* what follows is the genealogical history, a formula which marks off this and the other nine sections which make up the rest of the book of Genesis—an orderly division and succession, affording strong presumption of its unity of plan and singleness of authorship. Hofmann lays great stress on the Sabbatic pause at the close of the first narrative, as bringing out the principle of a distinction between the act of creation and the history of that which is created. And now what follows is the history of that which is transacted between God and man. He says it is impossible, upon a comparison of all the passages where the phrase is used (note especially Gen. xxxvii. 2), to think that it can ever refer to what has preceded (*Schriftbeweis*, i. 206). The passages are Gen. v. 1, vi. 9, x. 1, xi. 10, xxv. 12, 19, xxxvi. 1, xxxvii. 2 ; see also Num. iii. 1.

[2] "Die eigentliche Menschenschöpfungsgeschichte." In the series of papers in his *Jahrbücher der biblischen Wissenschaft* (1848, 1849), entitled, "Erklärung der biblischen Urgeschichte." In the first two papers of the series he discusses the double creation narrative of Genesis. So also Sir J. W. Dawson, in an article on "Early Man and Eden," in *The Expositor*,

Both narratives speak of the origin of man, and here, indeed, is their real point of unity and connection. We do not say that there are no difficulties in harmonising the two. It is not clear whether the plants and animals, the formation of which is described along with that of Adam in the second chapter, are the same *flora* and *fauna* the rise of which is described as successive-creation acts in the sublime language of the first chapter. The main difficulties are the introduction of a vegetable creation along with man, and an apparently subsequent or simultaneous origination of beasts and birds. In both these points, the second narrative appears to diverge from the first. One explanation takes the *fauna* and *flora* of the second narrative as those of the present geological era, or of the human period. Those described in the former narrative are, on this hypothesis, held to belong to the past epochs of life on the globe, of which palæontology reads us the record laid up in stone. This belongs, however, to the style of interpretation against which we have already protested. Another explanation is that the former narrative contains the grand principles of the rise of life on the earth generally ; the latter the production and grouping of life, vegetable and animal, in the Edenic region, which took place along with the origination of man.[1] This is certainly the natural impression which the narratives respectively make on the reader's mind. But, as has been said, the second is not

---

April 1894 : "To a scientific reader the second narrative is evidently local in its scope, and relates to conditions of the introduction of man not mentioned in the general account of creation." See the same author's *Meeting-place of Geology and History*, p. 112 (Lond., 1894).

[1] On this point see further discussion, pp. 33–37 *infra*.

strictly a creation-narrative, except as it bears on the introduction of the human being. So far as man and his origin are concerned, the coincidence of the two narratives is plain. Lay them side by side at this point, and their relation becomes clear.

The first narrative gives us man's place in the succession of being and life upon the globe. On that grand opening page of the Bible stands a cosmogony which fitly prepares for all that follows in the book, and which shines with its steady light to-day in presence of the torch of science, as it shone on the Hebrew mind for centuries before Christianity came into the world. After the march of the elements—light and sky, water and earth—after the preparation of the great platform of life, comes life itself, and that in the regular ascent which modern science has taught us to look upon as a law of nature. First vegetable life, then the creatures of the deep, then the fowls of the air, and, last of all, the animals of the land. At the summit man appears, the apex of the pyramid of earthly being., Who can doubt for a moment that we have in this arrangement a point in which theology and science meet? It matters little whether you read the arrangement as one of history or one of classification. If the account of the Creation in that chapter be taken, in its more obvious sense, as chronological, then you have the convergence of two independent witnesses—science and Scripture—to the fact that man comes last and crowns the series; his creation on the sixth day, at the close of the production of the land animals generally, corresponding with his place, as ascertained by observation, in the latest of the

geological epochs "A writer of fiction would probably
have exalted man by assigning to him a separate day,
and by placing the whole animal kingdom together in
respect of time. . . . Geology and revelation coincide in
referring the creation of man to the close of the period
in which mammals were introduced and became pre-
dominant, and in establishing a marked separation between that period and the preceding one, in which the
lower animals held undisputed sway."[1] On the other
hand, were that chapter taken merely as a pictorial classification, a clothing of cosmic principles in dramatic garb,
the result would be still the same. Man crowns the
edifice of nature and life—a principle attested by the
researches of biology and comparative anatomy, as much
as by those of geology and palæontology, namely, that
man is a compendium of nature, and of kin to every
creature that lives,—that man, in the words of Oken, is
the sum total of all animals, the equivalent to the whole
animal kingdom.[2] In either case you have a position as
to which revelation and natural knowledge are consciously
at one—a fact at once of religious and of scientific importance, for to give man his true religious or theological
place is to give him also his true natural or scientific place.
The obvious supremacy of man in the natural orders of
the animal kingdom corresponds with the central and final
place assigned him in the revealed system of religion.

Let us next note how the creation of man is made to
stand out of or above the line of the other creative acts.

---

[1] Dawson, *Origin of the World according to Revelation and Science*
(Lond., 1877).
[2] Quoted by Hugh Miller, *Footprints of the Creator*, p. 279.

This representation of man as "the paragon of animals,"
this account of him appearing in line with the other
living beings of God's making, though at the summit of
the line, is further heightened by a stroke of description
which places man far above the other creatures.   In the
march of animated being previous to man there is a
formula employed which indicates both mediate creation
and generic distinction: "And God said, Let the waters
bring forth abundantly the moving creature that hath life;
. . . Let the earth bring forth the living creature after
his kind."   But when we come to man, the formula is
suddenly and brilliantly altered.   Immediate rather than
mediate origination is suggested.   It is not, "Let the
waters or the earth bring forth," but God said, "Let us
make man."   It is no longer "after his kind," on a typical form of his own; far less is it after the type of
an inferior creature.   God said, "Let us make man in
our image, after our likeness."   Reserving all that has
to be said about the divine image as descriptive of man's
nature and destiny, let us here note simply how much
distinction the narrative attributes to his origination.
For this distinction appears in the very form of the
announcement.   As to all the other products of creative
power there is recorded in this first narrative simply a
fiat with its *factum est*—"Let it be," and "It was."   But
in the case of man there is a purpose with its fulfilment;
and that fulfilment is recorded with such majesty of
language, with such threefold repetition, "a joyous tremor
of representation,"[1] as to show how great stress the book
laid upon this fact: "So God created man in His own

[1] Ewald, *ut supra.*

image, in the image of God created He him, male and female created He them."

To these three leading features of distinction in man's creation,—the divine council and decree concerning it, the divine type after which he was formed, and the immediate divine agency exercised in his production,—the rest of the chapter adds some details illustrative of man's original state. There is not here, as in the second narrative, any special account of the creation of woman. But the creation of both by the divine hand is carefully emphasised. That it is of the same type is implied, and by subsequent Scripture writers inferred, though the description is generic, in keeping with the whole character of the narrative. The term *Adam* is used to include both sexes—"Male and female He created them ; and blessed them, and called their name Adam in the day when they were created."[1] The blessing of God pronounced over them (ver. 28) does not, in the terms referring to propagation and production, differ from those used of the lower animal orders in ver. 22. But now it is addressed *to* mankind as in conscious fellowship with the Supreme, and not merely spoken *of* them. It is further grandly distinguished as conveying to mankind the gift or office of dominion over the earth and all creatures in it. The subordination of all living creatures to man, and his subdual of the earth and them, is stated in the form of a divine donation or charter, significantly connected by its place in the context with the Divine Image in which he is formed.[2] This is followed by the grant to man of the seed-bearing

[1] Gen. v. 2.   [2] See *infra*, pp. 143, 146.

herbs and the fruit-bearing trees for food, while to the
beasts, birds, and creeping things, lower forms of vegetation
are reserved. That is to say, besides the dominion over
all living things for all uses,—food no less than other,—
man receives, in accordance with his superior intelligence
and ability, the use of grain and fruits capable of
cultivation ; to the inferior animals only the green herb,
as naturally produced, is given.[1]

Clearly, the great features of this first description are
the solemn preparation of all things for man's introduction, and then his formation after the Divine Image.
Here the Bible view of his origin and nature follows the
law of consistency. Man is an animal among the
animals, breathes the breath of life as they do, yet is
represented as occupying a different position from that
of all the other creatures, not only in relation to them,
as supreme over them, but in relation to God his Maker.
With all this the special account of his creation coincides.

When we pass to the second narrative the point of
view is changed—a fact noted long ago by Josephus
when he bids us mark how, at Gen. ii. 4, "Moses begins
to physiologize," *i.e. naturam interpretari*, to explain the
nature of things. The remark is especially applicable to
the account which follows of the production of man.
Even the words describing the mode of the divine action
are different. Instead of *Bara*, " to create," so prominent
in the former narrative, we find here *Yatzar*, " to form or
knead," as the potter his clay. Further on, in the detailed

[1] See Quarry, *Genesis and its Authorship*, pp. 82–84 (Lond., 1866), whose
strong masculine sense carries this exegesis as clearly preferable to the
fanciful and overdrawn view that Gen. i. 28 and Gen. ix. 3 are different
decrees.

account of woman's formation, another verb still, namely, *Banah*, "to build," is employed. The same general principle is maintained in this narrative as in the first —that of closely connecting man with earth and with the whole system of life. The order of arranging the facts, however, is here the converse of the former. In the first, the rise of the animated world is described in a continuous line, with Man for its end or climax. This one has Man for its centre. The other creatures are ranged round him in a circle. So that, not the order or succession of their becoming is the thread of connection, but the relation of living nature, vegetable and animal, to his uses. Thus what is said in this narrative concerning the plant world (chap. ii. ver. 5) has to do only with those forms of vegetation which are subject to his tillage. What is said of the animal world (vers. 19, 20) has reference to man's cognisance of them, and his association with them, rather than to the order or mode of their production. The point of junction is suggested in the evident derivation of his name (ver. 7) "Adam," from *Adamah*,—the ground, out of which he and they are alike formed or kneaded. But in this classic verse, two distinctive features of man's nature are universally allowed to be indicated, and these are the special contribution of this second narrative to the topic in hand. "*Jahveh Elohim formed man—dust from the ground, and breathed into his nostrils the breath of life.*"

This account of the formation of man's nature on one side, from the earth, makes more emphatic than did the former narrative his kinship with the animals. To this agree other passages of Scripture which speak of man as

"dust" (*aphar*, Gen. iii. 19; Eccles. iii. 20, xii. 7) and
"clay" (*chomer*, Job xxxiii. 6); as "of the earth,
earthy."[1] Yet even here there is not wanting a note of
distinction. "*Dust from the ground*" may be held to
denote not a solid mass, a clod of the earth, but the
finest derivative from earthy material. Some exegetes,
indeed, hold that not only *aphar* "dust," but *adamah*
"ground,' and *chomer* "clay," are special in their meaning
in this connection: "red earth," "virgin soil," "potter's
clay." At all events, there is suggested in this popular
phraseology something akin to what research has made
good as to the human frame.[2]

The other detail peculiar to this narrative is that into
the nostrils of the form so moulded—"this quintessence
of dust,"—the Lord God Himself "breathed the breath
of life" or "lives," and "man became a living soul," an
animated being. In this particular, also, there is something which connects man closely with the rest of
animated nature. For although the "breath," or "spirit,"
with which he is endued is expressed by a word
(*Neshamah*), which does often signify the human spirit,
yet it is sometimes (*e.g.* Gen. vii. 22) used both of men
and animals. And the word employed to denote the
result of this inbreathing, namely, "a living soul" (*Nephesh
hayyah*) has been used in the former narrative (Gen.
i. 30) of all living creatures. For these reasons, we

---

[1] ἐκ γῆς χοϊκός, 1 Cor. xv. 47.

[2] It is well known that the animal body is composed, in the inscrutable
manner called *organisation*, of carbon, hydrogen, oxygen, nitrogen, lime,
iron, sulphur, and phosphorus,—substances which, in their various
combinations, form a large part of the solid ground"—Macdonald, *Creation
and Fall*, p. 326.

cannot build the distinction between man and the other animals, plainly implied in this account, on the use of the word "spirit" or "breath" (*Neshamah*), which is by some groundlessly asserted to be the "specific designation of the human soul-life,"[1] or to be "invariably applied to God or man, never to any irrational creature."[2]   Neither can we base it on the formation of man's body by the Creator Himself, for the same phrase, that "He formed them out of the ground," is used here (ver. 19) concerning the beasts and the fowls.   Yet though we may not place the distinction on formation from "the dust," nor in the animating "soul" which man possesses, we are entitled to base it on the divine act of "inbreathing into his nostrils."   That is to say, the communication of life in the case of man is described as a peculiar and direct act of God.   That this is the point of distinction intended may be seen by the way in which it is taken up and emphasised in other Old Testament passages.   "There is a spirit in man, and the breath of the Almighty (*Nishmath Shaddai*) giveth them understanding."[3]   "The spirit of God hath made me, and the breath of the Almighty giveth me life."[4]   All the while my breath is in me, the spirit of God (*Ruach Eloah*) is in my nostrils."[5]   "God Jehovah is He that giveth breath (*Neshamah*) unto the people upon the earth, and spirit (*Ruach*) to them that walk therein."[6]   The inference plainly is that the immediate divine origination of man's breath, spirit, understanding constitutes a special connec-

---

[1] Beck, *Umriss*, p. 7 (note).
[2] Murphy, *Critical and Exegetical Commentary on Genesis*, p. 92.
[3] Job xxxii. 8.   [4] *Ibid.* xxxiii. 4.
[5] *Ibid.* xxvii. 3.   [6] Isa. xlii. 5.

tion between the Creator and this, the chiefest of his works. We may interpret this remarkable expression, as to the divine inbreathing, as meaning " that the spirit and soul of man are not the mere individuation of the general life principle, but a gift bestowed on him expressly and directly by the personal God. . . . The spirit-soul of man is self-conscious and capable of infinite development, because it is God-descended in another and higher manner than that of the inner nature of animals."[1] In other words, we may infer that this special divine act " was the foundation of the pre-eminence of man, of his likeness to God, and of his immortality ; for, by this, he was formed into a personal being, whose immaterial part was not merely soul, but a soul breathed entirely by God, since spirit and soul were created together through the inspiration of God."[2]   Combining both these distinctive notes, then, we conclude—(a) that on the one side of his nature, even the lower side, man's formation is here presented as the prime thing of earth, its highest excitation, the climax of animal structure ; (b) on the higher side, the communication of life to man is described as the peculiar and direct act of God, the climax of His creative activity, in which He appears as more than Creator, even Progenitor, and mankind is, in a sense, His offspring. This latter distinction, no doubt, corresponds in the second narrative to that point in the first where was signalised man's formation after the divine likeness.

This second account of man's creation, then, while

---

[1] Delitzsch, *New Commentary on Genesis*, i. 120 (Clark, 1888).
[2] Keil, *Biblical Commentary on the Pentateuch*, i. 80 (Clark, 1864).

giving prominence to the details of his structure, while making still clearer than the first his affinity to earth and the kinship of the animal world to him, is as emphatic as the former in declaring his superior nature and his lordly position. Indeed, if we mark how it describes the preparation of the earth for man,—how it assigns the garden, and the trees, and the animals to his care and use; how it expresses not merely, like the former, a commission of man to rule, but an actual knowledge of and rule over the creatures on the part of the first man,—we shall not wonder that some consider it, with Ewald, as bringing out the pre-eminence of man even more distinctly than the former. At all events, the relation of the two accounts becomes very clear when we place them side by side. The first may be called typical, the second physiological. The former is the generic account of man's creation—of man the race, the ideal; the latter is the production of the actual man, of the historic Adam. The former spoke of the creative *fiat* which called man into existence; this speaks of the plastic process through which the Creator formed both man and woman—him from the dust of the ground, her from the bone and flesh of man. The former spoke of them as to their type—in the image of God; this, of the elements in which that type was realised—a material frame, informed by a divinely-inbreathed spirit. The former spoke of mankind at the head of the creatures, ruling over the earth and them; this speaks of the home provided for him, the work committed to him, the relationships formed for him, and, finally, of the moral law under which he was placed in his relation to God.

And no unbiassed reader can see anything but unity in these two accounts—a real and reasonable harmony, as distinguished from literal or verbal dovetailing; nor can we doubt that the master hand which knit into that marvellous whole—the book of Genesis—various paragraphs of precious tradition, enshrining the highest spiritual truth, has placed these two accounts of the creation of man side by side for the mutual light which they shed on each other without absolute contact, and certainly without contradiction.

The results of this twofold biblical account of man's becoming are clear, definite, and intelligible. His origin is not emanation, but creation—formation out of existing materials on the one side of his nature, out of the blessed fulness of the divine life on the other. His becoming is in the line of the natural order of animated beings, but at its climax. His position among them is central and supreme, but his nature stands distinguished from them all, in that it is formed after the Divine Image.

To examine the psychological value of the words in Gen. ii. 7, describing man's formation, will fall appropriately to our next chapter. What elements in man's nature are denoted by his bearing the Divine Image will form the subject of a later chapter. Meantime, a word is required in leaving this Bible account of man's origin, as it confronts some ideas of our own age.

Upon the expounder of the biblical doctrine of Creation contradictory demands are apt to be made relative to recent scientific speculation. There is, on the one part, an expectation that he should supply some *modus vivendi* between the commonly received findings of Scripture and the so-called views of science. On the other part, it is rather desired that he should prove the first chapters of Genesis to have excluded these theories from any claim to explain the beginnings of life and of the animated world. The true hinge of all such questions we have already postulated, namely, that wherever the Bible touches the origin and nature of things, its standpoint is primarily spiritual and religious. So it is here. The main scope of the creation-history of man is to teach his relation to the Creator and his place in the providential order of the world. When we take up this position, other questions will fall into their proper line, and find in due course their appropriate solution.

The Bible should not be committed to any theory of the origin of species. The record of Genesis does not imply local, special, or successive creations for the various orders of animated being. On the contrary, a continuous line of creative process is suggested by it. The principle of mediate production, rather than of immediate formation, is recognised in it. The earth and the waters are severally called upon to bring forth the living creatures appropriate to each.[1] The distinguishing feature of the biblical cosmogony is that it recognises two factors, a creative fiat, and a creative process,—absolute divine causation on the one hand, and on the other designed dependence of link upon link, in the actual production of the cosmos as it now appears. Thus it secures a pre-established harmony between faith and

[1] Gen. i. 20, 24.

knowledge.   Absolute origin it is the part of the former
to receive.   " Through faith, we understand that the
worlds were framed by the word of God."   Mode and
order in production it is the province of science to
investigate.

That account of the origin of species with which
Darwin, more than a generation ago, took captive the
scientific, and even the popular imagination of his time,
owed its predominance almost entirely to his brilliant
suggestion of " natural selection " as the mode or law by
which the supposed principle of " descent with modification " had produced the myriad forms of organic life.
In the words of one of his closest followers, " The
evidences which Darwin adduced in favour of ' natural
selection ' as a method have constituted some of the
strongest reasons which scientific men have felt for
accepting evolution as a fact." [1]   Already, however, the
method is discredited in scientific circles.   The suggested
cause is no longer admitted adequately to account for
the effects.   It has to submit to the help or rivalry of
several other proposed causes, such as the " physiological
selection " of Romanes himself, the " germ-plasms " of
Weismann, the " discontinuous variations " of Galton and
Bateson.   Under this disintegration of scientific opinions
the evolution hypothesis, which had gained, as has been
said, such vogue through the Darwinian suggestion,
threatens to fall back into the region of philosophic
speculation, where it has never been wanting since the
time, we may say, of Lucretius—certainly of Leibnitz.

In face of these recent confessions of the merely

[1] At p. 252, *Darwin and after Darwin*, by G. J. Romanes (Lond., 1893).

tentative character of the hypothesis, the lesson for the interpreter of Scripture is plain. For him to hasten to propound schemes of conciliation between the Mosaic account of Creation and the Darwinian pedigree of the lower animals and man would be to repeat an old and now unpardonable blunder.

The Scripture account of a special divine act in the origination of man cannot certainly be divested of the appearance of opposition to the modern theory, with all its various consequences. But if any *modus vivendi* is to be devised, it must come in the first place from the scientific side. Of such an adjustment there are some indications. Less frequently is the claim now made for the evolution hypothesis as a universal solvent of the question of origins. The Darwinian form of the theory takes its due place, at the head of others, as a working hypothesis for the explanation of a large range of biological facts. Its ablest scientific expounders have won for it the advantages of that position. But they do not expect it to explain the origin of life itself. Some of them, while believing it sufficient to account for the derivation of man's bodily structure from some of the lower animal forms, rather inconsequently confess that his higher powers " could not possibly have been developed in him by means of the law of natural selection." [1] For it is when it enters the region of man's

---

[1] Dr. Alfred Russell Wallace—acknowledged to be with Darwin the contemporaneous and independent author of the theory of evolution by natural selection—has always held this anomalous view, and continues, in his latest edition, to express it in unchanged terms ; see his *Darwinism*, pp. 472, 475 (Lond., 1889). Cf. also Calderwood's *Man's Place in Nature*, pp. 23, 24.

mental, moral, and religious history, that its want of success becomes conspicuous. And no wonder. It has, for example, to construct an entirely new psychology, in which all the complex processes of mind shall be evolved from elementary nervous movement in the animal frame. Its task in the domain of ethics is if possible still heavier. The rude outline of moral feeling in animals must be held to be the "germinal form" of all moral life. Out of struggle and self-preservation, which is its own chosen expression for the law of animal development, it must evolve the exactly opposite law of self-denial, which is the basis of human morality. It has to develop morality, that is to say, in a primarily non-moral animal by the gradual predominance of the social over the individual affections. When we come to account for civilisation and religion, its method is at least equally paradoxical. It gives its primary and chief attention to those unfortunate branches of the human family which have hitherto failed to become civilised. It endeavours to fill out its conception of primitive man from observation of those presently existing races which are exceptions to that course of development proved by history to be normal to mankind.[1] Not to go farther with this enumeration of difficulties, let us rest our attention on what is most germane to our subject, the view which this theory gives of the starting-point of the human family; and let this be contrasted with the account we have already gathered from the sacred records.

---

[1] See Principal Fairbairn's (of Oxford) *Studies in the Philosophy of Religion and History*, pp. 251, 252 (Lond., 1876).

Let us place the two delineations for a moment side by side. Look on this picture and on that. The ideal man of the Scripture, "made a little lower than the angels," the typal man of the first creation-narrative, is portrayed to us in the second creation-narrative as the actual father of the race. The scene is a garden, the time is the morning of the world—that golden age upon which all poetry draws as upon an unfailing deposit in every human imagination. The figures are two, male and female, the prototypes of their kind ; living a simple, primitive life, almost impossible for us to conceive, to whom all comfort is an art and the product of civilisation ; living in close fellowship with a pure and primitive nature in the vegetable and animal kingdoms, but standing out above all other created beings in actual converse with their Maker ; placed upon the way of ascent to a still higher moral and spiritual position by a relation to Him of law, of obedience, of love. The Bible takes the bold and original course of starting mankind neither with civilisation on the one hand, nor with barbarism on the other, but with an Eden of innocence and simplicity far removed from either.

Take now that other delineation, the " joint product of modern philosophy and of antiquarian research." Instead of a type higher than the animal, and only lower than the angels, there is presented to us the type of the anthropoid ape ; which itself is but a supposition, for this missing link between man and the quadrumana has never been found. Instead of regarding man as the goal of creation, and the earth as prepared and provided for him, you have to regard him as a variety in a certain animal family, coming to the front by accidental superiority to his fellows — the survivor of a struggle for existence. And instead of that picture of primitive humanity which satisfies reason, imagination, and faith, you have to accept as the ancestral specimen of the race "a coarse and filthy savage, repulsive in feature and gross in habits, warring with his fellow-savages, and warring yet more remorselessly with every living thing he could destroy, tearing half-cooked flesh, and cracking marrow bones with stone hammers, sheltering himself in damp and smoky caves, with no eye heavenward, and with only the first rude beginnings of the most important arts of life." [1]

Now let us ask which of the two beginnings accounts for man as he is? Can there be any hesitation? On the doctrine that he was made in the image of God, we can understand all that is best in him,—"how noble in reason! how infinite in faculty! in form and moving how express and admirable! in action how like an angel! in apprehension how like a god!" On this doctrine, too, coupled with that other Bible doctrine of a fall, we can explain his guilt, his vileness, the degradation worse than animal to which he can sink, on the familiar principle that the corruption of the best produces the worst. In short, the Bible view of man's beginning and early history explains at once his greatness and his misery. But the so-called scientific view accounts neither for what is best in him nor for what is worst; it is impotent to explain the rise of man as he is, from that which it supposes to have preceded him.

[1] Dawson, *Story of the Earth and Man*, p. 377.

It is clear enough that believers in the Bible are not called upon to make any adjustment of their faith to this theory of the origin of man. On the other hand, all who desire to understand the human soul, to read human history aright, to hope and to labour for the future of the race, find in the Bible account of man's beginning an intelligible position.

Let us never undervalue science, nor even scientific hypothesis. The gold of fact will form at length the perfect ring of truth when the crust of suppositions which have helped in its formation shall be dissipated into dust and ashes. Whatever is true in the development hypothesis will ultimately be seen to be in harmony with all other ascertained truth. It has already led scientific opinion to agree, with Theism and the Bible, that the world must have had a definite beginning and an ordered process of becoming. It may yet win its way to some position among ascertained laws of nature, and be proved to have had a place in the production and nurture of the human race. But this would be far from conflicting with the Bible. It would only more fully illustrate the idea of mediate creation which is so plainly indicated in the Bible cosmogony. It would only enlarge and enhance our idea of creative power that so much should be evolved out of so little, and thus be another and grander way of telling the glory of God. Meanwhile we have a revealed account of the origin of the world and of man which coincides with the instinctive beliefs of the human mind, with the plan of human history, with the faith and hope that are in God. With this account we can work and worship, and for

the rest afford to wait.   Knowledge and thought are
advancing.   "The world moves," and vainly do some seek
with bars of iron or crooks of steel to hold it ever the
same.   "The world moves," but "The word of the Lord
endureth for ever."

II

MAN'S NATURE: THE BIBLE PSYCHOLOGY

"Affections, Instincts, Principles and Powers,
   Impulse and Reason, Freedom and Control—
   So men, unravelling God's harmonious whole,
Rend in a thousand shreds this life of ours.

Vain labour!   Deep and broad, where none may see,
   Spring the foundations of that shadowy throne,
   Where man's one nature queen-like sits alone,
Centred in a majestic unity."

—MATTHEW ARNOLD.

Gen. ii. 7.—"And the Lord God formed man *of* the dust of the ground, and breathed into his nostrils the breath of life, and man became a living soul."

1 Thess. v. 23.—"And the very God of peace sanctify you wholly ; and *I pray God* your whole spirit and soul and body be preserved blameless unto the coming of our Lord Jesus Christ."

Heb. iv. 12.—"For the word of God *is* quick, and powerful, and sharper than any two-edged sword, piercing even to the dividing asunder of soul and spirit, and of the joints and marrow, and *is* a discerner of the thoughts and intents of the heart."

1 Cor. ii. 14.—"But the natural (*lit.* soulish) man receiveth not the things of the Spirit of God : for they are foolishness unto him : neither can he know *them*, because they are spiritually discerned."

1 Cor. xv. 44.—"It is sown a natural (*lit.* soulish) body ; it is raised a spiritual body. There is a natural body, and there is a spiritual body."

CHAPTER III

THE BIBLE PSYCHOLOGY IN GENERAL

[LITERATURE.—M. F. Roos, *Fundamenta Psychologiae ex S.S. Collecta*, 1769; German transl. (Stuttgart, 1857). Olshausen, " De Naturae humanae trichotomia," in his *Opuscula theologica* (Berlin, 1834). Böttcher, *De inferis . . . ex Hebraeorum et Graecorum opinionibus* (Dresden, 1845). J. T. Beck (of Tübingen), *Umriss der biblischen Seelenlehre*, 1843, 1871; English transl. (Clark, Edin., 1877). Gen.-Major von Rudloff, *Die Lehre vom Menschen begr. auf der göttlichen Offenbarung* (Leipzig, 1858). Franz Delitzsch, *System der biblischen Psychologie* (2te Aufl. Leipzig, 1861; Transl. Clark, Edin., 1867). H. H. Wendt, *Die Begriffe Fleisch und Geist im bibl. Sprachgebrauch* (Gotha, 1878). Alliott, *Psychology and Theology* (Congl. Lecture, 1854). Gorman, *Christian Psychology*, founded on Swedenborg (Lond., Longmans, 1875). Ellicott, " The Threefold Nature of Man," in *The Destiny of the Creature, and other Sermons* (Lond., Parker, 1863). J. B. Heard, *The Tripartite Nature of Man* (5th Edition, Clark, Edin., 1882). E. White, *Life in Christ*, " A Study of the Scripture Doctrine on the Nature of Man," etc. (Lond., Elliot Stock, 1878). Prof. W. P. Dickson, *St. Paul's Use of the terms Flesh and Spirit* (Glasgow, 1883). Consult also the *Old Testament Theologies* of Oehler and Schultz, and the *New Testament Theology* of Bernhard Weiss.]

LET us begin here with a summary of the principles on which all the psychological terms of Scripture are to be construed. " In this work," says the pioneer of

4

modern biblical psychology,[1] "I take it for my guiding
rule that everywhere in Scripture there reigns an
accuracy and validity worthy of God. The more
seriously and circumspectly a man is expounding any
subject, the more careful is he in the choice of words;
and shall we not allow as much to the Spirit of God
speaking by apostles and prophets?" We are willing to
accept this as our primary position. Holding the Bible
to be substantially identical with that word of God
which "pierces even to the dividing asunder" of the
constituents of man's nature (Heb. iv. 12), we are
prepared to give the utmost heed to its minutest shades
of expression. Yet this we do in accordance with the
views of inspiration already explained. As the chosen
vehicle of the divine speaker to men, the accuracy of
Scripture language appears in spiritual sharpness and
moral power. It is plain that in regard to psychology,
for example the Bible is marked by quite another kind
of exactitude than that of the schools. Indeed, its
purpose requires that its teachings be not cast in the
scientific form. According to the Talmudic maxim,
"The expressions used in the law are like the ordinary
language of mankind,"[2] it may be said of the whole
Bible that on all subjects it uses the language of
common life, a speech which men in all lands and
times can understand. It is one of its divine charac-
teristics that by means of such expressions it conveys

[1] Magnus Friederich Roos, in his *Fundamenta Psychologiae ex Sacrâ
Scripturâ Collecta*, 1769. See German version by Cremer, p. 4 (Stuttgart,
1857). The whole passage has been freely adapted by Beck in the preface
to his own *Umriss der biblischen Seelenlehre*.

[2] De Sola's *New Translation of the Sacred Scrip.* i. 19 (1844).

discoveries of human nature which commend themselves to every man's conscience in the sight of God. Yet on these very grounds the exact meaning and consistent use of these expressions demand our closest attention.

Again, the psychological ideas of Scripture must be construed by us according to the manner of thought, so far as we can apprehend it, of the writers themselves. Now the writers of the Old Testament, from whom those of the New derive in large part their phraseology, are like the tongue in which they write, non-philosophical. Their psychology is not analytic. The whole character of their thinking should warn us against expecting distinctions and divisions of human nature in an abstract form. Their tendency is to the concrete. Their expressions, sensuous and symbolic, are " thrown out " at mental and spiritual ideas. They use a large variety of terms for the same thing, according as it is viewed from different points or conceived under different emotional impressions. Considering our mental habits of analysis and abstraction, care must be exercised in rendering their terms into modern equivalents which are to have for us any intellectual validity. But to conclude on that account that the expressions do neither justify nor repay accurate study, is to fall into one of the shallowest blunders of the Rationalistic school.

Once more, we shall certainly be wrong if we persist in the old method of taking all parts of Scripture as equally valid for our purpose, and furnishing terms equally pliable and useful. We should thus repeat the old error of the proof-text system in theology, namely, that of finding all the doctrines in every part of Scripture alike.[1] We must be prepared to find growth in the use of psychological terms in Scripture, and that from two several causes. Acquaintance with culture outside of the Hebrew nation has left its evident impress on the New Testament writers, and even on the later Old Testament writers as compared with the earlier. There is growth from a more simple and popular to a more complex and philosophical view of man's nature. But the other source of growth is more important. There is a progress in the revelation of which Scripture is the record. The proper influence of this fact upon theology has become an axiom of all enlightened study of that science. The fruits of that influence are already seen in our rapidly multiplying essays in Old and New Testament theology. Its bearing on the study of the sacred languages is also obvious. Rothe has said that " we may appropriately speak of a ' language of the Holy Ghost.' For in the Bible it is evident that the Divine Spirit at work in revelation has always fashioned for Himself, out of the language of those nationalities in which the revelation had its chosen sphere, an entirely peculiar religious dialect, moulding the linguistic elements which He found to hand, as well as the already existing conceptions, into a form specially suited to His

---

[1] H. Schultz complains of several otherwise meritorious works on Biblical Psychology that they commit the error of regarding the entire biblical writings, without more ado, as material of equal relevancy for the study of man.—*Alt. T. Theologie*, i. 348. See also Böttcher's remark on Beck: "Nuperrime, subtilius caeteris, nullo tamen aetatis discrimine facto." —*De Inferis*, p. 14 (Dresd., 1845).

purpose. Most clearly does the Greek of the New Testament exhibit this process." [1] Cremer, who cites this passage, adds : " The spirit of the language assumes a form adequate to the new views which the Spirit of Christ creates and works." [2] Without attention to this element of progress, it is impossible to construct any adequate biblical psychology. This alone explains the transition from terms in the earlier Scriptures that are rather physical than psychical, to those in the later Scriptures that are more deeply charged with spiritual meaning. A progressive religious revelation is intimately connected with the growth of humanity, casts growing light upon the nature and prospects of man, will therefore be increasingly rich in statements and expressions bearing upon the knowledge of man himself, and especially of his inner being. It is in the latest records of such a revelation that the terms expressive of the facts and phenomena of man's nature should be correspondingly enriched, diversified, and distinguishable in their meaning.

Bearing in mind these simple maxims, we proceed to ask, What is the Bible view of man's constitution ? The announcement in Gen. ii. 7 is that which first claims our attention. Into this ground-text of biblical psychology the meaning of the various theories has been read, and round it numberless controversies have raged. The chief of these has been whether the passage, taken along with the allied expressions, entitles us to say that the Bible

[1] *Zur Dogmatik*, pp. 233, 234, 2te Aufl. (Gotha, 1869).
[2] Cremer's *Wörterbuch der N. T. Gräcität*, Vorrede, p. 5, 4te Aufl. (Gotha, 1886).

views man's nature as dual or tripartite in its constituents.   But before discussing the " sufficiently famous " [1]
trichotomy, as it is called, we must meet a question which
recent speculation has brought up.   Most advocates of a
trichotomy of man allow it to be based upon a more
radical *dichotomy*.   But the newest question is, whether
the Bible necessitates even this—whether, in short, we
may not interpret its accounts of man's nature on the
one substance hypothesis of modern positivism.   If any
part of Scripture seems in accord with this view, it is
the earlier passages of the Old Testament, and prominently the one which stands at their head.   Let us
consider these three questions in order, taking the last
first.

I. The *unity* of man's nature, according to Scripture.
The meaning of Gen. ii. 7, to a mind unprepossessed with
theories, is sublimely simple.   It declares that the Lord
God formed the man, dust from the ground, and breathed
into his nostrils the breath of life (or " lives "), and man
became a living soul.   Here are plainly two constituents
in the creation : the one from below, dust from the
ground ; the other from above, the breath of life at the
inspiration of the Almighty.   Yet from these two facts
results a unit.   Man became an animated being.   Nothing can be more misleading than to identify " soul "
here with what it means in modern speech, or even in
later biblical language.   " A living soul " is here exactly
equivalent to " a creature endowed with life," for the
expression in these creation-narratives is used of man
and the lower animals in common.   " Soul " in the

---

[1] Olshausen, *Opusc. Theolog.* p. 145.

primitive Scripture usage means, not the "immaterial rational principle" of the philosophers, but simply life embodied. So that in this primal text the unity of the created product is emphatically expressed, and the sufficient interpretation of the passage is, that the divine inspiration awakes the already kneaded clay into a living human being.[1] Here is an account of man's origin fitted to exclude certain dualistic views of his nature with which the religion of revelation had to contend.[2] Whether, indeed, the formation of his frame and the in-breathing of his life be taken as successive or as simultaneous moments in the process of his creation, the description is exactly fitted to exclude that priority of the soul which was necessary to the transmigration taught by Oriental religions, and to the pre-existence theory of the Greek schools. There is here no postponement or degradation of the earthly frame in favour of the soul, as if the latter were the man, and the former were only the prison-house into which he was sent, or the husk in which he was for a time concealed. According to the account in this text, the synthesis of two factors, alike honourable, constitutes the man.

That neither the familiar antithesis, soul and body, nor any other pair of expressions by which we commonly render the dual elements in human nature, should expressly occur in this *locus classicus*, is a fact which may help to fix attention on the real character of the earlier

[1] Cf. Ezekiel's resurrection-vision (chap. xxxvii.), where there is first, the reconstruction of the animal frame, bones, sinews, flesh, skin ; and only after this the "Breath" comes into them, and they live.

[2] "It directly contradicts the doctrine of the pre-existence of the soul." —Schultz, *O.T. Theology*, ii. 252 (Clark, Edin., 1892).

Old Testament descriptions of man. The fact is not explained merely by the absence of analysis. Rather is it characteristic of these Scriptures to assert the *solidarité* of man's constitution,—that human individuality is of one piece, and is not composed of separate or independent parts. This assertion is essential to the theology of the whole Bible—to its discovery of human sin and of a divine salvation. In a way quite unperceived by many believers in the doctrines, this idea of the unity of man's nature binds into strictest consistency the Scripture account of his creation, the story of his fall, the character of redemption, and all the leading features in the working out of his actual recovery from his regeneration to his resurrection.

All this, however, will not avail those who wish to identify the Bible view of man with that of the positive, or monistic philosophy. With some recent writers on Bible psychology it is a favourite assertion that the Bible treats humanity as an integer; that man is the true monad; that in the language of Scripture and of early Christian writers the soul is not the man, and the body is not the man, but man is the *tertium quid* resulting from their union. There is a sense in which these statements are correct. But they bring no support to the one-substance theory. To say that the Bible language on this point " agrees in an unexpected manner with the deductions of recent science," [1] is at the best only to overrate the accidental agreement of non-analytic language with the terms of a false analysis. To go farther, and say that the Bible has no notion of a

[1] Rev. Edward White, *Life in Christ*, p. 94.

separable soul and spirit in man, that it regards death
as the destruction of the man, is to place oneself in
hopeless antagonism to the facts. The Bible, which
regards man as possessed of a dual constitution, composed of a higher and a lower element, God-given and
earth-derived, attaches the personality to the higher, and
views human beings as capable of existence apart from
their present visible corporeity. When, however, the
assertions above referred to are intended to bring out the
Bible view of the oneness of man's nature, they are fitted
to do good service. It is certain that the Bible mode of
speaking of man's nature differs essentially from much of
the language which an alien philosophy has imposed upon
religion. To speak so exclusively of " the soul " as has
been so long the practice in religious and moral teaching, is to show much disregard of man's position in the
world, and strange inattention to the language of Scripture. It seems to have been forgotten that man's one
though complex nature is to be his nature for ever.
The Bible never loses sight of this, nor overlooks the
place of the body. According to it, man's creation begins
with the formation of the body, his salvation is crowned
with its redemption.[1] From this great first text which
describes man's original constitution, through those passages which speak of his dominion over earth and the
creatures, in all those which represent work done through
the agency of the body as divine service and human
victory, onward to those which represent the redemption
of the body as the climax of salvation, it is evident that

[1] See remarks on Ps. xvi., by the late Professor W. Robertson Smith,
in *Expositor*, Nov. 1876.

the Bible system of religion is based upon the unity of man's nature.

It is therefore quite just to regard all attempts in philosophy and in science to appreciate the real unity of our nature as in the proper sense a return to truth, and an agreement with Scripture. " This harmony between the outer and the inner man," says Mr. Heard," [1] " the interdependence of sense on thought and thought on sense, is the point on which our soundest physiologists are advancing every day. Discarding the old materialism, which made thought a secretion of the brain or blood, and the old spiritualism, which taught that the spirit of man was probably that of some fallen demon imprisoned for a while in flesh, we are advancing in the right direction when we maintain the separate existence of the mind and body, and yet regard the former as perfectly pervading the latter, nay, as being the formative principle by which it is constructed and adapted to our nature and use. The goal to which modern research is tending is the point where the old dualism between mind and body will not disappear, but combine instead under some higher law of unity which we have not as yet grasped. Physiology and psychology will not stand contrasted then as they do now, but rather appear as the two sides of the same thing seen in its outward and inward aspect. The resurrection of the body, which at present is a stumbling-block to the spiritualists and foolishness to materialists, will then be found to be the wisdom of God as well as the power of God, and so the Scripture intimations of the unity of man's

[1] *Tripartite Nature of Man,* 5th Edition, p. 84 (Clark, Edin., 1882).

true nature in one person will be abundantly vin-
dicated."

11. The *duality* of human nature, however, is as clearly
expressed in Scripture, in another aspect, as the unity
of his being is conserved in the former. But let us
carefully note how these dual elements are conceived of
and set forth. The anthropology of the Greek, and of
some other ethnic schools, rested on a dualistic scheme
of the universe. Soul and body, mind and matter, were
the representatives in man of contrary opposites in the
nature of things. For them, man, so far from being a
unity, was a paradox—a mirror in little, of that universe
at large, in which God and the world, the real and the
phenomenal, were eternal opposites. But the Bible
philosophy of God, of the world, and of man, rests on
its grand and simple idea of creation proper—an idea so
familiar to us that we forget how originally and essentially biblical it is. Its simplicity must by no means
lead us to confound it with the pantheistic doctrine of
emanation; for not out of God's own essence or nature,
but as the creation of His expressed free will, do all
things arise. As little is its duality to be confounded
with the dualism of the ethnic systems, acording to
which the world is not created, but only framed or
fashioned, and exists therefore eternally in contradistinction and counterpoise to the framer of it. A duality,
however, in the Bible philosophy there is. In that
sublime revelation of all things as the result of free will
and word in God,—" He spake, and it was done,"—it is
plain that the things made, good and perfect though
they are, stand in a line apart from and beneath their

Maker.   This primal and fundamental antithesis runs
through all Bible thought,—antithesis of the Creator
and the creature, the infinite and the finite, the invisible
and the visible.   This prepares us for the duality of
terms in which the ground-text (Gen. ii. 7) describes the
origination of man's nature.   It pointedly presents two
aspects of it, the earthly and the super-earthly, *that*, on
the one side, which allies man to the animal creation,
namely, that like the lower animals he is formed from
the ground; *this*, on the other, which represents man
alone as receiving his life by the immediate in-breathing
of the Lord God.

We shall import into the passage a later meaning if
we insist on these contrasted aspects as a material and
an immaterial element in the modern sense of the terms,
if we identify the duality off-hand with that of body and
soul, much more if, led away by mere verbal parallelism
(*aphar*, *nephesh*, *neshamah*), we read into it the later
trichotomy of body, soul, and spirit.   The antithesis is
clearly that of lower and higher, earthly and heavenly,
animal and divine.   It is not so much two elements, as
two factors uniting in a single and harmonious result,—
" man became a living soul."   Here, then, we have a
dichotomy no doubt substantially agreeing with that which
has been current wherever man analyses his own nature,
but depending upon an antithesis native to the Scriptures.   If we neglect this antithesis, if we identify it at
once with the later philosophical contrast between matter
and mind, we shall miss the special light which it is
fitted to throw upon the Scripture doctrine of man.

The pervading dual conception of man in the Old

Testament, beginning from this account of his creation, is that he is alternately viewed as fading flesh on his earthly side, and on the other as upheld by the Spirit of the Almighty; but this contrast of flesh and spirit is primarily that of the animal and the divine in man's first constitution. It is not to be identified with the analysis of man's nature into a material and an immaterial element. The antithesis—soul and body—in its modern, or even in its New Testament sense, is, strictly speaking, not found at all in the Old Testament. Early biblical usage had no fixed term for the human body as a living organism. An assemblage and alternation of terms were employed, such as " trunk," " bones," " belly," " flesh "; the last by far the most common, perhaps because it supplies form and colour to the body. In later Old Testament writings, we have such metaphorical expressions as " houses of clay," [1] or, as in the post-biblical writings, " earthly tabernacle." [2] In the latest, we have words which suggest a hollow, a frame-work, or a sheath, favouring the Greek idea of the body as the husk or clothing of the soul.[3]

As little was there at first a fixed term for the inner or higher part of man's twofold nature. " Soul," " heart," " spirit," are each used upon occasion as the counterpart of the lower, and as together with it, making up the whole man.[4] Thus " soul " and " flesh " are used in

---

[1] Job iv. 19.   [2] *Sap. Salom.* ix. 15.

[3] *Guphah*, 1 Chron. x. 12 (for a corpse) ; *Geshem* and *Nidneh*, found in Dan. iv. 33, v. 21, vii. 15, are Chaldee words, the latter meaning literally the sheath of a sword.

[4] The original terms are *Nephesh, Lebhabh, Ruach* ; and for " flesh," *Basar.*

combination, *e.g.* "My soul thirsteth for Thee, and my flesh longeth for Thee" (Ps. lxiii. 1); "My flesh in my teeth, and my life (soul) in my hand" (Job. xiii. 14); "His flesh hath pain and his soul mourneth" (Job xiv. 22). A land entirely stripped of its trees and of its crops is said to be consumed "soul and body" (*lit.* "flesh," Isa. x. 18). Equally characteristic is the conjunction of "flesh" with "heart" for the whole human being. Aliens wholly unfit for God's service are described as "uncircumcised in heart and in flesh" (Ezek. xliv. 7, 9). The man whose whole being is given to pleasure "searches in his heart how to cheer his flesh" (Eccles. ii. 3). "Remove sorrow from thy heart and put away evil from thy flesh" (Eccles. xi. 10). The *summum bonum* of human life is when "a sound heart is the life of the flesh" (Prov. xiv. 30), an expression reminding one of the classic, *mens sana in corpore sano.* This dualism of the Old Testament is clinched in the memorable description of its final form "when the dust returns to the earth as it was, and the spirit to God who gave it" (Eccles. xii. 7).

The distribution of parts, however, is not invariably nor rigidly dualistic. For, along with such as those now quoted, we have also various trinal phrases, *e.g.* "My soul longeth . . . for the courts of the Lord: my heart and my flesh crieth out for the living God" (Ps. lxxxiv. 2); "My heart is glad and my glory rejoiceth; my flesh also shall rest in hope" (Ps. xvi. 9); "Mine eye is consumed with grief, yea my soul and my belly" (Ps. xxxi. 9). Yet, dual or trinal though the terms may be, the intention is to express, in man, the inner and the outer, the higher and the lower, the animating and the animated,—all resting upon the primal contrast of what is earth-derived, with what is God-inbreathed. So soon as we pass to the New Testament, we come upon those antithetic expressions which we ourselves familiarly use, —soul and body, flesh and spirit,—Greek words moulded by Greek thought, but still derived directly from the Septuagint, used therefore with their Old Testament force, rather than with any reference to the philosophical analysis of the Greek schools.

We are sometimes told, in this connection, that the antithesis of material and immaterial was not developed till late in the progress of thought; that the ancients, and even the Fathers of the Christian Church, had no notion of an immaterial essence; that the soul was to them a gas,—a finer kind of matter than the body, but matter still. Dr. Bain, on the ground that the "sole theory of mind and body existing in the lower stages of culture is a double materialism," holds that this was the prevailing tenet even in the Christian Church down to the fifth century. He asserts that though a beginning for the notion of the immaterial or spiritual had been made in the Greek schools, it "received no aid either from Judaism or Christianity." [1] Such writers as Lüdemann, Holsten, and Pfleiderer try to force the same construction even upon S. Paul's psychology. The Pauline *pneuma*, they tell us, implies a conception of material substance, of a non-earthly sort,—" a transcendent physical essence, a supersensuous kind of matter, which

[1] *Mind and Body*, pp. 143–158, by Prof. Alex. Bain, of Aberdeen (1876).

is the opposite of the earthly, sensuous materiality of the *sarx*." [1]

Now we are not concerned to defend the Christian Fathers on such a point. Many of them had been pagans before their conversion, and carried with them into Christianity the crudeness of pagan philosophy, instead of the purer psychological ideas of the Old Testament. So far as the Pauline passages are concerned, it is enough to refer to Wendt's convincing demonstration, on exegetical grounds, that the "pneumatic" in these places means not a special kind of substance, but that which is animated by the *Pneuma, i.e.* by a newly infused principle of divine life.[2] In regard to the biblical dualism generally, and that of the Old Testament in particular, the statements above quoted are singularly beside the mark. That dualism we certainly distinguish from the philosophical one of material and immaterial. But instead of being, therefore, a lower conception, like that of the ethnic peoples, it is other, because in a sense higher. If we grasp the notion of the Bible antithesis between the earthly and the super-earthly in man, if we note how it rests upon his unique origin as there revealed, we shall know how to account for the absence from the earlier Scriptures of the Greek antithesis between matter and mind, and see how this other supplied its place. Its motive, indeed, was religious, rather than philosophical. Spirit and spiritual, as thus

[1] Pfleiderer, *Paulinism,* i. 201, Transl.

[2] Wendt *Die Begriffe Fleisch und Geist im biblischen Sprachgebrauch,* pp. 139-142. Cf. Dr. Dickson's summary of Wendt's argument in Appendix to his Baird Lecture, *St. Paul's Use of Flesh and Spirit* (Glasgow, 1883).

contrasted with flesh and earthly, is not an antithesis of substances, rather of origin and force. It is not the pitting against each other of two sorts of material,—a lower and a higher, a coarser and a finer. Neither is it, in point of form, the antithesis of the corporeal and the incorporeal, though it may nearly agree with that in fact. Yet it does not follow that this religious duality of the ancient Scriptures had no influence in forming the philosophical conception of immateriality which now rules all our thinking. The Old Testament conception of God is really that of " spirit " in the highest sense of the term,—that of the illocal, impalpable, immaterial,— " without body, parts, or passions,"—while it rises above even this in its further idea of Him as living, intelligent, transcendent, and absolute Personality. Nothing but wanton disregard of fact is shown in saying that Old Testament religion contributed nothing to the metaphysical idea of " spiritual substance as recognised by us." [1] The grandeur of its conception of God speaks for itself. The idea of God as one of whom His worshippers saw no similitude, of whom they were to make no likeness, who has no image but that which He Himself has formed in his intelligent offspring, whom no temple could contain, and who is to be worshipped everywhere in spirit and in truth,—this surely has done much to ripen a notion of immateriality which coincides with our highest intellectual conceptions, and rises to the dignity of our purest moral ideals.

[1] Bain, *ut supra.*

CHAPTER IV

THE TRIPARTITE VIEWS EXAMINED

HAVING considered the *Unity* which Scripture attributes to the human constitution, and the *dual* elements acknowledged by it, in common with almost all human psychologies, we have now to inquire whether this duality has to be further modified in favour of a *three-fold* division of man's nature. Here, as before, everything turns on interpretation of terms. There is a pair of expressions for the inner or higher part of man's nature which occurs plentifully in the Old Testament, as *Nephesh* and *Ruach*, in the Greek Scriptures as *Psyche* and *Pneuma*, in the modern languages as *Seele* and *Geist*, SOUL and SPIRIT. The distinction implied in this usage may be said to be the *crux* of biblical psychology. The controversy concerning it has been, not unnaturally, though rather unfairly, identified with that concerning the possibility of a Bible psychology at all. On the other hand, the revival of this whole science in recent times is coincident with the recall of attention to the fact of a distinction in Scripture between these two terms. The real controversy, however, concerns the precise force of that distinction. Does it indicate two separable natures, so that, with the corporeal presupposed, man may be said to be of Tripartite Nature? Or, is it rather such a view of the inner nature of man as sunders that nature into two functions or faculties? Or, finally, is it a nomenclature to be explained and accounted for on principles entirely peculiar to the biblical writings? We shall here sketch the theory of Tripartition, and in next chapter point out the historical explanation of the scriptural usage.

I. THE THEORETICAL CONSTRUCTIONS.—The Trichotomy of body, soul, and spirit held an important place in the theology of some of the Greek Christian Fathers; but, in consequence of its seeming bias towards a Platonic doctrine of the soul and of evil, still more because of its use by Apollinaris to underprop grave heresy as to the Person of Christ, it fell into disfavour, and may be said to have been discarded from the time of Augustine till its revival within a quite modern period. It has recently received the support, or, at least, the favourable consideration, of a respectable school of evangelical thinkers on the continent, represented by such names as those of Roos, Olshausen, Beck, Delitzsch, Auberlen, and Oehler. In our own country, such writers as Alford, Ellicott, Liddon, and Lightfoot fully recognise the importance of the Trichotomic usage in Scripture, but none of them has investigated its real meaning. Most of them adopt the mistaken interpretation that the distinction between soul and spirit is that between a lower and a higher essence or nature, and accordingly lean to the foregone conclusion of this exegesis, namely, that Scripture is committed to the affirmation of a tripartite nature in man. Yet their utterances on this point are little more than *obiter dicta*. Not one of these authors has seriously or consistently taken up this peculiar psychology. There exists among us a small school of writers who have done so. Their leading representative is Mr. J. B. Heard, whose *Tripartite Nature of Man* has now been before the public for some considerable time.[1] This psychology has been largely adopted by those who maintain the peculiar eschatological position known as that of Conditional Immortality, although Mr. Edward White, the main exponent of this view, makes comparatively little of the Trichotomy. That it has furnished a favourite scheme of thought for mystics and sectaries has not helped its fair investigation in our theological schools. The pretension put forth for it by some of its votaries, that as a theological panacea it would heal the strife of centuries, has had the effect on the professional mind which is always produced by the advertisement of a quack remedy, not without that other effect on the common apprehension that, after all, there is probably something in it. Its crudest and most frequently quoted form is that which, taking *body* for the material part of our constitution, makes *soul* stand for the principle of animal life, and *spirit* for the rational and immortal nature. This is plainly not the construction which any tolerable interpretation can put upon the Scripture passages, though it is often presented in popular writing as an account of the Trichotomy. It is not unusual, indeed, to identify the whole topic with this boldly unscientific statement.[2] But such a tripartition can hardly be

---

[1] Fifth edition (T. & T. Clark, Edin., 1882). See also his *Old and New Theology*, and his Hulsean Lecture of 1892–93, *Alexandrian and Carthaginian Theology Contrasted*.

[2] *E.g.* Dr. Charles Hodge's account of the Trichotomy consists in so describing it. His refutation of it as unbiblical would accordingly be

attributed to any theologian of repute. The views of most of those named above are greatly more creditable attempts to frame a theory which will cover the biblical use of the terms. Let us briefly examine them.

Divergence from the track of valid biblical science may be measured by the degree in which a real Trichotomic usage in Scripture has been mistaken for the assertion of a tripartite nature. M. F. Roos (1769), already alluded to as the pioneer of this inquiry, has wholly avoided this error. He distinguishes the terms soul and spirit in their natural sense, and has carefully marked the spiritual import of their contrasted usage in the Pauline Scriptures. But he goes no farther.[1] Olshausen, the well-known commentator, in an academic address (1825), entitled " The Trichotomy of Human Nature adopted by New Testament Writers," takes the position so largely followed of distinguishing *pneuma* and *psyche* as higher and lower powers, though not without a glimpse of the real distinction. The leading sentence usually quoted from him is to this effect:—
" *Pneuma* signifies the power in man, superior, active, and governing, though it indicates, at the same time, man's divine origination. *Psyche*, again, signifies the inferior power which is acted on, moved, and held in check ; for it is thought of as placed midway between an earthly force and a heavenly one." [2]

Delitzsch holds both a dual and a trinal division of human nature to be scriptural. He contends for

entirely successful, if this were the only thing to be discussed. See *Systematic Theology*, ii. pp. 47–49.

[1] See especially pp. 41, 42, 53–62 of his work, as cited above.

[2] P. 154 of his *Opuscula Theologica* (Berlin, 1834).

three distinct or essential elements in man—soul and
spirit, though not distinct natures, being nevertheless
separable elements of the inner man, and these such
as to be substantially distinguished.[1]   This position
Delitzsch thinks of such cardinal importance to his
system that he signalises it thus: " The key of biblical
psychology lies in the solution of the enigma: How is
it to be conceived that spirit and soul can be of one
nature and yet of distinct substance?   When once I
was enlightened upon this enigma, my confused materials
for a biblical psychology formed themselves, as if
spontaneously, into a systematic whole." [2]   This light
he endeavours to convey to his readers, thus: " Soul and
spirit are of one nature but of distinct substance . . .
as the Son and the Spirit in the blessed Trinity are of
one nature with the Father, but still not the same
hypostases.   The soul is related to the spirit, as the
life to the principle of life, and as the effect to that
which produces it; as the brute soul is related to the
absolute spirit which brooded over the waters of chaos." [3]
He quotes from Justin that as the body is the house of
the soul, so the soul is the house of the spirit; from
Irenæus, that the soul is the tabernacle of the spirit;
but his main and favourite analogy is that the human
soul is related to the human spirit, as the divine *Doxa*
is related to the triune divine nature.   The spirit is
the in-breathing of the Godhead, the soul is the out-
breathing of the spirit.   The spirit is *spiritus spiratus*,
and, as *spiritus spirans*, endows the body with soul.

[1] *System der biblischen Psychologie*, 2te Aufl. pp. 90–92 (Leipzig, 1861).
[2] *Ibid*. Vorrede, p. 5.   [3] *Ibid*. p. 96.

The spirit is the internal of the soul, the soul is the external of the spirit. In the Old Testament the soul is also called simply " the glory " (*Chavod*),[1] for the spirit is the image of the triune Godhead, but the soul is the copy of this image, and relates itself to the spirit as the "seven spirits" (Rev. iv. 5) are related to the Spirit of God.[2]

So much for his explanations and analogies. The main proofs he adduces for a scriptural trichotomy in the sense now explained are the two classic passages, 1 Thess. v. 23 and Heb. iv. 12. On the first of these, he virtually gives up the tripartite view. " If any one prefers to say that by *pneuma* and *psyche* the apostle is distinguishing the internal condition of man's life, and especially of the Christian's life in respect of two several relations, even this would not be untrue. For the three constituents of our nature, which he distinguishes, are in no wise three essentially distinct things. Either spirit and soul, or soul and body, belong to one another, as of like nature, and the apostle's view is thus, in the final result, certainly dichotomic. Yet it would scarcely be consistent to attribute to him the meaning that spirit and soul are only two several relations of that essentially similar inner nature, and not two distinct constituents. It is certain that Paul distinguishes three constituents of man's nature, to each of which, in its way, the work of sanctifying grace extends."[3] On Heb. iv. 12, he makes the exegetically happy suggestion that there is

---

[1] Gen. xlix. 6 ; Ps. vii. 6, xvi. 9, xxx. 13, lvii. 9, cviii. 2 (*orig.*).

[2] Pp. 97, 98 of *Bibl. Psych.*, or pp. 117, 119 of Clark's Transl.

[3] *Ibid.* p. 91 ; cf. Transl. p. 110.

a parallel in the passage between the sensuous and the supersensuous in man, and that both are here represented as bipartite; "soul and spirit," in the one standing, over against "joints and marrow," in the other. "I maintain," he says, referring the reader to his commentary, *in loc.*, "that the writer ascribes to the word of God a dividing activity of an ethical sort which extends to the whole spiritual-psychical, and corporeal constitution of man; and that he regards as bipartite the unseen and supersensible constituent, as well as that which is sensuous and apparent to the senses, inasmuch as he distinguishes soul from spirit in the former, and in the latter, 'the joints,' which minister to the life of motion, from 'the marrow,' which ministers to that of sensation."[1] Clearly this exegesis favours the conclusion that soul and spirit are two several functions or aspects of the inner life of man, as the organs of motion and sensation are distinguishable parts of his corporeal being, but not distinct natures. Delitzsch has thus declared himself against the Tripartite theory. He even goes further, and guards against the current misapprehension that soul and spirit are intended to represent lower and higher divisions of the mental faculties. "The distinction," he says, "of so-called higher and lower powers of the soul has, no doubt, its substantial truth, witnessed for also by Scripture; but, for the rest, the false trichotomy consists exactly in that way of distinguishing soul and spirit, which refers these two to distinct departments of being. There is no special need of a refutation of this trichotomy from

[1] *Bibl. Psych.*, p. 92; Transl. p. 111.

Scripture, for it is absolutely incapable of being established on scriptural authority. Since *psyche*, according
to the *usus loquendi* of all the Bible books, frequently
denotes the entire inward nature of man; frequently,
also, the 'person' designated according to the whole
inner and outer life; since it oftener says that man
consists of body and soul, than that he consists of body
and spirit, the soul (in the Bible sense of the word)
cannot possibly belong to the nature-side of man as a
thing of distinct essence of the spirit. . . . We maintain
the dualism of nature and spirit as strenuously as we
maintain the dualism of God and the world, and accordingly regard the body and the spirit of man as being of
distinct natures. But the soul belongs to the side of
the spirit. To maintain an essential distinction between
a human nature-soul and the thinking human spirit is a
construction contrary to Scripture and to experience." [1]
All this is clear and convincing. How the author
reconciles it with his repeated assertion that soul and
spirit, though of one nature, are yet distinct substances,
it is not for us to say.

The late Dr. J. T. Beck, of Tübingen, was much earlier
in this field than Delitzsch, the substance of his treatise
—*Outlines of Biblical Psychology*—having been delivered
to a semi-academic audience more than fifty years ago.
The work, rendered accessible in English so late as 1877,
appears to have undergone very little modification since
its first issue in 1843. It abounds in subtle and original
remarks. The exegesis is keen and accurate; but the

---

[1] *Bibl. Psych.*, pp. 93, 94; cf. Transl. pp. 113, 114 (which, however,
requires frequent correction).

historical method of treating Scripture and its ideas is entirely disregarded. The Bible is throughout quoted as if the whole had been written contemporaneously, and as if every text, in which a psychological word occurs, bore with equal directness on the nature of the soul. He, like Delitzsch, feels that the Scripture view of man's nature is at root dichotomic, but his account of the tripartite usage is clearer and more attractive. Man is, according to him, made up of " body " and " spirit," but the unity or personality thus formed is in the Bible designated by " soul." The following paragraphs give his view in brief: Body and spirit are the two radically distinct elements or principles. Soul is that which unifies them: derived from the inbreathing of the spirit, formed by the union of the breath of God's Spirit with the body (Gen. ii. 7), it yet constitutes, or is identical with the human personality. Man *is* soul ; he possesses body and spirit. " So even for the individual life, spirit forms the principle and the power by which life persists ; soul forms the seat, guide, and holder of it, while body is its vessel and organ. The three are specifically different, but they exist only in connection with one another. The proper foundation of human nature, formed as it is out of spirit and earth,—the Ego or Subject in the strict sense of the word,—is the soul, which connects the inward vital power of the spirit with the outward vital organ of the body, forming the two into one living individuality." [1]

Again : " The soul has the spirit in and above it, the body by and about it. Thus there is a double

[1] *Umriss der bibl. Seelenlehre*, p. 35.

sphere of life and activity (a spiritual and a corporeal) existing together in one organism and in one economy. This indicates a point of unity, as the life-centre which forms a meeting-place and source for the life-streams as they flow from within outwards, and from without inwards, in their fulness and force, both spiritual and corporeal. From this function, the centre-point has its significance and its special organic property. This office Scripture ascribes to the heart." [1] Similarly, Oehler speaks, and with still greater distinctness : " In the soul which sprang from the spirit and exists continually through it, lies the individuality—in the case of man his personality,—his self, his Ego ; because man *is* not *Ruach* (spirit), but *has* it,—he *is* Soul. . . . From all it is clear that the Old Testament does not teach a trichotomy of the human being, in the sense of body, soul, and spirit being originally three co-ordinate elements of man ; rather the whole man is included in the *Basar* (flesh) and *Nephesh* (soul) which spring from the union of the *Ruach* with matter. The *Ruach* forms partly the substance of the soul individualised in it, and partly, after the soul is established, the power and endowments which flow into it and can be withdrawn from it." [2] It is plain, then, that even defenders of a biblical trichotomy so strenuous as Beck and Delitzsch do not understand it to imply a tripartite nature. It is not two separate inner natures or essentially distinct life-principles that they find in soul and spirit. " We thoroughly agree,"

---

[1] *Umriss der bibl. Seelenlehre*, p. 70.

[2] *Theology of the Old Testament*, vol. i. pp. 218, 219 (Clark, Edin., 1874).

says Delitzsch, "in this respect with Aquinas, when he
declares it to be impossible that in one man there can
be several essentially different souls. There is one only
which discharges the function of growth, sensation, and
intellect." [1] Thus their position does not practically
differ from that of the large number of writers, both in
this country and on the Continent, who understand the
biblical distinction between soul and spirit as expressing
two aspects or functions of man's one inward nature.

As has been already indicated, the writers who in this
country entirely carry out the Tripartite scheme of interpretation are neither many nor of great weight. Their
contention is, moreover, connected with certain theological views which they seek to ground on their peculiar
exegesis. This theology will call for remark at several
points of our subsequent discussion. Here it is relevant
to give a brief account, once for all, of their scheme,
drawn chiefly from the work of Mr. Heard,—a book
abounding in vigorous strokes of thought, and of considerable value on one important aspect of our theme,
notwithstanding the extremeness of the thesis which it
seeks to maintain. This author claims that "the trichotomy of human nature into spirit, soul, and body is part
of that wisdom 'hidden' from man, till it was taught us
by God in His Word." [2] He claims further to have made
out from Scripture, that the trichotomy amounts to a
divine discovery that "Man is a tripartite hypostasis—
a union of *three*, not of *two* natures only." [3] With this
simple key he proposes to unlock the main positions of

---

[1] Quoted, *Bibl. Psych.* p. 94.
[2] *Tripartite Nature* (Preface), p. 10.　　　[3] *Ibid.* (Summary), p. 388.

Scripture as to man's Original Standing, the Fall, Regeneration, the Intermediate State, and the Future Glory.

Out of the union of three natures in one person result two tendencies, the flesh and the spirit. "Soul," the union point between "spirit" and "body," was created free to choose to which of these two opposite poles it would be attracted. The equilibrium between flesh and spirit is the state in which man was created, and which he lost by the fall. Adam was created innocent and capable of becoming holy, endowed with inherent capacities for becoming spiritual, capable of becoming pneumatical through the native powers of the *pneuma*. This was the sense in which man was made in the divine image.

The fall was an inclination given to the whole nature of Adam in the direction of the flesh, by which the spirit or image of God was deadened in him; and this bias to evil descends to his posterity. There is also transmitted the germ or remains of the fallen *pneuma* (variously described by our author as a dead organ, a rudimentary organ without corresponding function, or a bare spiritual capacity); an integral part of man's nature which could not be destroyed by the fall, and which still makes itself felt as conscience. It is proposed by this theory to resolve the quarrel of fourteen centuries' standing between the Augustinian and Pelagian view of man's present natural state. It proposes a return to the position on this subject said to have been held by the Greek Fathers in consequence of their attending to the distinction between *pneuma* and *psyche*—a position lost to Latin theology by the obliteration of the distinction, and which the Reformers, Lutheran and Calvinistic alike, failed to restore.   Any account of original sin from a dichotomic point of view is held to make more difficulties than it solves.   Upon the bipartite hypothesis of man's being, if original sin be something positive, it must be a transmitted *virus*, which, like a physical disease, should either have worn itself out or should wear out the race.   The *reductio ad absurdum* of the Augustinian position was the view of Flacius Illyricus that original sin corrupted the nature of the soul.   The negative or privative idea of birth-sin is quite sufficient to explain the facts of the case, but still only upon the tripartite view of man. For the privative idea when applied on a bipartite psychology results in the utterly insufficient theory of the Pelagian.   A far more serious defect, than Pelagians allow, can alone account for the facts of human nature as we see them ; that is, the defect of the *pneuma*.   When Adam fell, God withdrew from him the presence of His Holy Spirit, and thus the *pneuma* fell back into a dim and depraved state of conscience toward God.   We need not suppose more than this fatal defect allowed to continue, and Adam to propagate a race under the unspiritual condition into which he had fallen, and we have enough to account for the condition of man as we see him now.   Original sin is by the help of this psychology seen to be privative only, but so serious in its privation as defect of the regulative or sovereign *pneuma*—a defect which sufficiently accounts for universal depravity.

This dormant existence of the *pneuma* in the natural man is further insisted on as giving us assurance of the possibility of regeneration or conversion, and insight into its method. Were the *pneuma* in man supreme, as by his constitution it ought to be, there would be no need of regeneration. As Butler says of it under the name of conscience, " had it power as it had manifest authority, it would absolutely govern the world "; on the other hand, were it wholly obliterated, regeneration would be impossible. Men would be beyond the reach of redemption, as devils are with reason supposed to be. Thus the rudimentary existence of the *pneuma* in all men in their unconverted state is the ground of the possibility of their recovery by grace. In the same way this theory suggests the possibility and mode of sanctification. The Evangelical view of fallen human nature is said to land in a dilemma those who hold man as a compound of soul and body only. For if the immaterial nature of man is wholly corrupt, desperately wicked, and that nature is a unit, no *nidus* in human nature is reserved into which the Divine Spirit can descend and purify all within. How can a good thing come out of an evil ? Upon this view the heart is desperately wicked, and remains so, even in the regenerate, who nevertheless are led by the Spirit of God, and walk not after the flesh but after the Spirit. How this can be is as unexplained as how a deaf man can hear, or a lame man can walk. Let but the distinction between *psyche* and *pneuma* be seen, and all is clear and consistent. The *pysche* is like the flesh prone to evil, and remains so even in the regenerate. But the *pneuma*—the God-like in man—is not prone to evil, indeed it cannot sin. Its tendency is naturally upwards to God. Regeneration, then, is the quickening of this *pneuma*. Sanctification is the carrying on of that which conversion began. Conversion may be dated either from the first moment of conviction by the law (Rom. vii. 9), or from the time when the *pneuma* is practically acknowledged to be the master principle, and our members are yielded as instruments of righteousness unto God. The gradual character of sanctification and the conflict implied in it thus explains itself. It is the working out of that which was begun at conversion, The seminal principle, then quickened, grows and asserts its presence by asserting its mastery over the lower part of our nature, until the true harmony of man's constitution, spirit, soul, and body, overturned by the fall, is completely restored.

When it enters on questions connected with the future life, this tripartite theory breaks up in confusion. Its supporters are hopelessly divided among themselves. Mr. Heard treats the moral and metaphysical arguments for a future life with respect. He considers them to be presumptions, and presages rather than proofs, intimations more than arguments. But to Mr. Edward White,[1] the doctrine of the soul's immortality is the root of all evil in theology. Since the Fall, man naturally goes to nothing at death. Mr. Heard knows that when the early Fathers speak of the mortality of the *psyche*, they may fairly be taken "to mean no more than this, that the existence of the wicked in the place of punishment depends on the appointment of God, not on the necessary immortality of the soul." Of the soul as the seat of self-consciousness, he will affirm neither mortality nor immor-

[1] *Life in Christ*, 3rd Edition (Elliot Stock, 1878).

tality. He thinks the soul or self-consciousness can only exist through its union with the spirit or God-consciousness, so that the proof of the life everlasting must rest, not on the argument for the natural immortality of the *psyche* (who argues for this ?), but on the gift of eternal life to the *pneuma*, when quickened and renewed in the image of God. But he admits that there may be an evil-possessed *pneuma* in man as well as a divinely quickened *pneuma*. The duration of punishment and malignity of evil must bear some proportion to each other. So far, therefore, from denying eternal punishment, he declares that Universalism seems to shut its eyes to all those passages which speak of spiritual wickedness. He wishes to discover some middle truth between the Augustinian theory of a *massa perditionis*, the undistinguishable misery of all out of Christ, and the Universalist doctrine that all punishment is remedial. He concludes with Bengel that the doctrine of final retribution is not one fit for discussion.

All this is treated in a much less tentative way by Mr. White. Having started with the proposition that the Fall changed man's constitution to one perishable at death, like the lower animals; having set out with the bold general denial of man's natural immortality, and yet being loyal enough to Scripture to preach judgment to come for all mankind, he is in sore straits to find a ground for the survival of the impenitent. For the eternal life of the saved he finds sufficient ground in their union to Christ, the act of regeneration having changed their constitution from mortality to immortality. But for the rest, he is compelled to say that it

6

is the incarnation and work of the Redeemer which
secures their reservation to future punishment, though
there is for them no continuous or immortal existence in
the world to come.   Some disciples of the school seem
to imagine that the trichotomy affords ground for a solution of the terrible problem.   They apply it in a very
crude and simple fashion.   Since natural men have only
the *psyche*, and since the *pneuma* is added or bestowed
only in regeneration, immortal existence belongs to those
alone who are possessed of the *pneuma*.   All others by
and by pass into nothing by the very law of their nature.
But this denial of the *pneuma* altogether, as an element
of being, to natural men, this addition of it as a faculty
in the case of the regenerate, this attempt, in short, to
construct an eschatology out-of-hand, upon the basis of
the tripartite theory, is too obviously irreconcilable with
fidelity to Scripture to command the support of the
present leader of the school.   He is aiming at the same
conclusion, namely, that none but those who are in Christ
live for ever.   But he cannot be content so to snatch at
it.   How little Mr. White really makes of the trichotomy
will be seen in his succinct and fair statement of the
question at pp. 274–279 of his *Life in Christ*.   He sees
clearly that no ontological distinction is implied in the
difference between *psyche* and *pneuma* ; consequently he
is shut up to assume that by the *pneuma* in regeneration
our Lord meant the " spiritual and eternal *life* secured
by the indwelling of the Holy Spirit, not the addition of
a wholly new faculty to humanity."

The great fault of this scheme of thought is that no
ground is laid for these revolutionary conclusions in any

careful synopsis of Bible usage in regard to the terms
soul and spirit. That there is a meaning in the usage
is seen, and more than a glimpse is got in Mr. Heard's
treatise of the distinguishing feature in biblical psychology, namely, the supreme place it assigns to *spirit* in the
human constitution, and the close relation of " spirit " in
man to the Spirit of God. But there is no attempt
made to justify the assumption that Scripture intends
by these two terms two essentially distinct natures or
elements in man's inner being. Consequently the whole
scheme is built up in defiance of exegesis. What conception of the trichotomy pervades the treatise is not
certainly the coarse one often attributed to the school,[1] but
is more akin to that of Beck. Often no more appears
to be claimed for the distinction between soul and spirit
than one of poise, or point of view ; but this is only one
of many inconsistencies in the treatment. What is made
out of the scheme, theologically, has all the character of
a foregone conclusion, supported by reasonings that are
largely " special pleadings."

Since, then, this endeavour to found a rigid tripartition of human nature upon the biblical antithesis of
" soul " and " spirit," breaks down, let us turn to those
interpretations of it which are satisfied with less. But
when we examine the views of those who maintain that
the distinction, though something less than that of two
separate natures, is yet something like that of two
departments in man's inner nature, we find much
diversity in the mode of construing the distinction.
Some tell us, with Liddon, that *pneuma* represents the

[1] See *ante*, p. 68.

higher region of self-conscious spirit and self-determining will, *psyche*, the lower region of appetite, perception, imagination, memory; the former that which belongs to man as man, the latter that which, in the main, is common to him with the brute.[1] Bishop Ellicott puts it thus : " The spirit may be regarded more as the realm of the intellectual forces, and the shrine of the Holy Ghost; the soul may be regarded more as the region of the feelings, affections, and impulses, of all that peculiarly individualises and personifies." Body, soul, and spirit he holds to be " the three component parts of human nature."[2] Similarly, Bishop Lightfoot holds that spirit, as the principle of the higher life, is distinguished from the soul, the seat of the affections and passions.[3] Lünemann thinks that *pneuma* describes the higher and purely spiritual side of the inner life, elsewhere called by Paul the *nous*, or reason; *psyche*, the lower side, which comes into contact with the region of the senses.[4] All these writers, it will be noticed, follow the idea of Olshausen quoted above, that the distinction is one of a higher and lower faculty in the mental or incorporeal region. Others, again, make all three members of the trichotomy to be figurative differentiations of internal human phenomena. They take the term " body " to indicate those appetites which we have in common with the brutes ; " soul," to denote our moral and intellectual faculties, directed only towards objects of this world; and spirit for the same, directed towards God and

---

[1] *Some Elements of Religion*, p. 92 (Lond., 1873).
[2] *Destiny of the Creature*, p. 123.   [3] See on Phil. i. 27.
[4] See on 1 Thess. v. 23, in his New Testament Commentary (Meyer's).

heavenly things.[1] Not greatly different from this last, but more succinctly expressed, is the view of Auberlen: "Body, soul, and spirit are nothing else than the real basis of the three ideal elements of man's being—world-consciousness, self-consciousness, and God-consciousness."[2]

Now, it would be easy to confute each and all of these proposed biblical trisections of human nature, by confronting them with numerous passages of Scripture which will not consist with them. Especially is this the case with the above-quoted attempts to find a psychological analysis in the use of the two leading terms of the trichotomy. That "soul" and "spirit" denote distinct natures in man, or, as Delitzsch has it, separable elements of one nature, or even, as the well-known commentators above quoted seem to say, distinct faculties, or departments of the inner man, implies a kind of analysis which is out of harmony with biblical thought, and will not stand upon an impartial examination of the whole Scripture usage. On the other hand, to assume that, in the special passages to be explained, we have nothing more than rhetorical accumulation of terms, will not satisfy the facts. It is easy to prove, from the Old Testament Apocrypha, and from the writings of Philo and Josephus, that, by their time, a definite use of the terms "soul" and "spirit" had passed into psychological language, and even into current popular speech. In the New Testament usage of these terms, therefore, we must recognise a real meaning for

---

[1] Dr. T. Arnold, as quoted by Heard, *Tripartite Nature*, p. 175, Note.
[2] Art. "Geist," Herzog, *Real Encyc.* (1st Edition, iv. 729).

which the old parallelism of Hebrew poetry will not alone account.[1] Before proceeding to examine the origin and explanation of this usage, we may here sum up what has already appeared on the face of Scripture to be its mode of viewing human nature as *one*, as *dual*, or as *trinal*. There is evidence enough to show that while maintaining with strong consistency the *Unity* of the human being, Scripture confirms the usual *dual* conception that his two natures are flesh and spirit, or soul and body, yet makes use quite consistently of a *trichotomy* depending on a distinction between soul and spirit, which distinction, in some New Testament passages (especially the Pauline), is charged with a religious or doctrinal significance. "Anyone who does not force on Scripture a dogmatic system, must acknowledge that it speaks *dichotomously* of the parts viewed in themselves, *trichotomously* of the living reality, but all through so as to guard the fact that human nature is built upon a plan of unity."[2]

---

[1] In commenting on 1 Thess. v. 23, Lünemann says: "The totality of man is here divided into three parts. We are not to assume that this trichotomy has a purely rhetorical signification, since, elsewhere, Paul also definitely distinguishes *pneuma* and *psyche*. The origin of the Trichotomy is Platonic, but Paul has it, not from the language of Plato and his scholars, but from the current language of society, into which it had passed out of the narrow circle of the schools."

[2] From a lecture of Dr. von Zezschwitz, *Profangräcität und biblischer Sprachgeist* (Leipzig, 1859), repeatedly referred to by Delitzsch in his *Biblical Psychology* ; quoted also by Prof. Dickson in a Note at p. 177 of his Baird Lecture (Glasgow, 1893).

CHAPTER V

THE so-called Trichotomy rests, as we have seen, not so much upon the comparatively rare use in Scripture of the three terms together—body, soul, and spirit—as upon the pervading use of the two latter terms for the interior life. This usage, therefore, requires explanation. The too common attempt to render them analytically, as discriminating lower and higher faculties, has broken down. It is plainly not justified by consistent exegesis. Thus, baffled exegetes usually retreat upon the unsatisfactory explanation that there is nothing more in the usage of "soul and spirit," than poetic parallelism. Let us try the historical, instead of the analytic method. Let us trace the rise and current of the usage. It can be shown how the simpler and more popular antithesis, in the Hebrew Scriptures, passed at length into a sharper and more theological discrimination, in the New Testament Epistles, of "soul" and "soulish," from "spirit" and "spiritual." Thus we shall arrive, not only at the exact force of the distinction, but at the causes and uses of it, and see how such writers as St. Paul adapted this Old Testament phraseology to express the enlarged ideas with which the spirit of New Testament revelation had furnished them. We come therefore to—

II. THE HISTORICAL EXPLANATION.—Let us begin with the use of both terms in their primary sense, or in relation to physical life. To this, both *Pneuma* and *Psyche*, like *Ruach* and *Nephesh*, of which they are the Greek equivalents, originally refer. *Ruach* and *Nephesh* are easily distinguished in this primal reference. *Nephesh* is the subject or bearer of life. *Ruach* is the principle of life; so that in all the Old Testament references to the origin of living beings, we distinguish *Nephesh* as life constituted in the creature, from *Ruach*, as life bestowed by the Creator. The life indicated by both these terms is that of man and the lower animals alike. A " living soul " is a living creature in general, or an animated being. It is used in Gen. i. 30 of every creature that has life, and in Gen. ii. 7 to express the result, even in man, of the divine creative breath. So also *Ruach* and its kindred term *Neshamah* are used for the principle of life, in man and brute alike. It is the " *Nishmath* of life " that makes man a living soul (Gen. ii. 7). It is the " *Ruach* of life " that animates all the creatures who were threatened by the flood (vi. 17), and all those who entered into the ark (vii. 15). It is the " *Nishmath-ruach* of life " which denotes those who perished in the waters (vii. 22). These passages prove that no distinction is made in Genesis between the life-principle in animals generally and in man. But, what is of more importance, they call attention to a usage which is practically uniform, of putting " spirit " (*Ruach* or *Neshamah*) for the animating principle, and " soul," or "living soul" (*Nephesh hayyah*) for the animated result. This primary distinction of the two terms, when applied to physical life, has passed over from the Hebrew of the Old Testament to their Greek equivalents in the New Testament, and suggests a reason for their respective employment, even where the meaning goes beyond the merely physical. If *psyche* thus means the entire being as a constituted life, we see why it is used in such an expression as that of John x. 11, "He giveth His life (*psyche*, not *zoe* nor *pneuma*) for the sheep." If *pneuma* is the life-principle bestowed by and belonging to God, we see its propriety in John xix. 30, "He gave up the ghost (*pneuma*)."

When we pass from this primary application of these two terms to a higher, in which they refer not to physical life merely, but to the life of the mind, both denote almost equally and indifferently the inner nature of man as distinguished from the corporeal. For this purpose they are used throughout the Old Testament, and generally even in the New Testament, with no sharp distinction, but are, rather, freely interchanged and combined to express the whole inward nature. This appears upon examination of three classes of passages: (*a*) Those where each term is used alone, as, "Why is thy *spirit* (*ruach*) so sad?" "Why art thou cast down, my soul (*nephesh*)?"[1] "Jesus was troubled in spirit" (*pneuma*). "My soul (*psyche*) is exceeding sorrowful."[2] (*b*) In those where either term is joined with body to express entire human nature: "To destroy both soul (*psyche*) and body"; "The body without the spirit

---

[1] 1 Kings xxi. 5; Ps. xlii. 11.   [2] John xiii. 21, Matt. xxvi. 28.

(*pneuma*) is dead." [1] (*c*) Those in which the two terms occur together, in the manner of other parallel terms of Hebrew poetry: "With my soul (*nephesh*) have I desired Thee in the night; yea, with my spirit (*ruach*) within me will I seek Thee early." [2] "My soul (*psyche*) doth magnify the Lord, and my spirit (*pneuma*) hath rejoiced in God my Saviour." [3] "Stand fast in one spirit (*pneuma*), with one soul (*psyche*), striving for the faith of the gospel." [4] These last passages render it quite impossible to hold that "spirit" can mean exclusively or mainly the Godward side of man's inner nature, and "soul" the rational or earthward. The terms are parallel, or practically equivalent, expressions for the inner life as contrasted with the outer or bodily life; and the usage, on the whole, makes for the ordinary twofold view of human nature, and not at all for any tripartite theory.[5]

No doubt the underlying distinction found in the primary or physical application of the two terms gives colour and propriety to their usage, and, when firmly grasped, prepares us to understand the expanded meaning which they receive in the special or Pauline passages yet to be considered. All through Scripture, "spirit" denotes life as coming from God, "soul" denotes life as

---

[1] Matt. x. 38, Jas. ii. 26. [2] Isa. xxvi. 9.
[3] Luke i. 46, 47. [4] Phil. i. 27 (R.V.).
[5] After examining the terms as we have done, Weiss, in his *New Testament Theology* (vol. i. pp. 123–125, Clark's transl.) concludes thus: "It follows that the nature of man is conceived of as dichotomous, and that all distinctions between *psyche* and *pneuma*, in the sense of a trichotomy such as Delitzsch had adopted, are arbitrary. Similarly, Oehler, as quoted *ante*, p. 75, who, however, holds the distinction between soul and spirit which we are now tracing to be real, and of value.

constituted in the man. Consequently, when the individual life is to be made emphatic "soul" is used. "Soul," in Scripture, freely denotes persons. "My soul" is the Ego, the self, and when used, like "heart," for the inner man, and even for the feelings, has reference always to the special individuality. "Spirit," on the other hand, seldom or never used to denote the individual human being in this life, is primarily that imparted power by which the individual lives. It fitly denotes, therefore, on occasion, when used as a psychological term, the innermost of the inner life, the higher aspect of the self or personality. While therefore we see that the two terms are used over the breadth of Scripture as parallel expressions for the inner life, there is never wanting a certain difference of poise, which can be accentuated when required. The inner nature is named "soul," "after its special, individual life," and "spirit" "after the living power which forms the condition of its special character." [1]

Thus far there is no apparent design in the use of these two terms, throughout the Scripture generally, to analyse the constituents of man's inner being into two parts, natures, or elements. Not only would such analysis be foreign, as we have said, to the Bible way of thinking, but the usage has now been sufficiently accounted for, without the violent hypothesis of the " Tripartite" nature. The purpose of the double phrase, " soul and spirit," is, at most, to present the one indi-

---

[1] These two phrases are quoted by Oehler from von Hofmann (*Schrift-beweis*, i. p. 296), who uses *bedingtes Einzelleben* for "soul," and *bedingende Lebensmacht* for "spirit."

visible thinking and feeling man in two diverse aspects, according as these two terms originally suggest his life viewed from two different points. Their use, therefore, in the older Scriptures and generally, cannot be held as giving us a psychological analysis of human nature. It is quite certain, however, that in the period between the production of most of the Old Testament writings and those of the New Testament, a use of *psyche* and *pneuma* had sprung up, under the Alexandrian influences, which led some of the apocryphal writers—as well as the Seventy—to attribute to the sacred books such an analysis of man's nature—a trichotomy, in short, corresponding to that of Plato, though not identical with it. It is as undoubted that these combined influences—the Greek philosophy and the later Jewish schools—led the Christian writers of the early centuries to adopt the analysis as if it had been sanctioned by Scripture; hence also its revival in the cruder forms of recent biblical psychology.

Apart from this historical origin, and far more worthy of attention, is the fact that in a special set of New Testament passages there emerges a particular usage of the two terms and their congeners in a religious application, not unconnected with their original force, but fraught with a distinct and additional meaning. In these passages—mainly though not exclusively Pauline —it is plain, first of all, that the adjective *psychic*, or " soulish," [1] has taken on a meaning, not obvious in its root-word. It has acquired a force almost equivalent to " carnal." In Jas. iii. 15 (*e.g.*) a wisdom is spoken which

---

[1] $\psi\upsilon\chi\iota\kappa\delta s$.

is " earthly, soulish (sensual, R.V.), devilish." Of certain predicted opponents of the gospel it is said, in Jude 19, that " they are soulish (sensual, marg. *natural* or *animal*, R.V.), not having the Spirit." St. Paul terms the unregenerate, who cannot discern the things of the Spirit of God, " a soulish man " (1 Cor. ii. 14). The " body " which we wear at present—" the body of our humiliation," as he once calls it (Phil. iii. 20),—that which is of the earth earthy, is a " soulish " body, and shall be sown in the grave as such (1 Cor. xv. 44). On the other hand, the corresponding adjective " pneumatic," or " spiritual,"[1] has, in the parallel passages, come to denote, not what belongs to the natural, human *pneuma*, but what belongs to the *Pneuma* in the religious sense, the Spirit of God or the spirit of the regenerate life. Indeed, this word in its frequent use throughout the New Testament always denotes life and activity that are under the influence of the Spirit of grace.[2] In the classic Pauline passages, however—1 Cor. ii. 11–16 and xv. 42–47—it is used as the antithesis, not to *sarkic* or carnal, as sometimes elsewhere, but to *psychic* or soulish. It is this usage which specially claims attention and requires to be accounted for. No doubt, even in St. Paul's Epistles, " spirit " also occurs in the older meaning. For example, in the same context (1 Cor. ii. 11), the natural human *pneuma* is referred to as the faculty of self-consciousness in man, corresponding to the Divine *Pneuma* as the self-searching and self-explaining Power within the Godhead.

---

[1] πνευματικός.

[2] With the single exception of Eph. vi. 12, where " spiritualities " of exactly the opposite moral character are spoken of.

But the contrast or antithesis with which we are dealing is plainly one between human nature in its own
native elements and human nature under the higher
power which has entered it in the New Birth. The
former is *psychic*, the latter is *pneumatic*. The psychical
or "soulish" man is man as nature now constitutes him,
and as sin has infected him. His own mere wisdom may
therefore be "psychic" as allied to earthly, or even
worse (Jas. iii. 15). As such, he is unable to receive the
things of the Spirit of God, for these are only spiritually
discerned. The pneumatic or spiritual man, again, is
man as grace has re-constituted him, and as God's Spirit
dwells in him and bestows gifts upon him (1 Cor. ii. 15).
He is able to judge spiritual things. He receives
spiritual blessings in the heavenlies (Eph. i. 3). He is
to increase in spiritual understanding (Col. i. 9). He
is to offer spiritual sacrifices (1 Pet. ii. 5). In the progress of redemption, he shall exchange a body "psychical" or "natural," which he has in common with all men
as derived from Adam, for a body spiritual or glorified,
adapted to his new nature, and fashioned like unto the
glorious body of his Lord. For the first head of the
race was made a living *psyche*; the Second Adam is a
life-giving *Pneuma* (1 Cor. xv. 44–47).

Thus far the contrast between psychical and spiritual
in these special passages is an undeniable and intelligible
usage. The last quotation suggests that the antithesis
thus peculiarly conceived and applied had come, in the
mind of some New Testament writers, to extend its force
back to the older and original antithesis between "soul"
and "spirit" as constituents of man's created nature.

Such passages as Heb. iv. 12 and 1 Thess. v. 23 may therefore be explained upon the same implied antithesis. The "Hebrews" passage will then mean, either that the word of God divides and discriminates between what is psychical and what is spiritual; or, that it penetrates both regions of human nature. The "Thessalonians" passage will mean that the Christian is to be sanctified wholly in his threefold life, the physical life of the body, the individual life of the soul, and the inner life of the spirit.

Now comes the question, whence this undeniably religious or theological distinction, in these passages, between the psychical or natural and the spiritual or regenerate? The Old Testament use of soul and spirit was non-analytic and simple, as opposed to philosophical, and this use is followed by our Lord and the New Testament writers generally.[1] The special or Pauline usage (as it may be called) may no doubt have been influenced by the would-be philosophic usage of these terms by Josephus and Philo,—must have been so, indeed, if, as is commonly alleged, that use had become a habit with cultured Jewish writers of the period. But though St. Paul may be said to have adopted this cultured language of the Jewish schools, he was, in point of fact, redeeming the Old Testament terms out of their hands for his new purpose. The parallel between his trichotomy and that of the Platonists and Stoics is appreciable, but the differ-

---

[1] Weiss points out that the psychological ideas directly borrowed from the Old Testament are the same in the whole of the New Testament, "*Up till the peculiar transformation which they undergo in the Pauline system,*" *N. T. Theologie*, 1 Theil, sec. 27, a sentence curiously mistranslated in the English edition.

ence is more important. Their tripartition was a mode of accounting for divergent moral forces in man, for the subjugation in him of what is best by what is worst. It did so by assuming that there was in his constitution a physical element eternally opposed to the divine. In the Old Testament terms adopted by St. Paul there was no such taint. They were fitted to do a better thing than account for man's moral failure, namely, to express the new force that had entered into humanity for its redemption. One of these terms especially, "spirit" (*pneuma*), had never been debased by ethnic thought. It was never used in the Greek psychology. Even Plato's highest human principle is not *pneuma*, but *nous*, and its derivatives. While therefore the ethical distinction between "soulish" and "spiritual" may have had some dim parallel in Græco-Jewish philosophy, the terms themselves were biblical. The meaning was true at once to the older biblical psychology, and enlarged with the fulness of the new revelation. Instead of being rooted in a philosophical analysis of the constituents of human nature, the idea sprang from two disclosures of Christ's own teaching. One is His clear revelation of the personality of the Holy Spirit; the other is that of the spiritual union of redeemed humanity with God, through Jesus Christ.[1] The new life or nature thus originated, St. Paul variously terms "the new man," the "new creature," "the inner man," but especially "the spirit" and "spiritual," as contrasted with the psychical or carnal. Why this last term became technical or signal in this topic is evident. With a rare felicity the same

[1] See John xiv. xv. xvi. *passim.*

word (*ruach* of the Old Testament, *pneuma* of the New Testament) serves to denote the Spirit of God Himself, and the new spirit or life-power which He creates in the regenerate. This Pauline usage is an instance at once of the elevating influence of revelation upon language, and of that insight into the capacities and destinies of man which the progress of the revelation makes possible. According to this explanation, we do not base the Pauline psychology upon any school distinctions, Platonist, Philonian, or Stoic.[1] We recognise it as an essential part of the apostle's inspired insight into the relations of man's nature under the Christian dispensation of grace. Nevertheless, we thus see how the use of the terms "soul" and "spirit" in the Old Testament, and in the current language of the New Testament, prepared the way for this new meaning which Pauline Christianity has poured into them. The natural life as organically instituted,—the personal living being had always been denoted by the term Soul—(*nephesh* or *psyche*); life as emanating from the fountain, the divinely derived energy of the creature by the term spirit (*ruach* or *pneuma*). Thus, when a further distinction became necessary, man, as he is now produced in nature, could be described as psychical or soulish; man as born from above, pneumatical or spiritual. That is to say, the same word which expressed the God-derived natural life came to express the principle of the regenerate life, the identity of the terms answering to an underlying biblical idea, namely, that the immediate

[1] This is confirmed by such keen inquirers as Lüdemann, *Die Anthropologie des Apostels Paulus* (Kiel, 1872), and Pfleiderer, *Paulinism.* See also the vigorous argument of Dr. Dickson, *St. Paul's Use of the Terms Flesh and Spirit,* pp. 70-72, 274, 275 (Glasgow, 1883).

7

divine origination of man's being in creation lays a ground for the immediate divine renewal of his nature in redemption.[1]

NOTE TO CHAPTER V

THE TRICHOTOMY IN ITS HISTORICAL CONNECTIONS

PROCEEDING on the general principle that the historical method is the right one for the elucidation of the psychological terms of Scripture, I have endeavoured to show that a close observation of Old Testament usage will enable us to understand how the trichotomic language of the New Testament arose, and what is its exact force. But a great deal that is interesting in the way of collateral illustration of the Bible trichotomy might be got together. I am only able to add a few scattered notes on the various ancient sources which shed light on the Pauline or sacred trichotomy either by contrast or by resemblance.

As indicated in the chapter (pp. 95, 96; also *infra*, p. 129), the main parallels in ancient philosophy, though differing all of them essentially from the scriptural trichotomy, are those of the Platonic and the Stoic schools before the rise of Christianity, and of the Neo-Platonic after it. Even in the Stoic psychology, however, I am unable to find any exact parallel, except in a writer subsequent to Paul, namely, the Emperor Marcus Aurelius.

Some profess to find a trichotomy indicated by Pythagoras. If we may believe Diogenes Laërtius (viii. 20), the highest power in man according to that philosopher was that designated by the Greek term φρένες. He says: τὴν δὲ ἀνθρώπου ψυχὴν διαιρεῖσθαι τριχῆ, εἴς τε νοῦν καὶ φρένας καὶ

---

[1] Since this was first written, it has received confirmation from the exegetical acumen of the above-named scholar in his Baird Lecture, both as to the distinction between soul and spirit, and as to the originality of the latter term as a psychological factor in the biblical philosophy, see pp. 193 and 196 of *St. Paul's Use of Flesh and Spirit*.

θυμόν. Νοῦν μὲν οὖν εἶναι καὶ θυμόν καὶ ἐν τοῖς ἄλλοις ζώοις, φρένας δὲ μόνον ἐν ἀνθρώπῳ. But Olshausen, who gives this reference, adds: "I can hardly persuade myself that Pythagoras would attribute νοῦς to all living creatures." He also quotes Stobæus (*Ecl. phys.* p. 878), who assigns quite another division to Pythagoras, namely of man, εἰς λογισμον, θυμόν, καὶ ἐπιθυμίαν; but this is clearly Platonic. It is best to confess that no one knows what Pythagoras held on these subjects.

The Platonic tripartition is familiar. It consists in the assertion of three principles as constituting the inner nature of man, τὸ λογιστικόν, τὸ θυμοειδές, τὸ ἐπιθυμητικόν, the rational, irascible, and concupiscible; often also represented by ὁ λόγος, ὁ θυμός, αἱ ἐπιθυμίαι. At first sight this appears to be only a trichotomy of the soul, leaving the body out of account. It does not seem to be inconsistent with the ordinary dichotomic language which Plato also freely uses of our whole nature as made up of body and soul. But as he goes on to teach that the rational or intelligible part of the soul is immortal, necessarily partaking of eternity with those eternal ideas which it contemplates, while the two others, the irascible and concupiscible parts are mortal, we see how it has been usual to attribute to him the doctrine of three souls. Again, when we observe him saying (*Timæus*, 72 D) of the soul that a certain part is mortal and another part divine, we may more properly speak of him as teaching a doctrine of two souls in one body. Finally, when he speaks of a tripartite universe made up of νοῦς, ψυχή, σῶμα, we may consider that man, who is an image or copy of it in little, consists of the same three parts. Thus we arrive at a Platonic tripartition of man's nature into Reason, Soul, and Body.

In the *Republic*, book iv. (440, Steph.), will be found a passage where the threefold division of the soul is insisted on, τὸ λογιστικόν, τὸ θυμοειδές, τὸ ἐπιθυμητικόν. The object of the reasoning is to prove that the *second* of these principles sides with the first; that it is at war with the *third*, and is clearly distinct from them both (Οὗτος μέντοι, ἔφην, ὁ λόγος σημαίνει τὸν θυμὸν πολεμεῖν ἐνίοτε ταῖς ἐπιθυμίαις ὡς ἄλλο ὂν ἄλλῳ);

that this spirit or courage (θυμός) is on the side of reason (ξύμμαχον τῷ λόγῳ γιγνόμενον τὸν θυμόν); that the contrary is never known to take place, namely, that θυμός should be on the side of the desires when reason decides the other way. At first sight, τὸ θυμοειδές may appear to be of the order of the desires ; but now we should say the contrary, that much rather in the conflict of the soul it takes arms for the rational principle (πολὺ μᾶλλον αὐτὸ (τὸ θυμοειδές) ἐν τῇ τῆς ψυχῆς στάσει τίθεσθαι τὰ ὅπλα πρὸς τοῦ λογιστικοῦ). Still further, he goes on to make sure that τὸ θυμοειδές is distinct from τὸ λογιστικόν ; that it is not merely a kind or species of reason (λογιστικοῦ τι εἶδος), but that, as there are three classes in the state,—traders, auxiliaries, counsellors,—so there are three principles in the soul, and that this third element of courage or spirit must be distinct, and is, when uncorrupted, an auxiliary of reason (οὕτω καὶ ἐν ψυχῇ τρίτον τοῦτό ἐστι τὸ θυμοειδές, ἐπίκουρον ὂν τῷ λογιστικῷ φύσει, ἐὰν μὴ ὑπὸ κακῆς τροφῆς διαφθαρῇ). This is plain when we prove that courage (θυμός) is distinct from reason (λόγος), as we have already proved it distinct from desire (ἐπιθυμία) ; and this is proved by the case of children, who from the very first have spirit (θυμός), though they may never have reason (λόγος).

In these passages πνεῦμα never once occurs—as, indeed, it could not, having in classical Greek a totally different meaning of a merely physiological kind ; and as for ψυχή, it is used by Plato for the whole inward nature of man, as appears from the use of σῶμα for its correlative. The two master-principles above named, τὸ λογιστικὸν and τὸ θυμοειδές, as counsellor and warrior combined, are said to rule and defend the whole soul and the whole body (ὑπὲρ ἁπάσης τῆς ψυχῆς τε καὶ τοῦ σώματος). It is also evident that the τὸ λογιστικόν here does not correspond with the New Testament πνεῦμα in any sense, though it may with νοῦς. Τὸ θυμοειδές may be more like the לב, καρδία, of the Scriptures, but this too may be questioned. The parallel between αἱ ἐπιθυμίαι and the τὰ μέλεα of Paul is a good deal more close ; and an interesting question of possible parallelism arises when we take this Platonic division as on the whole a division into higher and lower powers of the soul.

Beside the above let us place that other passage in the *Republic*, book ix. (589, Steph.), where, in allegorical fashion, Plato pictures the soul as a human figure containing within it a hydra, a lion, and a smaller man. He then reasons that the noble course is that which subjects the beast to the man, or rather to the divine in man, the ignoble, that which subjects the man to the beast (τὰ μὲν καλὰ τὰ ὑπὸ τῷ ἀνθρώπῳ, μᾶλλον δὲ ἴσως τὰ ὑπὸ τῷ θείῳ τὰ θηριώδη ποιοῦντα τῆς φύσεως, αἰσχρὰ δὲ τὰ ὑπὸ τῷ ἀγρίῳ τὸ ἥμερον δουλούμενα), and asks, how would a man profit who should take money to enslave the noblest part of him to the worst? The two beasts and the inner man here, all covered by the outward form of man, answer to the three principles of the former passage. There is a slight contradiction; for he supposes here that the two lower (hydra and lion) may combine against the higher, the man, but says the wise will seek an alliance with the lion-heart. Again, the exquisite figure in the *Phædrus* (246, Steph.), where the nature of man is compared to a charioteer driving two winged horses, one of them noble and of noble origin, the other ignoble and of ignoble origin, may be held to illustrate his theory of the composite and even paradoxical constitution of man. It is usually assumed that the *Phædrus* was an early treatise. And this allegory does not easily fit into Plato's more mature scheme of man's composition. Nevertheless the passage is extremely characteristic. When taken along with the reasonings based upon the allegory, *e.g.* that such a constitution cannot be intended to be immortal, it contrasts strikingly with the simple biblical idea of the unity of man's nature. Besides these divisions of the whole inner nature of man into three principles, we find in the *Timæus* (30, Steph.), a division into νοῦς, ψυχή, and σῶμα (νοῦν μὲν ἐν ψυχῇ, ψυχὴν δὲ ἐν σώματι ξυνιστὰς τὸ πᾶν ξυνετεκταίνετο). It is true that this is given in connection with the *anima mundi*, but commentators have always understood it as referring to the human being as well. Delitzsch seems, therefore, to be mistaken in ascribing this division first to Plotinus. For the full Platonic doctrine of two souls in one body, *vide Timæus*, 69, 70.

An Aristotelic trichotomy is sometimes spoken of (*e.g.* by Delitzsch, p. 93), but it is plain that Aristotle differed fundamentally from Plato in his view of man's constitution. His subtle and profound doctrine of the ψυχή has pervaded philosophic speculation ever since his own day. He meant to conceive of ψυχή as a principle manifesting itself in an ascending scale through vegetable, animal, and human life. But his theory of its vegetative, sensitive, and noetic functions by no means favours a trichotomy. Much rather, his view of ψυχή as "the simplest actuality (ἐντελέχεια) of a physical body potentially possessing life" laid the foundation for the strict philosophical dualism which has prevailed through all the centuries of Christian thought. It may, with some appearance of plausibility, be even held to favour the monistic view of modern Positivism. It is to be noted, on the other hand, that Aristotle finds in man νοῦς παθητικός and νοῦς ποιητικός, a passive and an active intellect. And as Plato claimed immortality only for that highest of his two souls which as λόγος or νοῦς constituted the real man, so Aristotle says (*De Anim.* iii. 5), τοῦτο (*i.e.* ἀπαθὴς νοῦς) μόνον ἀθάνατον, . . . ὁ δὲ παθητικὸς νοῦς φθαρτός. Still with him these are only two modes of reason. They are not, as for Plato, several souls. According to Aristotle, the active or creative reason (νοῦς ποιητικός) is apparently impersonal. Its survival of death, its everlasting existence, is not the continued personal existence of the man. [For the bearing of Aristotle's view on the question of a future life, see Westcott's *Gospel of the Resurrection*, pp. 147–152.]

The psychology of the early Stoics seems to have been of a ruder and lower kind than either of the preceding. They assimilated man's rational activity to the activity of the senses. But they upheld the oneness of the soul's being with greater vigour than did either Plato or Aristotle. Reason, τὸ ἡγεμονικόν (otherwise called διανοητικόν, λογιστικόν, or λογισμός), is with them the primary power. From it the other parts of the soul are only derivatives. From it, like the arms of a cuttle-fish, the seven divisions of the soul reach to the body. At a later period, among the Stoics, and also among the Epicureans, this scheme appears

to have become that of the ascription to man of a rational
and an irrational, or of an intelligent and an animal soul
—a tendency which stretched far on, as we shall see, into
the philosophy of modern Europe. The most remarkable
parallel to the biblical trichotomy is that found in the
writings of the last of the Stoical philosophers, the
emperor M. Aurelius Antoninus. In his only extant
treatise, Τῶν εἰς ἑαυτὸν, βιβλία ιβ', he says : " What I am consists entirely of the fleshly and spiritual, and the chief
part," ὅ τί ποτε τοῦτό εἰμι, σαρκία ἐστὶ καὶ πνευμάτιον, καὶ τὸ
ἡγεμονικόν (lib. ii. § 2).   Again : " Body, soul, mind ; to thy
body belong senses ; to thy soul, affections ; to thy mind,
assertions (decreta)," Σῶμα, ψυχή, νοῦς· σώματος αἰσθήσεις,
ψυχῆς ὁρμαί, νοῦ δόγματα (lib. iii. § 16). Once more : " There
are three parts of which thou art composed,—the bodily,
the spiritual, and the mind," Τρία ἐστὶν ἐξ ὧν συνέστηκας,
σωμάτιον, πνευμάτιον, νοῦς (lib. xii. § 3).   It is not possible to
agree with T. Gataker (the scholarly editor, 1652) when
he says, in a note on the second of the passages quoted,
" Parilis distributio et in sacris literis reperitur 1 Thess.
v. 23, σῶμα, ψυχή, πνεῦμα qui et νοῦς, Rom. vii. 25 " ; nor
with Sir A. Grant (Ethics of Aristotle, vol. i. Essay vi.
p 297), who thinks that we find in Aurelius " the same
psychological division of man into body, soul, and spirit as
was employed by St. Paul."   To make this out it is necessary to say, as the last-quoted writer does, that the πνεῦμα
of St. Paul answers to the νοῦς or ἡγεμονικόν of Antoninus.
Now any one who follows the line of investigation we
have indicated, will see at a glance the differences between
these two trichotomic schemes.   St. Paul would totally
deny that the νοῦς is the ἡγεμονικόν.   The real governing
principle according to him is πνεῦμα, and πνεῦμα in a sense
entirely different from that in which it is used by Aurelius.
For though πνευμάτιον in the Stoic scheme is an addition to
the Platonic language, there is no change or advance upon
the Greek idea which identifies πνευμάτιον and ψυχή, whereas
everything in the scriptural scheme turns upon the natural
and moral distinction between ψυχή and πνεῦμα.   Lastly,
the σῶμα and the σάρξ of the two schemes are only seem-
ingly parallel.   The Stoic depreciates the σῶμα, considers

τὰ σαρκία as the mere prison of the mind; but there is nothing in the stoical σάρξ answering to what St. Paul understood by that term in relation to the depraved nature of man. His conception is wholly biblical.

This particular form of the Stoic psychology is later than Paul. But of any influence exercised even by earlier Stoical schools upon the Pauline psychology it is vain to speak. An Alexandrian influence would have been more probable. But Philo's trichotomy is purely Platonic, and differs, therefore, essentially from that of the apostle. Older and simpler influences, as we have seen, sufficiently account for the rise of this last. The idea of a trichotomy was rendered familiar to Paul, as to other Hebrews of his time, by the current language of philosophy, both Stoic and Alexandrian; but the form and contents of that which appears in the New Testament were moulded by Old Testament psychology, while its special terms were prepared in the Greek of the Septuagint. The Seventy were doubtless familiar with the philosophical language of the Greek schools, yet they have remained entirely true, in their translation, to the genius of the Hebrew Scriptures. Accordingly, the term νοῦς, so prominent in Greek philosophy for the higher aspect of the soul, never occurs in the Septuagint in that connection (see *infra*, p. 137). Πνεῦμα and ψυχή are of constant occurrence,—the former as the uniform translation of רוּחַ, and sometimes of נְשָׁמָה (which is also, at times, rendered by πνοή); the latter as the equivalent of נֶפֶשׁ and חַיָּה, sometimes of כָּבוֹד. The general names for body are σῶμα and σάρξ. The terms of the simple trichotomy, spirit, soul, and body, are evidently thus provided for in that version of the ancient Scriptures with which Paul was so familiar, and need not be sought in any extraneous source whatever. The application of it in the Christian system belonged to the new revelation.

It would be overstrained to build much on occasional traces of philosophical influence in the language of the Septuagint, *e.g.* Job. vii. 15, Ἀπαλλάξεις ἀπὸ πνεύματός μου τὴν ψυχήν μου, where our present Hebrew text has no such distinction; or Ps. li. 12 (Heb. ver. 14; Sept. l. 12), πνεύματι ἡγεμονικῷ στήριξόν με, where we have probably a purely undesigned coincidence with the philosophical ἡγεμονικόν. It is clearer, however, that Josephus had a favour for the current trichotomy when he paraphrases Gen. ii. 7 thus : Ἔπλασεν ὁ Θεὸς τὸν ἄνθρωπον, χοῦν ἀπὸ τῆς γῆς λαβών· καὶ πνεῦμα ἐνῆκεν αὐτῷ καὶ ψυχήν (Antiqq. I. i. β), instead of giving the simple and untechnical rendering of the Septuagint. A similar favour for what became the New Testament trichotomic usage is traceable in the Wisdom of Solomon, in such passages as xv. 11 : ῞Οτι ἡγνόησε τόν πλάσαντα αὐτὸν, καί τὸν ἐμπνεύσαντα αὐτῷ ψυχὴν ἐνεργοῦσαν, καὶ ἐμφυσήσαντα πνεῦμα ζωτικόν ; and xvi. 14 : ἐξελθὸν δὲ πνεῦμα οὐκ ἀναστρέφει, οὐδέ ἀναλύει ψυχὴν παραληφθεῖσαν. In the Apocrypha generally, the leading psychological terms are used with much the same latitude as in the Old Testament. But among other traces of Greek influence, we may reckon the more pronounced dualism of "body and soul" which begins to appear in these writings : e.g. σῶμα, ψυχή, Wisd. i. 4, 2 Macc. vi. 30, xv. 30 ; πνεῦμα, σπλάγχνα, Baruch ii. 17 ; a hint of pre-existence, Wisd. viii. 20 ; and most noticeably, the Greek notion of the body as the fetter of the soul, Wisd. ix. 15,—this last passage containing also the very terms of the later Greek trichotomy, σῶμα, ψυχή, νοῦς.

The only other illustration of a trichotomy which it is necessary to adduce from non-Christian philosophy is that of the Neo-Platonists. This was rather a trinity of the universe, however, than a tripartition of human nature. The first principle of the universe was the One (τὸ ἕν), a mysterious unity, out of which all things emanated. The second principle is that which contemplates the One and requires only it to exist. This is pure intelligence (νοῦς). The third principle is the universal soul (ψυχή), which is produced by and reposes on intelligence, as intelligence derives from the original Unity. The soul in the very power of its weakness forms to itself a body, endows blind matter with form and thought. (For an account of this tripartition, see Archer Butler's *Lectures on the History of Ancient Philosophy*, ii. p. 354 et seq.) When this scheme is applied to human nature, the soul is reckoned as the image and product of intelligence, and inferior to it, though divine. Then, the soul permeates the body as fire permeates air. It is more correct to say that the body is in the soul, than that the soul is in the body. The soul contains the body. The divine extends from the One to the soul. We might identify this system with the Stoic trichotomy, σῶμα, ψυχή, νοῦς, but the character of the Plotinian thinking was theosophic rather than philosophic. It was a bold jumble of all the philosophies, pervaded by mysticism, and intended to rival Christianity,—a mere inflated imitation, which owed all that was really new in it to the sacred thought which it obviously parodied.

To trace the history of the trichotomy in the hands of early Christian writers would be a difficult task. The whole subject of the psychology of these writers is obscure and uncertain. That the Pauline trichotomy does not appear in the Apostolic Fathers proves nothing against its acceptance in the early Church, for the range of topics and therefore of Scripture quotation, in their extant writings, is necessarily very limited. In the Greek Apologists, on the other hand, the use of a trichotomy is frequent. The Pauline terms even are easily traced. But though they use the scriptural *pneuma* and *psyche*, their thinking is really Platonic or Stoic. They protested against the results of the Platonic psychology (see Note to our final Chapter), but they could not shake themelves free of its influence. Accordingly, they are ruled by the notion of two principles in man, a lower and a higher; a creaturely soul (*psyche*), and a divine or incorruptible spirit (*pneuma*). This was undoubtedly an unscriptural view, and it soon led to such results—Gnostic, Manichæan, Apollinarian— as drew forth the protest of the Church in her general councils. How great was the influence of the ancient philosophy, even with Christian writers, may be seen in Clemens Alexandrinus and Origen, both of whom favour the Platonic trichotomy. Even Tertullian is disposed to accept it as not alien to the faith (*De Anima*, xvi.), while he disparages the biblical distinction between soul and spirit.

Long after these early controversies were forgotten, the Aristotelic philosophy perpetuated the distinction between a vegetative and a rational element in the human ψυχή.

The distinction was promoted by William of Occam (d. 1347), into a doctrine of two souls differing in substance from one another,—the sensitive soul joined to the body *circumscriptivè*, so as to dwell in separate parts of it ; the intellective soul separable from the body and joined with it *diffinitivè*, so that it is entirely present in every part. A similar view is ascribed to the Italian philosopher Bernardinus Telesius (1508–88). But it is of more interest to find something akin to it in the writings of the father of modern inductive science. Lord Bacon suggests a trichotomy of man's nature in this way : having observed that " there were two different emanations of souls in the first creation of them, namely, one that had its original from the breath of God, and another from the matrices of the elements," he proposes to distinguish these in man as the *spiracle* or *inspired substance* on the one hand, and the *sensible* or *product soul* on the other. It is in connection with his consideration of the former, in proposing to ask whether it be native or adventive, separable or inseparable, mortal or immortal, how far it is tied to the laws of matter, how far not, and the like, that he utters the suggestive sentiment that there are questions in philosophy which must be bound over at last unto religion [see extract given on title-page of Division I.]. In speaking of the second, he says that this is in beasts the principal soul, whereof the body of beasts is the organ ; but in man this soul is itself an organ of the rational soul, and should bear the appellation, not of a soul, but rather of a spirit. His trichotomy then would be soul, spirit, and body,—*soul* denoting the divine spark, the inbreathed principle of rationality ; *spirit*, the unreasonable soul, " which hath the same original in us as in beasts, namely, from the slime of the earth." This is a tripartite theory, for it seems to demand a rational principle ruling over two distinct organs or organisms, the animal soul and the animal body.—*De Augmentis*, lib. iv. cap. iii.

From the time of Lord Bacon, the trichotomy may be said to have fallen greatly out of sight, until the revival of biblical psychology in the end of the last and beginning of the present century. There is probably no instance since the ancient councils in which a psychological article has been introduced into church symbols, except that of the later Helvetic Confession. In this document the strict dualism of the human constitution is insisted on in words which reflect some forgotton controversies: "Dicimus autem constare hominem duabus ac diversis quidem substantiis, in una persona, anima immortali, utpote quæ separata a corpore, nec dormit, nec interit, et corpore mortali, quod tamen in ultimo judicio a mortuis resuscitabitur, ut totus homo inde, vel in vita, vel in morte, æternum maneat. Damnamus omnes qui irrident, aut subtilibus disputationibus in dubium vocant, immortalitatem animarum, aut animam dicunt dormire, aut partem esse Dei."—*Conf. Helvet. posterior*, c. vii.

CHAPTER VI

FLESH, HEART, AND OTHER TERMS

No⊤ less important for biblical psychology and theology
than the terms soul and spirit, is the term FLESH (*Basar*,
Sarx).[1] It will be necessary to note its use in two
broadly distinct regions. There is (A) a natural
meaning, admitting of various shades of application,
which runs through the whole Scripture. It bears
also (B) a very definite ethical significance in certain
well-known doctrinal passages of the New Testament,
especially of the Pauline Epistles.

Under the first head (A), there are four shades
of meaning which we may conveniently distinguish.
There is (1) its literal meaning, *substance of a living
body*, whether of men or beasts. From this radical
meaning it comes to be a designation of the creature
on one side, as " living soul " is on the other. If " soul "
(*nephesh*) be an embodied life, " flesh " (*basar*) is ensouled
matter; though we must never construe it as merely
material, for in the life-principle which makes it flesh
a higher element than matter is presupposed. Under

---

[1] שְׁאֵר is sometimes used as equivalent to בָּשָׂר even in its psychological
sense ; see Ps. lxxiii. 26. More usually the relation of שְׁאֵר to בָּשָׂר is
like that of κρέας to σάρξ ; see *e.g.*, Ps. lxxviii. 20, 27, comp. with ver. 39.

this use it denotes all terrestrial beings possessing life.[1]
From this there arises (2) its application to *human nature
generally,* and the personal life attached to it.   Man as
clothed in corporeity is contrasted under the name
" flesh " with purely spiritual being, and especially with
God.   Hence with reference to the weak, the finite,
the perishable being which man is, this expression
pervades both the Old and New Testament as a phrase
for human kind.[2]   The New Testament has the additional
expression " flesh and blood " (*sarx kai haima*) [3] to
designate human nature on its earthly side, in contrast
with the supersensible and the divine.   The phrase,
though without an exact equivalent in the Hebrew of
the Old Testament, is doubtless expressive of the Old
Testament idea, " The life of the flesh is in the blood."
Its special force, however, lies in contrasting human
nature with something greater than itself.[4]   This can
hardly be made too emphatic in our exegesis, for it is
the prevalent force all through the Bible of the term as
applied to mankind.   Man is " flesh," from his creaturely
nature, or from his nature on its creaturely side.

When we come (3) to use " flesh " as a term for one
constituent of human nature in contrast with the others,
it naturally stands for *the corporeal or lower element.*
In the Old Testament it is used along with " heart "
or " soul " to express the entire nature of man.   So far,

---

[1] *E.g.* Gen. vii. 21.

[2] *E.g.* Gen. vi. 3 ; Job xxxiv. 15 ; Ps. lvi. 5, lxxviii. 39 ; Isa. xl. 6–8 ;
Jer. xvii. 5 ; 1 Cor. i. 29 ; 1 Pet. i. 24.

[3] σὰρξ καὶ αἷμα.

[4] *E.g.* Matt. xvi. 17 ; 1 Cor. xv. 50 ; Gal. i. 16 ; Eph. vi. 12 ; Heb. ii.
14, to which may be added John i. 13.

however, is "flesh" from being despised in contrast with
these higher elements, that it is joined with them in the
relation of the whole man to God and to his future
hopes.[1] In the New Testament its use in this psychological sense for the lower element in man without any
disparagement, though not very frequent, is quite clear.
In a sufficient number of passages it occurs coupled with
spirit (*pneuma*), to show that flesh and spirit are used
for the whole of man, the simple natural elements of
which he is made up, exactly as "flesh and soul," "flesh
and heart," are in the Old Testament.[2] It is of considerable importance to point out that even within the Pauline
writings, where we are afterwards to find the specifically
ethical meaning of flesh so current, a quite unethical
use of "flesh" for the outward or sensuous part of man,
in contrast with the inner and spiritual, is undeniable ;[3]
and even when the sinful state of man is the subject
under consideration, the whole of man is designated by
"flesh and mind" in one Pauline passage, and by "flesh
and spirit" in another, where simply our entire nature
is meant.[4] The New Testament has other pairs of
expressions for the same thing. It uses freely the Greek
duality which has become the modern one, "soul and

---

[1] Ps. lxiii. 1, lxxxiv. 2, xvi. 9 ; Job xix. 26. A good example of the
two, *basar* and *nephesh*, used as the sole and even separable constituents
of human nature, like soul and body, is Job xiv. 22.

[2] Matt. xxvi. 41 ; Mark xiv. 38 ; comp. Luke xxiv. 39.

[3] Rom. ii. 28 ; 1 Cor. v. 5, vii. 28 ; 2 Cor. iv. 11, vii. 5, xii. 7 ; σάρξ
is also used by Paul of corporeal presence cognisable by the senses, as
contrasted with spiritual fellowship, ἐν πνεύματι, 2 Cor. v. 16, Col. ii. 1, 5,
and, indeed, of the earthly life of man without any moral qualification ;
e.g. Gal. ii. 20, "The life which I now live in the flesh" ; so also
Phil. i. 22.

[4] Eph. ii. 3 ; 2 Cor. vii. 1.

body." And though the Old Testament "soul and flesh" does not recur, "body and spirit" can take its place.[1] These phrases afford additional proof that the biblical view of man's constitution is truly dichotomic. It may also be observed that the use of "flesh and spirit" as really equivalent to "body and soul" is an incidental confirmation of the view already advanced, that there is no distinction of *natures* between soul and spirit, though there is an obvious propriety in the ordinary form of these dual combinations, where the inner and the outer nature of man are respectively designated according to fixed aspects of each. "Soul and body" links the individuality with the organism; "flesh and spirit" links the earthly substance in which life inheres with the divine spark or principle of life. The last use (4) of the term "flesh" in its merely natural significance needs no more than to be named. It is that so common in both Old and New Testament for *relationship* or *connection*, by marriage, more usually by birth; kinship—tribal, national, or universal.[2]

It is clear that in the four uses now considered there is nothing directly ethical, at least nothing which identifies the flesh with the principle of evil. "Not a single passage in the Old Testament can be adduced wherein *basar* is used to denote man's sensuous nature as the seat of an opposition against his spirit, and of a bias towards sin."[3] It is true that "flesh," used for

---

[1] 1 Cor. vi. 16, 17, vii. 34. 1 Cor. v. 3, like "flesh" and "spirit" in Col. ii. 5.

[2] *E.g.* Gen. ii. 23, xxix. 14, xxxvii. 27; Judg. ix. 2; Rom. ix. 5, 8; 1 Cor. x. 18; Eph. v. 29.

[3] Müller, *The Christian Doctrine of Sin*, i. p. 323 (Clark's Translation, 2d Edition).

human kind in contrast to higher beings and to God, brings out the frailty and finitude of man. It is also true that "flesh" as a constituent of human nature means the perishable, animal, sensuous, and even sensual element of it; but which of these ideas is prominent in any passage must be learned from its connection and context. It is further true that in its meaning of "natural kinship" there is often an implied contrast with something better, as, *e.g.*, "Israel after the flesh." But the conclusive proof that nothing of moral depreciation is necessarily implied in this use of it, is its application to our Lord as designating his human in contrast to His divine nature : "Who was manifest in the flesh, justified in the Spirit," "made of the seed of David according to the flesh." [1]

(B) It is evident, however, that another, and a morally unfavourable use of the term occurs in the Pauline Epistles. In certain well-known passages, "flesh" denotes the principle, or the seat of the principle, which in fallen human nature resists the divine law, which is contrasted with "the mind" or man's own higher nature consenting to the law, and which even in the regenerate makes war against the "spirit." Here we have a very marked ethical significance given to the word. Nor is it the only term of its kind used to denominate the evil principle in man's nature as now under sin. "The old man," "the body of sin," "the body of the flesh," "the law in the members," "our members which are upon earth," are kindred expressions more or less closely denoting the same thing, although "flesh" in its counter-

---

[1] 1 Tim. iii. 16 ; Rom. i. 3.

poise to " the mind " [1] and to " the spirit " [2] respectively,
is the leading expression. Now, although it is not
usual to construe these phrases as asserting that the
literal flesh or the bodily organism is the seat or
principle of sin, although a metaphorical turn is generally
given to them, yet it must be admitted that it is exactly
the current and allowable character of the metaphor
which needs explanation. How is it that the terms
properly denoting the lower or corporeal element in
man's nature should come to denote the being of sin in
that nature? The answer that it is because the sensuous
is either, the main seat or, the original source of sin in
man, although it long contented negative divines, has
become too obviously shallow and incorrect even for
some of them. As to the elements in man's nature
where sin has (a) *its seat*, these are plainly not the
sensuous or sensational alone. There are sinful desires
of the " mind." There is defilement of the " spirit." [3]
There are works called " of the flesh " which have
nothing to do with sensuality ; *e.g.* " hatreds, variance,
emulation, heresies." [4] The apostle calls by the name
of " fleshly wisdom " what was evidently speculative
tendency derived from the Greek schools.[5] And
there were heretics at Colossæ whose ruling impulse
he calls their " fleshly mind," though they were

[1] νοῦς, in Rom. vii.

[2] πνεῦμα, in Rom. viii. and Gal. 5.

[3] διανοιῶν (Eph. ii. 3); πνεύματος (2 Cor. vii. 1).

[4] Gal. v. 20 ; comp. also 1 Cor. iii. 1, 3, where the charge is "strife,
division," etc., not sensuality ; yet it is said, " Are ye not carnal ? "

[5] Comp. 1 Cor. i. 21, 22, Ἕλληνες σοφίαν ζητοῦσιν, with ver. 26, σοφοὶ
κατὰ σάρκα. The phrase σοφία σαρκική occurs in another connection,
2 Cor. i. 12.

evidently extreme ascetics attached to some form of Gnosticism.[1]

It might, indeed, be maintained that if we assume the sensuous nature in man to be (*b*) *the principle* or *source* of evil in him, it is easy to understand how the whole man under its influence should receive the denomination of " the flesh," or the " body of sin." But this is an assumption which will not tally with the treatment of man's corporeal nature in the sacred writings. Any view implying the inherent evil of matter is radically opposed to the whole biblical philosophy. To derive moral evil in man from the bodily side of his nature is as opposed to the Scripture account of its beginning in the race as it is to our experience of its first manifestations in the individual. In Genesis the first sin is represented as the consequence of a primary rebellion against God.[2] The first outbreaks of moral evil in children are selfishness, anger, and self-will. Again, that the corporeal nature is necessarily at strife with the spiritual is a view which cannot be reconciled with the claims made upon the body in the Christian system—with such precepts as that believers are to " yield their members instruments of righteousness unto God,"[3] to present their bodies a living sacrifice,[4] to regard their bodies as the members of Christ and as the temple of the Holy Ghost,[5] that the body is for the Lord and the Lord for the body.[6] Still more impossible is it to reconcile with such a view

---

[1] Col. ii. 18 ; comp. vers. 21, 22, 23. See Lightfoot's dissertation on "The Colossian Heresy," prefixed to his *Commentary* on that epistle, 2d Edition, 1876.

[2] See Chap. X. *infra*. [3] Rom. vi. 13. [4] Rom. xii. 1.
[5] 1 Cor. vi. 15, 19. [6] . Cor. vi. 13.

the Christian revelation concerning the future of the redeemed, and the consummation of redemption.   If sin were the inevitable outcome of man's possession of a body, redemption ought to culminate in his deliverance from it, instead of in its change and restoration to a higher form.[1]   To say that the matter of the body is or contains the principle of sin, and then to say, as Paul does,[2] that the last result of the Redeemer's Spirit indwelling in us shall be to quicken these mortal bodies, would be flat self-contradiction.   But the truth is, the view which connects sin with the material body is neither Hebrew nor Christian.   It is essentially alien to the whole spirit of revelation.   Nevertheless, at a very early period in Christian history, chiefly through the influence of the Greek and some of the Latin Fathers, it obtained such hold of Christian thought that it continues to colour popular modes of conception and speech to the present day.   One of its most obvious examples is that men imagine they are uttering a scriptural sentiment when they speak of welcoming death as the liberation of the soul from the body, the sentiment of Paul being exactly the reverse, when he declares that even the redeemed who have the first-fruits of the Spirit groan within themselves, waiting for the adoption, *i.e.* for the redemption of their body.[3]   Two additional reasons why Paul cannot be held as tracing man's evil to the corporeal element may be summed up in the words of Julius Müller: " He denies the presence of evil in Christ, who was partaker of our fleshly nature,[4] and he

---

[1] Phil. iii. 21.   [2] Rom. viii. 11.
[3] Rom. viii. 23.   [4] Gal. iv. 4 ; Heb, ii. 14.

recognises it in spirits who are not partakers thereof.[1]
Is it not, therefore, in the highest degree probable that
according to him evil does not necessarily pertain to
man's sensuous nature, and that *sarx* denotes something
different from this ? " [2]

When, however, those who successfully refute this
mistaken derivation of the ethical force of *sarx* come to
give their own explanation of it, they fall for the most
part into mere tautology. If we say with Neander that
it represents " human nature in its estrangement from
the divine life, " [3] or with Müller that it is the " tendency which turns towards the things of the world and
is thereby turned away from God," [4] or with Principal
Tulloch that it means " all the evil activity of human
nature,"[5] we attain the profound conclusion that the
flesh is sinful human nature ! If " flesh " be a designation for sinfully-conditioned human nature, whence comes
it that the term is appropriate ? When *sarx* is defined
as " the sinful propensity generally," or as " love of the
world," it is quite fair to ask, as Pfleiderer does,[6] " how
it would sound to say, ' In me, that is, in my tendency
to sin in general, or in my love of the world, dwelleth
no good thing.' " " If the ' flesh ' be nothing else than
just this condition of man's nature as we find it, this
condition which is to be explained, then the whole of

---

[1] τὰ πνευματικὰ τῆς πονηρίας, Eph. vi. 12.

[2] *The Christian Doctrine of Sin*, i. p. 321.

[3] *Planting of Christianity*, i. p. 422 (Bohn's Edition).

[4] *Ut supra*, i. p. 326.

[5] Croall Lecture, 1876, p. 154. Dr. Tulloch also employs Neander's
phrase.

[6] *Der Paulinismus*; ein Beitrag zur Geschichte der urchristlichen Theologie, p. 54, note.

Paul's subtle and acute deduction would be nothing but the most wretched argument in a circle. People would give anything to explain away the idea of an impersonal principle of sin contained in the nature of man that precedes every sinful manifestation, and is the ultimate cause which infallibly produces it; and yet this is just the pith of the whole passage." [1] It is quite certain that Paul means to posit a principle of sin in man,— "the sin that dwelleth in me, the law in my members." It is further clear (notwithstanding the occasional use of the one for the other, *e.g.* "the flesh lusteth against the Spirit"), that the law or principle of sin is one thing, and the flesh or native constitution of man in which it inheres is another. And it is certain that he as little develops the principle of sin out of the mere physical flesh as he identifies the one with the other. It is impossible to deny a very pointed reference to the lower element of human nature in this important key-word of the Pauline theology; but what misleads contending exegetes is the supposition that the lower and higher elements in man were conceived of by Paul as by the Greeks or by ourselves,—that the antithesis, material and immaterial, is at the basis of the distinction. So long as this idea prevails, it will be impossible to get rid of the suspicion that in the "flesh" of the Pauline Epistles we have something which connects sin essentially with the material element in man's constitution. Dismiss that antithesis, substitute for it the proper biblical antithesis,

---

[1] *Der Paulinismus*, p. 58. This book, which is now in a second edition (Edin., 1890), occupies vols. xiii. and xv. of the Theological Translation Fund Library (Williams & Norgate, 1877). See Chap. XIV. *infra*, for further reference to Pfle``erer's own position.

—earthly and heavenly, natural and supernatural, that "flesh" is what nature evolves, "spirit" what God in His grace bestows,—then we can see how the idea of "flesh," even when ethically intensified to the utmost, is appreciably distinct from the notion of evil as necessarily residing in matter. The great word of John iii. 6 is the source of the apostolic doctrine on this subject: "That which is born of the flesh is flesh." "Flesh" has become the proper designation of the race, as self-evolved and self-continued. Human nature as now constituted can produce nothing but its like, and that like is now sinful. "Flesh," therefore, may be appropriately used for the principle of corrupt nature in the individual man, for the obvious reason that it is in the course of the flesh, or of the ordinary production of human nature, that the evil principle invariably originates and comes to light. Thus the phrase is some explanation of the condition of man's nature, which it describes. It is no objection to this view, but rather a confirmation of its correctness, that it grounds the Pauline use of *sarx*, for sinful human nature, on the underlying doctrine of hereditary corruption,—the primary assumptions of apostolic doctrine regarding man being always, that "God made man upright," and that "by one man sin entered into the world." This view is well expressed by Professor E. P. Gould,[1] thus: "What, then, is the reason of this use of *sarx* to denote man's sinful nature? . . . Humanity, which on the natural side owes its continuance to the *sarx* is itself called *sarx*. Natural and sarkikal are therefore convertible terms in reference to man. On the

---

[1] In a brief article on Σάρξ in the *Bibliotheca Sacra*, Jan. 1875.

other side, the spirit is that through which man is connected with the divine and supernatural, and specially in the new birth. It is there that the Divine Spirit works, implanting the germs of a new life; and so 'spiritual' and 'divine or supernatural' are also convertible terms in regard to man. To this let it be added that the natural man, connected with the race through the *sarx*, is sinful, while the new man, connected with God through the *pneuma*, is holy; and does it seem strange that *sarx* should itself be used to denote the sinful natural man, and *pneuma* the holy renewed man? It is simply resolved into this: 'flesh' is that through which man, in his natural state, is descended from a sinful race, and inherits a sinful nature, and the term is used to denote that nature; while 'spirit' is that through which and in which God implants a new divine life of holiness, and the term, therefore, is used to denote that life."

We thus see how the secondary, *i.e.* the ethical or theological meaning of *sarx*, has a certain reasoned connection with its primary or natural meaning. But we make no apology for any want of complete continuity in the transition. It is not our view of the thoughts and language of the Bible that the religious or spiritual is developed by the human writers of it out of the natural or philosophical language of their time, and that critics can trace the development. We hold it a worthier view that the Spirit of revelation poured new and intenser meanings, as revelation advanced, into the earlier and simpler language. The rise of the Pauline phrase, "the flesh," for human nature under sin, is in our view another striking instance of this method of the inspired writers, or rather of the Spirit of inspiration in them.

The only other leading term in biblical psychology which requires detailed notice is HEART (*Lebhabh, Kardia*). This term is the one least disputed in its meaning, and which undergoes the least amount of change within the cycle of its use in Scripture. Indeed, it may be held to be common to all parts of the Bible in the same sense. It only concerns the modern reader to note what that sense is, and to distinguish it, in one or two particulars, from the modern use of the word. Its prominence as a psychological term in the Bible and in other ancient books is due, doubtless, to the centrality af the physical organ which it primarily denotes, and which, according to the view of the ancients, bulked so much more in the human frame than the brain. Since, in Bible phrase, "the life is in the blood," that organ which forms the centre of the distribution of the blood must have the most important place in the whole system. By a very easy play of metaphor, therefore, "heart" came to signify the seat of man's collective energies, the focus of the personal life. As from the fleshly heart goes forth the blood in which is the animal life, so from the heart of the human soul goes forth the entire mental and moral activity. By a sort of metaphorical anticipation of Harvey's famous discovery, the heart is also that to which all the actions of the human soul return. In the condensed language of Roos, *In corde actiones animœ humanœ ad ipsum redeunt*. In the heart the soul is at home with itself, becomes conscious of its doing and suffering as its own. "The heart knoweth the bitterness

of its soul," or, " of its self." [1]   It is therefore the organ
of conscience, of self-knowledge, and indeed of all knowledge.   For we must note well that, in contradistinction
to modern usage, " heart," in Bible speech, includes tne
rational and intellectual as well as all other movements
of the soul.   It is only in the later scriptures that the
Greek habit of distinguishing the rational from the emotional finds a place in the sacred language.

Now, because it is the focus of the personal life, the
work-place for the personal appropriation and assimila-
tion of every influence, in the " heart" lies the moral
and religious condition of the man.   Only what enters
the heart forms a possession of moral worth, and only
what comes from the heart is a moral production.   On
the one hand, therefore, the Bible places human depravity in the heart, because sin is a principle which has
penetrated to the centre, and thence corrupts the whole
circuit of life.   On the other hand, it regards the heart
as the sphere of divine influences, the starting-point of
all moral renovation: " The work of the law written in
their hearts"; [2]   " A new heart will I give you ;" [3]
" Purifying their hearts by faith." [4]   Once more, the
heart, as lying deep within, contains " the hidden man," [5]
the real man.   It represents the proper character of the
personality, but conceals it; hence it is contrasted with
the outward appearance, and is declared to be the index
of character only to Him who " searches the heart and
tries the reins of the children of men." [6]

[1] Prov. xiv. 10.   [2] Rom. ii. 15.
[3] Ezek. xxxvi. 26.   [4] Acts xv. 9.   [5] 1 Pet. iii. 4.
[6] 1 Sam. xvi. 7 ; Jer. xvii. 10, xx. 12.   On " the heart" as the seat of

It is impossible, in so rapid a sketch as this, to trace the introduction and history of less prominent terms, such as Mind, Understanding, Conscience,[1] which the greater analytic perfection of Greek thought, with its attention to the intellective element in man, has brought into the language of the New Testament through the medium of the Septuagint. The Old Testament did not distinguish that element by a radical term, as it did Spirit, Soul, Heart, but only by derivatives, such as (*binah*), Understanding,[2] and even this with the effect of giving to "knowledge" the turn "prudence" or "good sense." Such, moreover, was the influence of the Old Testament spirit on the Seventy, and much more on the writers of the New Testament, that although the above-named words of greater precision are introduced, yet *Kardia* retains in the Greek of both Testaments the old Homeric breadth of meaning, and largely represents the corresponding term, *Lebhabh*, of the older scriptures.

One of the most obvious examples of both these facts, namely, that *Kardia* is retained in the New Testament with much of its archaic force, and yet that need was felt of terms more distinctly marking out the *rational* in man, is to be seen in the various Greek renderings of the great commandment, "Thou shalt love the Lord thy God with

sin, see *infra*, Chap. XI. The whole subject is well discussed by Oehler in *Herzog*, art. "Herz"; also in his *Old Testament Theology*, i. pp. 221–227; by Roos, *Grundzüge der Seelenlehre*, pp. 89–175; and by Beck, *Biblische Seelenlehre*, pp. 70–126.

[1] νοῦς, διάνοια, σύνεσις, συνείδησις.

[2] בִּינָה from the verb בִּין.

all thy heart, and with all thy soul, and with all thy might." [1]

Mind, Reason, Understanding,[2] are not used with any psychological refinement in the sacred writings. It is quite impossible, for example, to follow Olshausen [3] when he attempts to show that *Nous* and *Synesis*, with their corresponding verbs, as used in the New Testament, represent the Kantian distinction between *Vernunft* and *Verstand*, familiarised to us in English by Coleridge as that between Reason and Understanding,—the former being the higher intuitive or spiritual perception, the latter the lower or dialectic judgment. It is quite plain, from a glance at the passages, that the terms are really interchangeable.[4] Some more abstract terms, such as [5] "thought," "minding," "thinkings," are used very much at convenience, to represent the contents or products of the inner life, what the Old Testament calls

---

[1] In the original of Deut. vi. 5 the three terms are . . . לְבָב‎, נֶפֶשׁ‎, מְאֹד‎,

In the Septuagint they run thus: διάνοια, ψυχή, δύναμις.

In Matt. xxii. 37, with noticeable change . . . . . καρδία, ψυχή, διάνοια.

Mark has two renderings, { xii. 30 καρδία, ψυχή, διάνοια, ἰσχύς.
{ xii. 33 καρδία, σύνεσις, ψυχή, ἰσχύς.

Luke x. 27 . . . . . καρδία, ψυχή, ἰσχύς, διάνοια.

Godet (Comm. *in loc.*) calls attention to the Alexandrine variation in Luke, which, retaining ἐκ before καρδία, inserts ἐν before the other three terms. This he thinks emphasises καρδία as the *focus* of the moral life, and indicates the other three as its principal directions.

[2] νοῦς with its congeners, διάνοια, ἔννοια, νόημα ; also σύνεσις, διαλογισμός, etc.

[3] *Opuscula Theologica*, p. 156.

[4] Mark viii. 17 ; Matt. xiii. 14, 15. That σύνεσις cannot be confined to the things earthly is plain from Col. i. 9 ; Eph. iii. 3, 4 ; 2 Tim. ii. 7. In this last passage, νοέω and σύνεσις take almost the reverse force from that suggested by Olshausen.

[5] νόημα, φρόνημα, διαλογισμός.

the "imagination of the thoughts of the heart." [1] But
there is one special use of *mind* in the Pauline writings
which deserves notice. Paul's highest element in the
trichotomic expression of man's nature is undoubtedly
"spirit" (*pneuma*). But this entirely original biblical
phrase for the highest aspects of man's life is almost
inseparable from the idea of man's relation to God,
whether in creation or in redemption. Accordingly, when
he wishes to contrast man's own highest sense of right
or faculty of knowledge with other powers, sinful or
spiritual, he adopts the word *Nous*, which represents the
highest element in man according to the philosophers.
This is brought out in two leading passages, in one of
which, *Nous*, the "mind," is contrasted with the "flesh"
in the struggle against sin (Rom. vii. 23, 25); in the
other it is contrasted with "spirit," when *pneuma* represents the inner man under control of a spiritual or
prophetic afflatus (1 Cor. xiv. 14, 15, 19). Thus, *mind*
(*nous*) becomes a convenient and appropriate term for
highest natural faculty in man, moral and intellectual,
but so purely natural that it can be either "mind of the
flesh" (Col. ii. 18), or awakened by the law, which will
then be the "law of the mind" (Rom. vii. 23), or
renewed in the spirit (Rom. xii. 2; Eph. iv. 23).

Through a somewhat similar current of influences,
which may be expressed generally as the necessity for
greater analytic precision, what was in the Old Testament denoted by "heart," and by the several verbs for
the active side of man's inner life, has to appear in the

[1] Gen. vi. 5: יֵצֶר מַחְשְׁבֹת לִבּוֹ.

Greek of the New Testament as *will* and *conscience*.[1]
The word *conscience* takes its place in the New Testament
beside *heart*, as the critical or self-judging function of the
inner man ("hearts sprinkled from an evil conscience"[2]).
Therefore, as *mind* is the highest faculty of the soul, and
conscience of the heart, the intensest corruption of the
whole nature can be described as the defilement even of
the *mind* and of the *conscience*.[3]

To sum up: no one need be at any loss to grasp the
simple psychology of the Bible who keeps well in view
the original signification and subsequent growth of the
four leading terms SPIRIT (*Ruach*, *Pneuma*), SOUL (*Nephesh*,
Psyche), FLESH (*Basar*, *Sarx*), HEART (*Lebhabh*, *Kardia*).
These are the *voces signatæ* of the entire Scripture view
of man's nature and constitution.   They are all grouped
round the idea of life or of a living being.   The first
two, *soul* and *spirit*, represent in different ways the life
itself of a living being.   The last two, *flesh* and *heart*,
denote respectively the life-environment and the life-
organ; the former that in which life inheres, the latter
that through which it acts.   So much for their simple
and primitive meaning.   In their secondary meaning
(which again in the case of the first three—*spirit*, *soul*,
flesh—becomes the basis of a tertiary, namely, an ethical
or theological meaning in the latest development of inspired
thought) they are to be grouped as follows.   *Spirit*, *soul*,
and *flesh* are expressions for man's nature viewed from
different points.   They are not three natures.   **Man's**

---

[1] ἐθέλειν, θέλημα ; συνείδησις.

[2] Heb. x. 22.

[3] Tit. i. 15.   For further remarks on some of these psychological terms
of Scripture, see Note to this Chapter.

one nature is really expressed by each of them, so that each alone may designate the human being. Thus man is *flesh*, as an embodied perishable creature : " All flesh is grass." He is *soul*, as a personal being, an individual responsible creature : " All souls are mine " ;[1] " There were added about three thousand souls."[2] Once more, he is *spirit*. More commonly, however, he is said to have it, as his life-principle derived from God. He is of the spiritual order—that, namely, of God and angels. But " spirits " designates men only as disembodied : " The spirits of just men made perfect,"[3] " spirits in prison,"[4] exactly as we read " souls under the altar."[5] *Heart* stands outside of this triad, because man is never called " a heart," nor men spoken of as " hearts." *Heart* never denotes the personal subject, but always the personal organ.

Again, they may be grouped thus : *Spirit, soul, heart*, may be used each of them to indicate one side of man's double-sided nature, namely, his higher or inner life. Over against them stands *flesh*, as representing that nature on the lower or outer side, so that any one of the first three combined with *flesh* will express in dual terms the whole of man—" flesh and spirit," " flesh and soul," or " flesh and heart." Then, looking at the first three once more, not in relation to *flesh* but in their mutual relations to " life," we get that correct and convenient division suggested by Beck, and followed by most competent inquirers since,—a clear and intelligible result, which justifies itself throughout the whole Scripture, namely, that

[1] Ezek. xviii. 4.   [2] Acts ii. 41.   [3] Heb. xii. 23.
[4] 1 Pet. iii. 19.   [5] Rev. vi. 9.

spirit represents the principle of life, *soul* the subject of
life, and *heart* the organ of life ; definitions which will be
found to apply accurately to all the three constituent
lives which the human being can lead—(*a*) the physical,
(*b*) the mental and moral, (*c*) the spiritual and religious.

The general result is a view of man essentially
bipartite, corresponding to the generally accepted
position, which is native and almost instinctive to the
human mind, that man consists of flesh and spirit, or
of body and soul ; although the Scripture lays stress
upon the oneness of man's constitution, a truth obscured,
and sometimes betrayed, by the kind of dualism which
has prevailed even in Christian theology. Besides this,
however. it is undoubted, as we have shown, that a
trichotomic usage arose, which prevails in the Pauline
Epistles, where *soul* and *spirit* are represented as diverse
aspects of man's inner being—a division brought to
light mainly in consequence of the spiritual distinction
which is based upon it. The trichotomy of the sacred
writings, *spirit*, *soul*, and *body*, is to be distinguished
from that of Plato, from which it differs entirely both
as to content and form, Plato's being the ascription to
man of three souls, the *rational*, the *irascible*, and the
appetitive ; also from that of the Stoics, which in its
ripest form associated with the *fleshly*, a *psychic* or
pneumatic, and a *noetic* or governing principle, and
which in its simplest terms was a tripartition into *mind*,
soul, and *body*. Finally, it differs from the famous
Plotinian triad, the neo-Platonic offset to the Christian
Trinity, which consisted of the *One* or absolute principle,
the *mind* and the *soul*, " body " being the product of the

last.[1] Hence the important distinction in form as well
as in content which belongs to the Pauline or scriptural
trichotomy. That distinction lies in the use of *spirit*
for the highest element or aspect of man's nature. In
this the biblical psychology stands entirely alone, and
is thoroughly consistent with itself from first to last.
Pneuma is not so used by Plato, by Philo, by the earlier
Stoics, by Plotinus and the neo-Platonists, nor indeed
anywhere out of the circle of Bible thought. The
great and peculiar affirmation of Scripture in regard to
man's nature is this attribution to him, as the highest
in him, of that which is common to man with God.
What this *spirit* (*pneuma*) of the biblical psychology is,
however, we must be careful properly to state. Regard
to accurate Scripture interpretation forbids us to distinguish *pneuma* otherwise than as the God-given
principle of man's life, physical, mental, and spiritual.
To make *pneuma* a nature or life-element,—the spiritual,
for instance, in contrast to the other two, the physical
and the rational,—is to fall at once into a false and unbiblical analysis. The theory that *pneuma* is a separable
constituent of man's being, which can be wanting, dead,
or dormant on the one hand, restored or confirmed on
the other, so as to explain the fallen, regenerate, and
immortal states of man respectively, is temptingly
simple, as such arbitrary suppositions often are, but it
wants the foundation of fact, and leads to grossly
unscriptural conclusions. It is also a mistake, though
one by no means so serious, to make *pneuma* the faculty
of God-consciousness or the organ of religion in man,

[1] See Note to Chapter V.

deadened by the fall, awakened in regeneration, and perfected in the life to come. It is evident, on a general view of the facts, that we cannot assign religion to any single faculty or power in man as its exclusive function. The intellect, the affections, and the will are seen to be all concerned in it.[1] It is equally evident that no such use or application of *pneuma* marks the language of Scripture. It is not the *pneuma* only which in the words of the Psalms and Prophets is the organ of the spiritual or religious mind; heart, soul, and even flesh cry out for the living God. On the other hand, the functions of the *pneuma* are not confined to the religious consciousness or conscience toward God; it has the faculty of self-cognisance as well. Indeed, the whole character of the Bible psychology is mistaken in such attempts to distinguish spirit, soul, heart, as separate faculties. They are diverse aspects of one indivisible inner life.

In spite of these errors and exaggerations, it is important that we recognise what some of those who have fallen into them do with truth maintain, namely, that the distinctive feature of the biblical psychology lies in its doctrine of the *pneuma* in man. By this term the Bible indicates, as we have shown, (a) from the first, the divine origination even of his physical life; then (b), the innermost aspect of his inward natural life; finally, in the latest system of Scripture thought, (c) the regenerate or spiritual life in which man is linked anew to God through Christ Jesus. Parallel to this doctrine

---

[1] For some good remarks on this subject, see pp. 54–59 of Dr. Alliott's *Psychology a 'd Theology*, the Congregational Lecture for 1854.

of the *pneuma* in man runs a higher line of Bible teaching concerning God. He is the God of the spirits of all flesh, the Father of spirits. God is Spirit. *Pneuma*, with appropriate epithets, becomes the designation of the Third Person of the Trinity. And it is one of the central doctrines of Christianity concerning the theanthropic person of the Son, that He becomes, as head of the new humanity, a life-giving *Pneuma*, " a quickening Spirit.". At every point in the unfolding of the Bible anthropology, this doctrine of the *pneuma* in man will be seen to be peculiar to and distinctive of the whole revelation. It forms a central element of the Divine Image. It explains the nature of that moral movement which we designate the Fall. It enters into the psychology of Regeneration, and into the Scripture doctrine of man's Future Life. It is with these topics that our four remaining sections must be occupied.

NOTE TO CHAPTER VI

LEADING TERMS IN BIBLE PSYCHOLOGY

Some additional material on the interpretation of these terms.

SPIRIT (רִיחַ, נְשָׁמָה, πνεῦμα). — To begin with the New Testament word Πνεῦμα. The meanings in *ordinary Greek* are three,—(*a*) air or wind, (*b*) breath, the air we breathe, (*c*) life in general. " Thus in a *physiological* sense we often find it in the classics, especially in the poets and in later Greek ; in a *psychological* sense, as the element of human existence and personal life, never " (Cremer). It is only

in the LXX. and in the New Testament that πνεῦμα has
the sense of a spiritual being, or refers to man in his higher
mental aspects, and thus is a good example of the language-
building and enriching power of the religion of the Bible.
In the *Scriptures*, however, we find it used (A) in the
classical senses,—"wind," John iii. 8; "breath, breath of
life," Ezek. xxxvii. 8; Hab. ii. 19; "life" (in the physiological sense, but drawing rather to the meaning "soul"),
Luke viii. 55; Jas. ii. 26; Rev. xi. 11, xiii. 15. The
additional idea which is even on this side introduced into
the term is that it is life, or a life-principle, from God. So
in the LXX. as = רוּחַ or נְשָׁמָה, Isa. xlii. 5. Both of men and
brutes, Eccles. iii. 19, 21; Ps. civ. 29, 30. (B) The senses
special to the Scriptures are these:—(1) It denotes the
distinctive, self-conscious, inner life of man, 1 Cor. ii. 11,
v. 3, 5; Col. ii. 5; Matt. v. 3; Luke i. 80, ii. 40; Mark
viii. 12. (2) Connected with the former or physiological
sense, as life which is God-derived, comes the πνεῦμα in its
religious sense, Ps. xxxi. 6, xxxii. 2, xxxiv. 19, li. 12, 19,
lxxviii. 8; Prov. xvi. 2; Isa. xxvi. 9, xxix. 24, xxxviii. 16,
lxi. 3, lxvi. 3; Ezek. xiii. 3; Rom. i. 9. Then (3) its highest
and specially Pauline meaning of "the new nature," Rom.
viii. 2, 6, 10, 16; Gal. iii. 6, v. 16, 17, 18; Jude 19. See
the gradual rise of πνεῦμα in these three meanings traced
in Chap. V. pp. 88–95.

For the relation of πνεῦμα τοῦ ἀνθρώπου to τὸ Πνεῦμα τὸ
ἅγιον, τοῦ Χριστοῦ, the chief passages are Rom. viii. 16 (comp.
1 Cor. ii. 11, 12), and the whole context of Rom. viii. 1–17,
Gal. iii. 5; Philem. 25. "Inner assurance depends upon
the contact of the Spirit newly given of God with the
spirit in us which is ours conformably with nature; and
the vitality and power of this divine life-principle depend
upon the indwelling or communication of the Spirit of
Christ. We must always understand by πνεῦμα the divine
life-principle by nature peculiar to man, either in its
natural position within his organism, or as renewed by the
communication of the Spirit. But we must keep fast hold
of the truth that this newly given life-principle does not
become identical with the spirit belonging to men by
nature nor does it supplant it. It cannot be said of it, τὸ

ἐμόν, ὑμῶν πνεῦμα; and we must distinguish between the passages where it is spoken of as now belonging to man, and those where it appears as independently existing. Still this is not a difference of subjects, as if a different πνεῦμα were meant, but simply a difference in the relation of the πνεῦμα to man; so that when reference is thus made to the Spirit, though it be the personal Holy Spirit that is meant, yet He is regarded as the agent who in and for man accomplishes the work of redemption" (Cremer, *sub voce*). With some slight wavering, the opinion of Cremer on the whole appears to be, that in the Christian there is simply a natural πνεῦμα and the divine Holy Spirit, and that it is the divine Holy Spirit acting on the natural πνεῦμα in man which produces the quickened or renewed πνεῦμα. He seems to say that this renewed πνεῦμα must not be held identical with the πνεῦμα belonging to man by nature— that it is non-individual, that it is the Holy Spirit acting in the man. Is this a *tetrachotomy* of the Christian into body, soul, spirit, and the Holy Spirit?

To understand πνεῦμα, especially in its antithesis to ψυχή, attention should be given to the use of πνευματικός in the New Testament. With one exception (Eph. vi. 12), it always denotes that which belongs either directly to the Lord, the Spirit (*e.g.* 1 Cor. x. 3, 4), or to the renewed spirit in believers. 1 Cor. ii. 11–16 and xv. 42–47 are the two main passages determining its force. No careful reader of 1 Cor. ii. could avoid seeing that the distinctive character of the human πνεῦμα is present to the mind of the writer. The clear description of the πνεῦμα in ver. 11 as the self-conscious faculty in man, and its comparison with the τὸ πνεῦμα τοῦ Θεοῦ, make this undeniable. That in this connection the man blind to spiritual-divine things should be called ψυχικός, and the spiritually enlightened πνευματικός, is a clear recognition that in the writer's mind ψυχή and πνεῦμα have the respective values that have been accorded them in modern biblical psychology. The whole passage is moulded, like that in the same Epistle, xv. 42–47, upon the antithesis of ψυχή and πνεῦμα, and both passages would be unintelligible without the assumption of that antithesis. It might be possible to reckon 1 Thess. v. 23

rhetorical amplification, but Heb. iv. 12 and the two passages now named refuse to bend to such an hypothesis.

רוּחַ is the complete Old Testament equivalent of πνεῦμα. The Septuagint is on the whole faithful to this rendering. נְשָׁמָה is a strictly parallel expression in Hebrew. It can be used along with רוּחַ of the mere principle of life even in animals (Gen. vii. 22). Like רוּחַ, also, it can denote the innermost function of the human spirit (Prov. xx. 27). The LXX. have rendered it frequently by πνοή, especially when a parallelism with רוּחַ occurs in the original (e.g. Job xxvii. 3, xxxii. 8, xxxiii. 4; Isa. xlii. 5, lvii. 16), and this probably indicates accurately the distinctive shade of meaning. There does not seem to be the slightest foundation for the notion favoured by Beck, that נְשָׁמָה denotes the specific difference between the life of man and that of the brute (*Umriss*, p. 7, note: the passages cited by him, especially the verses Deut. xx. 13, 14, 16, seem to me to disprove the distinction). The idea is of Rabbinic origin. So also is the still less scriptural notion of making נְשָׁמָה and רוּחַ denote separate spiritual elements, or even distinct souls in man. We find the Rabbinical writers sometimes quoted as making three inner principles. Olshausen cites *Jalkut Rubeni*, fol. 15: " In homine est רוּחַ et נֶפֶשׁ et נְשָׁמָה, sed quando peccat, נְשָׁמָה ab eo abit et adscendit, נֶפֶשׁ et רוּחַ manent, ita ut homo adhuc vivere possit." But so arbitrary were these distinctions, that according to another form of the Rabbinical terminology, נֶפֶשׁ was the intelligent, immortal principle, נְשָׁמָה, on the other hand, the animal soul which passes away with the body (Delitzsch, p. 154, note). The more usual trichotomy of the Rabbins, נֶפֶשׁ for the lower soul, רוּחַ for the spirit of life, and נְשָׁמָה for the intelligent soul, may be noted as ministering to the confused usage through which, with some writers, *spiritus* came to signify the animal soul, and *anima* or *mens* the higher soul. See Lord Bacon's psychology as described in Note to Chap. V. p. 107.

SOUL (נֶפֶשׁ ψυχή).—The original use of נֶפֶשׁ is (*a*) for the

principle of life as embodied in individual instances, and
this either with חַיָּה, as Gen. i. 20, 30, or by itself, as Ex.
xxi. 23; Job. xxxi. 39; Jer. xv. 9. This life-principle is
viewed as seated in the blood, Gen. ix. 4; Lev. xvii. 11;
Deut. xii. 23. In this sense it is simply *anima*, the soul
of the flesh. Then (*b*) it becomes equivalent to *animus*, as
the subject of all activities, even of the highest in man,
Deut. iv. 29, vi. 5; Ps. xix. 8, xlii. 2; Isa. lxi. 10; and is
used also of God Himself, Jer. li. 14, on which the reader
may consult Origen, *De Anima* (Ante-Nicene Lib. x. 118).
We then advance to (*c*) its use to denote the individual
possessing life. This usage pervades the Scriptures. It
proceeds on the distinction that the נֶפֶשׁ or ψυχή is the
subject of that personal life, the principle of which is רוּחַ
or πνεῦμα. But " soul," in the Old Testament sense of the
word, does not of itself constitute personality. Delitzsch's
remarks on this point are acute and just (*Bibl. Psych.*
p. 153). The use of soul (נֶפֶשׁ) for a "dead body" is
peculiar to the Old Testament, Lev. xxi. 11; Num. vi. 6, ix. 6,
7, 10, xix. 13. It is most simply explained by Oehler on
the principle of euphemism, just as we speak of a "dead
person" without meaning to say that the personality lies
in the body. Delitzsch's idea, that it may allude to the
impression made by a corpse immediately after death, as
if the soul still lingered by it, is more fanciful. In the
Septuagint and in the New Testament the use of ψυχή is
wider and higher than that of נֶפֶשׁ in the Old, for it has
often to stand for the Old Testament לֵבָב, the heart.

The adjective ψυχικός originally signified in classical
Greek that which pertains to life; then it came to be
used in antithesis to σωματικός. In Old Testament Greek
it occurs only in 4 Macc. i. 32 (ψυχικαί over against σωματι-
καί), and in 2 Macc. iv. 37, xiv. 24 (in the adverbial form,
equivalent to "heartily"). In the New Testament it
takes the remarkable meaning of a contrast, not to σωματικός, but to πνευματικός. (See passages referred to above
under *Pneuma*.) On its peculiar use in Jude 19 the
remark of Cremer seems to be just, namely, that the ψυχι-
κοί are not denied to possess πνεῦμα as a constituent of

human nature, which would have been expressed by μὴ πνεῦμα ἔχοντες, but that they are not so possessed of the πνεῦμα as they might have been. Beck leans to a contrary conclusion (*Bibl. Seelenlehre*, p. 38). He says man, by becoming mere *man with soul*, loses the stamp of the spirit. This view of Beck probably arises from his identifying "soul" with the human ego.

Of the relation of "soul" and "spirit" to each other, we have spoken in Chap. V. pp. 90, 91. The following examples of the combination of רוּחַ and נֶפֶשׁ in the same context may be noted: Ps. xxxi. 6, 8 (Heb.); Isa. xxvi. 9 (with which may be compared the combination of לֵב and רוּחַ in Ex. xxxv. 21). The antithesis of רוּחַ and נֶפֶשׁ in Job. xii. 10, for human life as contrasted with life in other creatures, is entirely singular. The New Testament passages in which πνεῦμα and ψυχή stand together are the well-known ones, Luke i. 47 (with which compare 1 Sam. ii. 1), Phil. i. 27 (where the English has "spirit" and "mind"); 1 Thess. v. 23; Heb. iv. 12.

BODY (σῶμα).—Its Hebrew equivalents are very various. Böttcher, *De Inferis*, p. 20, arranges them as (1) proper, and (2) metaphorical. Under (1) he gives, as the oldest terms derived from the leading parts of the body, גְּוִיָּה, *truncus*, 1 Sam. xxxi. 10 ; עֶצֶם, *os, ossa*, Prov. xvi. 24; בָּשָׂר, *cutis, caro*, flesh, Gen. ii. 24. As the second and third stages, he remarks the use of a proper word for "body," גּוּפָה (*a cavitate*), 1 Chron. x. 12; גְּשֵׁמָא Dan. iii. 27 ; iv. 30 (Heb.); v. 21. He further notes, as an Old Testament usage, the employment of "flesh" and "bones" for the whole body, Gen. ii. 23, Job ii. 5. It is worthy of attention that "flesh and blood," which is not an Old Testament expression, first occurs in the Apocrypha, Sir. xiv. 18, xvii. 31 (see a conjectural emendation of this singular passage in Böttcher, par. 35), 1 Macc. vii. 17, and so passed into the current language of the New Testament. Under (2) there occur in the Old Testament only Job iv. 19, בָּתֵּי חֹמֶר (*houses of clay*), and Dan. vii. 15, נִדְנֶה, *a sheath*. But with these may be compared the New Testament οἰκία τοῦ σκῆνους (2 Cor. v. 1), ναός (1 Cor. vi. 19), σκεῦος (2 Cor. iv. 7). Of Flesh (בָּשָׂר, σάρξ) in its various uses we have spoken, pp. 109–112. The rise of the ethical meaning of σάρξ will probably remain the subject of considerable difference of opinion. That בָּשָׂר in its Old Testament meaning ever goes farther in an ethical direction than the physical weakness and fraility of human nature, has not been conclusively proved. Eccles. ii. 3 and v. 6 are quite insufficient proof. A philosophic origin has been asserted for the ethical force of σάρξ, and Lightfoot avers that such use of it has been traced to Epicurus (*On Philippians*, p. 285, note.)

MIND.—Noῦς is a word of which the scriptural use can be easily traced. It occurs very seldom in the Septuagint. In the few places where it does occur, it represents לֵבָב לֵב, except in Isa. xl. 13, where νοῦν Κυρίου stands for רוּחַ יְהֹוָה; and the rendering is retained in 1 Cor. ii. 16. The apocryphal writers have used it a few times, and in a sense more distinctively Greek. The passage Wisd. ix. 15 is singularly unbiblical, suggesting, as we have said, the Stoical trichotomy, σῶμα, ψυχή, νοῦς. In the New Testament the entire absence of νοῦς, with one exception (Luke xxiv. 45), from the Gospels and from the writings of the older apostles (leaving Rev. xiii. 18, xvii. 9, out of sight), shows how clearly they adhere to the Old Testament psychology, from which the very notion represented by νοῦς was absent. To note its frequent use by Paul, and that especially definite and almost delicate antithesis in which it contrasts with σάρξ in one connection (Rom. vii.) and with πνεῦμα in another (1 Cor. xiv.), will complete its history.

CONSCIENCE.—Συνείδησις is a word of late introduction into the Scriptures. As Old Testament Greek, it occurs once in the canonical books (Eccles. x. 20), where it renders מַדָּע, but obviously rather with the meaning "consciousness" than "conscience." The force of it in Wisd. xvii. 11 is more nearly our own. It does not occur in the Gospels, except in John viii. 9, a passage not usually

reckoned genuine. In the Epistle to the Hebrews and in
the epistles of Paul and Peter its occurrence is plentiful,
and its force equivalent to that which it has received in
modern speech. It is a function of πνεῦμα if we regard it
as self-consciousness, or of καρδία when regarded as moral
approval or disapproval. It may also be viewed as a
function of the renewed πνεῦμα in believers (see Rom.
ix. 1). The Old Testament לֵבָב covered what idea of conscience was akin to Hebrew thought. And it is to be
noted that St. John uses καρδία in a connection where
St. Paul would certainly have used νοῦς or συνείδησις (1 John
iii. 19–21). To trace the advance of the term from its
literal meaning of self-consciousness to its full ethical import would be of interest. Its clear recognition in the
latter sense in Pagan literature is also significant. Lightfoot speaks in somewhat strong terms of this word, as
" the crowning triumph of ethical nomenclature," which,
" if not struck in the mint of the Stoics, at all events
became current coin through their influence." He cites it
as a special instance of " the extent to which Stoic philosophy had leavened the moral vocabulary of the civilised
world at the time of the Christian era " (Essay on " St.
Paul and Seneca " in his *Commentary on the Epistle to the
Philippians*, at p. 301). On the place of conscience in
biblical psychology, see the slightly conflicting views of
Harless, *Christliche Ethik*, Pt. I. c. i. § 8, and Delitzsch,
Biblische Psychologie, III. iv ; Beck's remarks, *Umriss*, etc.,
§ 18, 22, are also worthy of attention.

III

THE DIVINE IMAGE, AND MAN'S PRIMITIVE STATE

Ἀλλὰ καὶ ἐὰν φῇς, Δεῖξόν μοι τὸν Θεόν σου· κἀγώ σοι εἴποιμι ἂν Δεῖξόν μοι τὸν ἄνθρωπόν σου, κἀγώ σοι δείξω τὸν Θεόν μου.—THEOPHILUS OF ANTIOCH, *Ad Autolyc.* lib. i. c. 2.

"In solâ creaturâ rationali invenitur similitudo Dei per modum Imaginis . . . in aliis autem creaturis per modum Vestigii."—AQUINAS, *Summa* I. q. 93, ar. 6.

"Whereas in other creatures we have but the trace of His footsteps, in man we have the draught of His hand."—BP. SOUTH.

GEN. i. 26.—"And God said, Let us make man in our image, after our likeness ; and let them have dominion over the fish of the sea, and over the fowl of the air, and over the cattle, and over all the earth, and over every creeping thing that creepeth upon the earth."

GEN. i. 27.—"So God created man in His *own* image, in the image of God created He him ; male and female created He them."

GEN. v. 1.—This *is* the book of the generations of Adam. In the day that God created man, in the likeness of God made He him."

GEN. v. 3.—"And Adam lived an hundred and thirty years, and begat *a son* in his own likeness, after his image ; and called his name Seth."

GEN. ix. 6.—"Whoso sheddeth man's blood, by man shall his blood be shed ; for in the image of God made He man."

JAS. iii. 9.—"Therewith bless we God, even the Father ; and therewith curse we men, which are made after the similitude of God."

EPH. iv. 24.—"And that ye put on the new man, which after God is created in righteousness and true holiness."

COL. iii. 10.—"And have put on the new *man*, which is renewed in knowledge after the image of Him that created him."

CHAPTER VII

THE DIVINE IMAGE: BIBLICAL AND THEOLOGICAL

[LITERATURE.—Seb. Schmidt. *De Imagine Dei in Homine ante Lapsum* (2nd Edition, Argentorati, 1701). Bp. George Bull, *State of Man before the Fall* (in Works, vol. ii., Oxford Edition, 1846), Macdonald, *Creation and the Fall*, Excursus at p. 296 (Edin., 1856). Grinfield, *The Image and Likeness of God in Man* (Lond., 1837). Harris, *Man Primeval: Constitution and Primitive Condition of the Human Being* (Lond., 1849). O. Zöckler, *Die Lehre vom Urstand des Menschen* (Gütersloh, 1879).]

THE doctrine of the divine image connects itself most intimately with the two questions already discussed, namely, with the Bible account of man's origin, and with the scriptural idea of man's constitution. In itself, indeed, it is the foundation of our entire theology and of revealed religion. For a religion in which God reveals Himself to man in order to reconcile and restore man to Himself, proceeds upon the fact that man was so constituted originally as to be capable of becoming the subject of such revelation and redemption.

The doctrine is found exactly where we should expect to find it,—on the forefront of the sacred records; and in its simplicity and grandeur it is worthy of the place which it occupies. We have to look at it, first, as a biblical definition of human nature, as expressing the type or ideal after which man was formed. Then we have to consider the Bible record of man's primitive state, that we may learn in what sense and to what extent the divine image was actually manifest in man unfallen.

Let us glance briefly (I.) at the leading Scripture passages in which the doctrine is expressed; and then detail (II.), in historical order, the doctrinal views which have been drawn from these.

I. The prime text, Gen. i. 26, 27, we have already discussed as an account of man's origin. Looking at it now as a descriptior of the moral type in which he was formed, we note especially two things brought out by its textual connection. Instead of the expression "after his kind," used of all the other creatures, it substitutes, as the archetype of man's formation, the image and similitude of God. Again, instead of the origination of an order of beings, each of which is a nameless specimen or example of its kind, what we find here is the origination of a person who holds a momentous place in the history of the world. As to the two terms, "image" and "likeness," it has only to be remarked that while both occur in ver. 26, "image" (*Tselem*) alone is twice repeated in ver. 27, and "likeness" (*Demuth*) alone is found in Gen. v. 1. This discourages the attempt of some ancient and modern writers to base important theoretical distinctions on the use of these words here. Especially futile is it to identify *Tselem* with the permanent, and *Demuth* with the perishable element in the divine image. The double expression belongs to the strength and emphasis with which the fact of man's creation in Godlikeness is set forth in this primal passage. Likeness added to image tells that the divine image which man bears is one corresponding to the original pattern.[1] For the rest, the light thrown on the contents of the divine image from the context is chiefly relational. The central and supreme place assigned to man among the other creatures is explanatory of his image on the one side, as the solemn and majestic record of his creation is on the other. By the latter is suggested man's nearness and kinship to his Maker; by the former, his superiority and supremacy over the things made.

The divine image, so far from being peculiar to the first man, or wholly lost to the race by his sin, is spoken of in Gen. v. 1–3 as natural and capable of transmission. The statement of this passage is, that Adam, whom God had created in His likeness (*Demuth*), begat progeny in his own likeness and image. Some, indeed, find in this an expression of man's degeneracy by the Fall. But,— not to insist on the fact that according to the documentary hypothesis, the Elohistic narrative is here resumed, in which, as yet, there has been no mention of a moral degeneracy of the race,—the real significance of the connection appears, when we observe the method of the narrative. It is done with the generation of Cain. That race is ruled out, and appears no more in the history. This chapter begins with a fresh "Book of Generations" (*Sepher Toledoth*) to carry on the account

[1] Oehler's *Theology of the Old Testament*, i. 211 (Clark, Edin., 1874).

of Adam's family by Seth—the genealogy of the pious, of those who " began to call upon the name of the Lord." Accordingly, it here recalls Adam's own creation in the likeness of God; exactly as Luke traces up our Lord's genealogy to Adam through Seth : "Which was of Adam, which was of God." The subject, then, as Hofmann says, is not the moral similarity of Adam's sons to their father, but the homogeneity of father and son, by virtue of which the race, so long as it propagated itself naturally, and not in the manner recorded in Gen. vi. 1, remains like itself, and as it was created by God at the first. This writer concludes that the Godlikeness suggested by the connection is not that of a morally holy being, but of a Lordship which could be transmitted even through one who had become sinful; that not of holy mankind but of man, simply as man, is it henceforth said in Scripture, that he bears the divine image.[1]

From passages such as Gen. ix. 6 and Jas. iii. 9, which unmistakably speak of man as he now is, it becomes clearer that the Image is the inalienable property of the race. To all generations, is it asserted in these two passages, that offence against our fellow-man, either by the murderous hand or by the slandering tongue, is an offence against the Divine Majesty; for man is made in the image, after the similitude of God. Gen. ix. 6 is valuable for its assertion that this image confers a sacredness on human life; that for this reason man is to protect and avenge the life of his fellow-man, and strive to secure the supremacy of his race over the

[1] *Der Schriftbeweis*, i. 287, 288.

earth. Thus it lays a foundation for those principles of jurisprudence on this subject which now rule the civilised world. It is not simply that human life is more precious than that of animals. It is not merely that man is brother to man. The principle here asserted rises far above that of blood-revenge in its most refined form. It asserts that man's life belongs to God: "At the hand of every man's brother will I require the life of man." It confers upon the execution of human justice, in the case of murder, the sacredness of a divine judgment. This very practical result from the idea of the divine image in man helps us to understand the idea itself; for murder assails man's personality, his sovereignty, and this the text declares to be that divinity which ought to hedge him about from the hand of his fellow.[1] Jas. iii. 9 bears a close resemblance in its effect to Gen. ix. 6. It refers to men as they are,—our brother-men, the children of the Lord and Father. It declares that the cursing tongue sins against that similitude of God which is inherent in mankind by creation.

In Ps. viii. the point of view is neither distinctively before sin nor after sin. It is one abstracted from moral history. This psalm, in praising the excellence of the divine name on earth, occupies itself chiefly with

---

[1] Note in this connection the Old Testament use of *Elohim* for judges (Ex. xxi. 6, xxii. 8, 27 (Heb.), and Ps. lxxxii. *passim*). Rulers are, in the New Testament, called Θεοῦ διάκονοι, λειτουργοί (Rom. xiii. 4, 6). They are God's delegates. In this primal passage (Gen. ix. 6), He transfers to mankind His own prerogative of blood-avenging (see the Cain story); therefore His representatives among mankind are also themselves called *Elohim*.

man. It boldly grapples with that constant problem of human thought, the apparent insignificance and the real centrality of man. It reconciles the two by throwing us back on his original constitution. First, his near approach to a divine standing. This mortal man has been constituted a little less than divine: "Thou hast made him (*or*, set him) a little lower than Elohim." If we take "Elohim" here as abstract, equivalent to "divinity" (*numen, göttliches Wesen*), we can see how the translation of the LXX. finds a legitimate foundation. If the meaning be that man, as spiritual, is of the same kind or order of being as God and angels, though subordinated to other members of that order in his degree, then it is conceivable how the expression could be rendered, "Thou hast made him a little lower than the angels," and also how the writer to the Hebrews found this expression exactly suited to his argument when he desired to set forth the dispensational subordination of man to angels at a certain point in his religious development; which point was occupied by Jesus when, as man's representative, He was under the law. The second assertion of man's original dignity in the psalm is that he is the representative of divine rule here below. Man is crowned a king, and the earth, with the works of divine wisdom which fill it, is his kingdom. Man's rule in it is described with much concentrated poetry—a rule extending from the domestic animals immediately around him to the remotest bounds of animate and inanimate creation. The Godlike in man, then, is his constitution "a little lower than divine," on the one hand, and his rule over the divine works on the other. The glory of God in man is brought out by man's greatness in littleness. The excellence which the psalm ascribes to Jehovah's name in all the earth, is that He should mirror Himself in such a one as man, and bring praises even out of the mouths of babes and sucklings. Now, though in all this there is no express mention of the image, yet these two things so exactly correspond to the likeness and the dominion in Gen. i. 27, 28, that we may well call the psalm, with Delitzsch, "a lyric echo of that account of man's creation."

A single expression of St. Paul condenses this interpretation, and illustrates the connection of Ps. viii. with Gen. i. 27. He speaks of man as "the image and glory of God."[1] True, it is "man," not "mankind,"[2] of whom this is affirmed; but the writer plainly has his eye also upon that second record[3] where the man is created first and directly, the woman through the man, so that whatever he is, she is more refinedly, for she is "the glory of the man." The combined expression, "image and glory," amounts then to this: the divine likeness is man's title to royalty on earth.[4] The dominion is that which manifests or reveals the fact that man bears the image of his Maker,—he is the glory of God.

Of the passages already considered, Gen. i. 26, 27 alone belongs to the section of Scripture history before the Fall. Ps. viii. is ideal, not historical. The other passages cited (Gen. v. 1, ix. 6; Jas. iii. 9) speak of

---

[1] 1 Cor. xi. 7.   [2] ἀνήρ not ἄνθρωπος.   [3] Gen. ii. 7–25.
[4] "Des Menschenkönigs Diploma," quoted by Oosterzee.

man as he now is, and clearly warrant the inference
that there is a sense in which the divine image is
inalienable from man.   It is further worthy of notice,
that of the many Scripture expressions denoting the
depth of man's fall, there is no one which describes
the effect of sin upon God's image in man.   St. Paul's
axiom, that "all have sinned and come short of the glory
of God," is the nearest allusion to it.   Indeed, the
formula never occurs in any description of man's now
depraved nature and fallen state.   It is when redemption
is the theme that Scripture resumes the language which
implies a correspondence and conformity between the
human and the divine.

Thus we come to the two classical texts on the
renewal of the image in man through Christ, namely,
Eph. iv. 24, Col. iii. 10.   These have the closest bearing
on the ethical contents of the image.   We must, however, repel the assumption that they were meant to
define primarily what the divine image was in Adam.
They treat expressly of the new man.   The distinct and
intended parallelism between the old man and the new
in both passages leaves us no room to doubt that the
creation signified is not the formation of man at the
beginning, but the new creation in Christ Jesus, and
that the result described is the "new creature"[1] of
2 Cor. v. 17.   That result consists in "righteousness,"
i.e. such rectitude as justice demands, and "holiness," i.e.
purity, the fulness of God in the soul; and both these
are "true" or "of the truth," as contrasted with the
"lusts of deceitfulness" in the old man, and are effects

[1] καινὴ κτίσις.

of " the truth in Jesus " and of renewal in the " spirit of
the mind." The expression, "after God," in Eph. iv. 24,[1]
denotes the divine ideal of the new creation, its formation in righteousness and holiness as contrasted with
the character of ordinary nature.[2] The Author or
Creator referred to in Col. iii. 10 [3] can be no other
than the God of grace, for the result is that new
creation where Christ is all in all. The image according to which is formed this new creation, where " all
things are of God in Christ Jesus,"[4] can be no other
than that " image of His Son,"[5] who, again, is the
" image of the invisible God." [6] But while the creation
of grace is thus the only direct subject of affirmation
in both these passages, the language fairly implies that
man was originally constituted in a divine image, of
which righteousness and holiness in truth or knowledge
were essential features. We are to guard against the
extreme view, which takes these texts as definitions of
the divine image in Adam, as implying that all the
features of the image borne by the new creature were
already in our first parents, so as to be lost by them.
When we content ourselves with the assertion that this
description of the " new man " presupposes corresponding
outlines in the first man which were broken off and
blurred by sin, and which are now for the first time fully
realised in man redeemed and renewed, a sound exegesis
will bear us out.

There are other passages referring to man's regene-

---

[1] κατὰ Θεόν. [2] κατὰ τὴν προτέραν ἀναστροφήν, ver. 22.
[3] τοῦ κτίσαντος. [4] Cf. 2 Cor. v. 17, 18 ; Col. iii. 10, 11.
[5] Rom. viii. 29. [6] Col. i. 15.

rated nature, where, though the image is not expressly
mentioned, the doctrine of it is assumed. The expressions in Matt. v. 48, Luke vi. 36, and 1 Pet. i. 15, 16,
in which believers are exhorted to be " perfect," " merci-
ful," " holy," as their Father in heaven, point to a
similarity or congruity between the natures that are
compared ; though interpreters, almost without exception,
remark that the Greek particles " as," " even as," [1] denote
not equality but similitude, likeness not in degree but in
kind. In 2 Pet. i. 4 it is said to be the aim of the
supernatural arrangement of grace that we might
become " partakers of the divine nature." [2] But this
appears from the context to refer not so much to the
presence of a divine element in the new creature, or to
the indwelling of the Divine Spirit in a regenerate heart,
as to the moral conformity which that " divine power "
produces. The expression, however, is valuable as showing that man's participation in the divine nature is
implied in his original constitution, and promoted by all
restoration and development of that constitution.

What light these texts cast on the thing meant by
this grand formula of the divine image is the main
question—one of " preponderating import not merely
for Anthropology, but also for Christology and Soterio-
logy, and one which in the course of centuries has been
answered in the most diverse ways." [3] We attempt an
answer, therefore, in connection with a rapid historical
sketch of those views.

---

[1] ὥς, καθώς.   [2] θείας κοινωνοὶ φύσεως.
[3] Van Oosterzee, *Christian Dogmatics*, p. 374 (Hodder & Stoughton,
1874).

II. Recalling our exact aim, which is to ascertain what ideas of man and his nature are involved in the biblical theology concerning his creation, fall, and redemption, we find that this first topic of his original image and primitive state has become much involved with dogmatic presuppositions.   Partly has this arisen from the brevity of the Scripture statements.   The primitive state of man became a favourite battle-ground of theologians, because it was like unexplored territory in maps, which the geographer can fill up at his pleasure. Theologians in their systems could draw up and deploy, in this comparatively empty space, the principles which they were afterwards to bring into action in more crowded departments.   The doctrine of the image became a great topic, so soon as sin and grace were the key-positions in theological controversy, because the idea formed of man's original nature and endowments had a direct bearing on the measure of the loss caused by the Fall, and upon the consequent necessity and nature of redemption.

From the earliest to the latest times, need has been felt of attaching a twofold meaning to the image ; and the double terms of the great proto-text seemed to give it express Scripture authority.   Justin Martyr and Irenæus refer image (*Tselem*) to the bodily form, likeness (*Demuth*) to the spirit.   The Alexandrian fathers prefer to understand *Eikon* of the rational basis of man's nature, *Homoiōsis* of its free development.   Augustine distinguished them as *cognitio veritatis* and *amor virtutis ;* the Schoolmen, as " natural attributes " and " moral conformity."   We have already said that the exegesis is incompetent.[1]　It is only another instance of the habit of interpreters to import dogmatic results into the simple and uncritical language of the earlier Scriptures.

The distinction itself, however, between a natural and a moral element in the image, between a constitutional potentiality and an ethical realisation, has proved itself valid at every stage of thought on the subject, though the form of the distinction has varied with the movements of theology. The great controversy concerning sin and grace, which, as we have said, first brought the doctrine of the image into prominence, for long determined that the distinction should turn on what remained after the Fall, and what was lost by the Fall. The Greek fathers had emphasised that which is permanent, and are accordingly said to place the image in the free-will and immaterial nature of man. The Latin fathers emphasise that in the image which perished by sin. When necessity arose of formulating into a dogma the relation between the two, that which the Schoolmen evolved for the Latin Church took the shape that man was created *in puris naturalibus* with a bent to religion; upon which was added, as a supernatural gift, original righteousness, to keep the lower nature in check, and to effect the production of actual holiness. The effect of the Fall upon each of these respectively was thus defined. Through sin the natural Godward bent was only weakened, the supernatural gift was quite lost.

When the strife concerning the doctrines of grace took a new departure at the Reformation, the Evangelical Church had to replace the mediæval view by a fresh

[1] See p. 142, *supra.*

assertion that the image of God was wholly created and natural; yet that a quite lost condition of innocence and holiness, the very power to recover which has departed from fallen man, formed an original element in it. This position Protestants had to maintain against Romish controversialists on the one hand, and Socinians on the other. These were not so much two extremes, as two diverse modes of Pelagianising. The more subtle is that of the Romanists, who seem to exalt the divine image in man by adding to it that peculiar feature which they call supernatural. But an endowment not essentially belonging to human nature, magically given and taken, passing soon away, could not be thought of as proper to the divine image. Hence Bellarmin, availing himself of the old verbal distinction, framed the well-known formula, " Adamum peccando non imaginem Dei sed similitudinem perdidisse." On this theory man is left by the Fall much as he was upon his natural creation, and before the bestowal of the *donum superadditum*,—that is, with u certain ability, though now damaged, to love and serve God. The other Pelagian tendency which the Reformers had to oppose was that which explained away the image into an expression of man's original or general superiority, together with his moral innocence. The Socinians, who, according to Principal W. Cunningham, " usually contrive to find in the lowest deep a lower deep," viewed it as consisting only in dominion over the other creatures. In contrast with this, it was necessary for evangelical divines to bring out the Scripture doctrine of the image, as embracing those features of perfect conformity to the divine character and law which were lost by sin, and which it is the object of redemption to restore. It concerned them to show that not merely a certain attained state of holiness, now lost, belonged to primitive man, but that an "original righteousness," which is now wanting, must have entered into his constitution as created.

With all this, Protestant theologians of both the great sections were careful to maintain both the wider and the stricter sense of the image. In the former sense, it stands for the essence of the soul endowed with the faculty of knowing and willing, the general congruity and analogy between the nature of God and of man, and man's dominion over the creatures. In the latter sense, it stands for that moral conformity to God which man lost by the Fall. The Reformed divines are somewhat more distinct than the Lutherans in maintaining that the image embraced those natural and indestructible features of likeness to God which survive the Fall. Calvin is clear that it includes all that excellence by which man surpasses all other species of living beings; though he argues that what holds the principal place in the renovation of the divine image must have held the like place in the formation of it at the first.[1] Turretin also is very clear that a certain part of the divine image must be held to belong to the substance of the soul, and hence is not lost by the Fall.[2] Divines of the evangelical school in the centuries following the Reformation

---

[1] "Principium quod nuper posui retineo, patere Dei effigiem ad totam præstantiam, quâ eminet hominis natura inter omnes animantium species." Again, "Dei imago est integra naturae humanae praestantia, qui refulsit in Adam ante defectionem."—*Instit.* I. xv. 3, 4.

[2] F. Turret. *Instit. Theologiae Elencticae*, Loc. V. Q. x. sec. 7.

continued to uphold this distinction between what was loseable in the divine image and what was not. When the great Puritan, John Howe, describes it in *The Living Temple* as now defaced and torn down, he says: " We speak not now of the *natural image* of God in man, or the representation the soul hath of its Maker in the spiritual, intelligent, vital, and immortal nature thereof, which image, we know, cannot be lost, but its resemblance of Him in the excellences which appear to be lost, and which were his duty,—a *debitum inesse*,—and could not be lost but by his own great default." [1] More accurately and philosophically it is expressed by Jonathan Edwards thus: " The *natural image* of God consists very much in that by which God in His creation distinguished man from the beasts, namely, in those faculties and principles of nature whereby he is capable of moral agency ; whereas the *spiritual and moral image*, wherein man was made at the first, consisted in that moral excellency with which he was endowed.[2]

The elements now commonly recognised by evangelical divines as forming the divine image, when they speak with special regard to the ethical content of the expression, are moral capacity and actual conformity—or, man's intellectual and moral nature on the one hand, and his original moral perfection on the other. It would, no doubt, have been very convenient and clear if Protestant divines could have agreed to say that the inalienable

---

[1] *Living Temple*, pt. ii. c. iv. sec. 2. *Debitum inesse* was a technical phrase for what was inherent quality of man's proper nature, *due to it*, because necessary to its completeness or perfection.

[2] *On the Freedom of the Will*, pt. i. sec. 5.

divine features in man constituted the *image*, and those actually lost by sin the *similitude*; but it was no mere superstitious dread of seeming to agree in phraseology with Romanists which prevented them. The fallacy of the Scholastic distinction between the *image*, as consisting in the natural attributes of the soul, which are retained, and the *similitude*, in the moral conformity, which was lost, had emerged in the course of discussion. For if we understand man's *moral capacity* as "perfect adaptation to the end for which he was made, and to the sphere in which he was designed to move," the Fall cannot be said to have left that *moral capacity* unimpaired, nor to have destroyed only the *actual conformity*. Neither will Protestant divines allow that the actual moral likeness was other than an essential part of the divine image in man. They will neither sublimate it with the Romanists to a supernatural and additional endowment, nor precipitate it with the Socinians to a mere natural innocency. They maintain that there was, from the first, an "uprightness" in man, a positive spiritual goodness, constituting the most important part of the divine image in which he was made. In this they are most true to the Scripture ideal of the dignity of man's nature, and, quite contrary to what is often supposed of them, are most interested in bringing out clearly the surviving vestiges of the divine image in man as now fallen. In other words, it appears that, however convenient the distinction in thought between the natural and the moral aspect of the image, it does not coincide with the actual division between that in the image which is permanent and that which has been lost by sin. For it is evident that man's entire moral and intellectual endowments, together with his place in creation, which constitute the divine image in the wider sense, are not unaffected by the Fall; while, on the other hand, his original possession of the divine similitude in righteousness and true holiness, or, the image in its stricter sense, is not so lost by sin but that man is capable of renewal in it through grace.

It would be easy enough to pass from all this with the remark that these are idle and obsolete battles about words. But it is not so. These controversies turn on deep and essential differences in the conception of man and creation. Hence their importance to our theme. The controversy between Romanists and Protestants, though seeming to hinge upon such questions as, whether man's original righteousness was concreated or subsequently bestowed, whether it was, in the strict sense, a natural endowment or a supernatural gift, is really a controversy between the Augustinian and the Pelagian view of human nature in its ruin and redemption. This controversy is oft misunderstood in its bearing upon the idea of man. Augustinians, whether Lutheran or Calvinistic, take the high view of man's original, and, in consequence, the dark view of man's fallen state. Pelagians of all shades—Romanist, Socinian, or Remonstrant—take the more liberal or flattering view of man's fallen state, but the low view of man's original nature. It is common, however, to represent the evangelical school of theology as that which vilifies human nature, the liberal as that which exalts it, whereas precisely the reverse of this is the fact.

The Pelagian theory, as represented, for example, by
Romish divines, is that the elements of human nature,
lower and higher, flesh and spirit, were from the first so
balanced against each other that an abnormal restraint,
in the form of a supernatural gift of original righteousness, was added in our first parents to keep the lower in
check.   This once set aside by the Fall, the constitution
of man fallen does not differ very greatly from that in
which he was created.   In other words, the nature of
man has not fallen far, because it had not far to fall.
The Augustinian maintains that man's original state is
one not of supernatural rectitude, but of uprightness by
nature; and, consequently, that when man in the exercise of his free will departed from God, a great shock
was given to the moral universe, a very great ruin befel
man's own moral constitution.   That is to say, the
underlying hypothesis of these two radically diverse
lines in theology is a low view of man's original nature
in the one case, a high view of it in the other; and the
low view belongs to those who make it their boast to
take a more favourable estimate of human nature than
their opponents.   But this is not all.   The origin of
these tendencies lies farther back.   They depend upon
views of the universe that are respectively dualistic and
ethnic on the one hand, monotheistic and scriptural on
the other.   To the Pelagian, evil seems as natural as
good.   His scheme of thought involves him in the Mani-
chæism from which Augustine had escaped, and which
he hated, or at least in the Neo-Platonism, which sees in
the universe a cosmos or order, evolved out of primary
ataxia or disorder, and finds evil something inherent and

inexpugnable.[1] The Augustinian view of the world is that which coincides with Scripture; namely, that a Being entirely good is the sole author of nature and the immediate originator of man. The Bible view of man's constitution fits into its exquisite picture of the primeval world. Nature is not evil, either in whole or in part. Pleasantness, innocence, perfection, are the features of the scene. "God saw everything that He had made, and behold it was very good." In the centre of that picture is man, made in the image of the Supreme Good Himself.

[1] Μεμιγμένη γάρ οὖν δὴ ἡ τοῦδε τοῦ κόσμου φύσις, ἔκ τε νοῦ καὶ ἀνάγκης. Καὶ ὅσα παρὰ Θεοῦ εἰς αὐτὸν ἥκει, ἀγαθά· τὰ δὲ κακὰ, ἐκ τῆς ἀρχαίας φύσεως, τὴν ὕλην λέγων τὴν ὑποκειμένην, οὔπω κοσμηθεῖσαν εἰ θεῷτο.—Plotini, *Ennead*, I. viii. 77.

CHAPTER VIII

MODERN FORM OF THE DOCTRINE

MODERN philosophical divines take a less strictly theological view of this great formula than did the Reformers, but make strenuous endeavours to interpret the divine image on its metaphysical and ethical sides. When we sift and summarise the views of Schleiermacher, Hofmann, Julius Müller, Oehler, Delitzsch, we find ourselves in a region of thought differing very considerably from that of the previous ages.[1] These more recent thinkers take their stand upon the permanent aspect of the divine image. Indeed, it has been successfully made out that this biblical definition of man's nature is given as his distinction among created beings, rather than as the distinction of man unfallen from man fallen. This can be maintained in perfect consistency with the Scripture view of the Fall; and, in truth, when properly handled, helps to explain the complex effects which follow upon the entrance of sin. But whereas at one period in the history of Reformed Theology it was important, in discussing the image, to direct attention to the greatness of the loss which human nature sustained by the Fall, it is now of more immediate moment to insist strongly on the

[1] See Note to this chapter.

divine image as man's original type and inalienable distinction from all other creatures on earth.

Delivered from the old strife as to how much of the image was lost by the Fall, and how much retained after it, theologians have less occasion to specify in what elements or constituents of man's nature the image resides. They are more free to look at the general analogy or congruity between God and man which Scripture presents, and therefore to proceed in the simple and non-analytic method of the Bible itself. Yet the subject has lost none of its importance. The greatest of modern controversies turns upon it; for the battle of the supernatural has the key of its position in the nature of man. Whether there be anything in the universe above mere physical causation and succession is the vital question for the philosophy and theology of our day. But the denial of a divine supernatural is logically impossible, so long as man's own being cannot be explained without allowing to it something which transcends mere physical nature. The Bible, by putting man in the rank of the *Elohim*, by co-ordinating the human and the divine so far as to make the one the image of the other, holds the citadel of this controversy, and shows us how great is its strength. Let us ask, then, how the Bible idea of God and the Bible idea of man cast light on each other.

The Scripture never speaks of the divine image in man, but always of man as formed after the divine image. And this indicates a profound principle of biblical thought. It presupposes God, to account for man. It never sets us the " Sisyphus task " of proving

11

God and the supernatural from man and nature.[1]   Thus,
by "the divine image," the Bible does not mean those
elements in man from which an idea of God may be
framed, but conversely those features in the Divine
Being of which man is a copy.   If we read what the
Bible says of God in relation to the world, and what of
God in Himself, we shall get leading lines for its delineation of man; always premising that of the Divine Idea
man is a created copy, not, like the Logos, an essential
image.

And, first, of the analogy between the relation of God
to the universe, and the relation of man to the other
creatures.   Students of revelation are but slowly learn-
ing to appreciate the magnificence and breadth of its
discovery of God.   Nowhere is this breadth more remarkable than in its description of the relation of God
to the world.   A true biblical Theism, avoiding the extremes in speculation of which Pantheism on the one
hand and Deism on the other are examples, yet gathering up all in these speculative views that is true, can
represent God as at once the Maker and the Upholder
of the world.   In other words, the Bible represents
God's relation to the world as at once immanent and
transcendent.   He is spoken of as creating it and ceasing, yet not ceasing to inform it; as in the world, but
not of it; as making all things for Himself, yet giving

---

[1] "It seems to me that both the sceptic and dogmatic schools of
thought alike assume erroneously that the true method of procedure is
this: 'Granting man and nature, to prove God and the supernatural,'—
a Sisyphus task which I am sure must for ever fail."—R. Holt Hutton,
Essays, Theological and Literary, vol. i. p. 219, 2nd Edition (London,
1877).

Himself to all things. Man, on the other hand, in relation to nature around him, is a created copy of God in
His relation to the universe. This is brought out by the
position assigned him in the order of creation. He
appears last, as the scope and end of all things earthly,
—the *terminus ad quem*,—and therefore as the similitude
of God, who is the " archetypal purpose of the universe." [1]
Still more clearly is it set forth by the place claimed for
him among the beings created, what theologians call
" his dominion over the creatures." As described in the
purpose and fiat of his creation at the first,[2] in the renewal of that commission after the flood,[3] in the ideal
picture of Ps. viii., in the redemption-victory fore-
shadowed in 1 Cor. xv. 22–28, man is set on earth as the
instrument and imitator of God, to appropriate nature
consciously and formatively to himself. To this world
of earth man is, in a sense, what God is to the world at
large. Its various grades of being lead to him and look
up to him. Its provisions and arrangements have respect to his use. Its forces and treasures serve his
purposes. He modifies its races of plants and animals.
He discovers and utilises its laws. He subdues nature
and her tribes. He makes earthly existence and human
toil things sacred to God, since he is God's vicegerent
and representative here below. He stands, in short, in
the midst of the material processes of nature and the
humbler denizens of the world as the divine shadow or
second self,—" the image and glory of God." At the
same time, these scriptures bring out the relation of

---

[1] Hofmann, *Schriftbeweis*, i. 290, etc.
[2] Gen. i. and ii.   [3] Gen. ix. 1–7.

man to Him who made the world.   The being who is set in the midst of the garden to till the ground, in the midst of the creatures to understand and name the animals, to dress the fairest of God's earth and keep it, is to carry back to God the praises of that world over which He has made him lord.   In reading the laws of nature, he is " thinking after Him the thoughts of God." In imitating the works of nature he is expressing the law of God written on his intellect; in subduing, improving, civilising, he is exercising towards God nature's best homage.   And he ought to go much farther.   As a living temple in the midst of nature, he ought to make its dumbness vocal and its voices articulate, to translate its animal gladness into intelligent thanksgiving, its irrational yet instinctive homage into a full-souled, high-hearted worship : " O Lord our Lord, how excellent is Thy name in all the earth ! "

Advancing from the Scripture view of God's relation to the world to its view of what He is in Himself, we find those grandly simple definitions of the Divine Being : God is " Spirit," " Light," " Love."   Let us see how these may find a parallel in man, the created copy.

It corresponds with all we have traced of the biblical psychology, that it is on the side of *Spirit* man should primarily exhibit an analogy with the divine nature. It is the only element in man's constitution which is properly ascribed to God.   He is Spirit.   Absolutely and supremely, spiritual existence is affirmed of God. He is said, moreover, to be the Father of spirits, and the God of the spirits of all flesh; indicating that the spiritual world, including man in so far as he is spiritual, stands in a closer relation to God than the corporeal. We have already sufficiently guarded against the Platonising form of this idea—a form given to it by some of the Greek Fathers, who made *pneuma* something physical connecting man with God. This form of statement easily leads to the conclusion, that through the Fall human nature has been constitutionally altered by the loss of a part or element; whereas the Bible doctrine is that man's nature is morally lowered by the loss of its purity. The standpoint of the Bible psychology is always that of the divine origination of man. His life—animal, intellectual, moral—is spiritual, because specially in-breathed of God. The " spirit in man " is the " inspiration of the Almighty," and man is spiritual in so far as he lives and acts according to his divine origin and basis of life. Thus does Scripture teach that the spiritual nature which man has, the spirit of man which is in him, affords a parallel or analogy to the absolute and supreme Spirit which God is.

We find, accordingly, that the Bible makes *Intellect* or *Rationality* in man—not only a function of " spirit " in him, but a function flowing from and corresponding to something in God. It is the breath of the Almighty that giveth man instruction and understanding. The scene in the garden, when the Lord God brought the animals to Adam to be named, presents this idea in a pictorial form. That " admirable philosophy lecture," as Bishop Bull has it, which Adam, appointed by God Himself, read on all the other animals, denotes the correspondence of divine and human intelligence: " Whatsoever Adam called any living creature, that was the name thereof."[1] "I think, O Socrates, that the truest account of these matters is, that some power more than human gave the first names to things, so as to make them necessarily correct."[2] Similar is the ascription to the artificers of the tabernacle, of wisdom, understanding, cunning workmanship, together with the Spirit of God.[3] Thus all scientific knowledge and artistic skill, all the results of reason, Scripture ascribes to divine assistance; not from a vague sentiment of piety, but in right of its consistent theory that the spirit in man corresponds to the Spirit of his Maker, and is sustained by it. Teaching like this is a foundation for the loftiest philosophy of man. It is at once an assertion of the preciousness of the individual and a prediction of the progress of the race. The true idea of human greatness we owe not to modern thought, but to the primary axioms of revelation. "It is indeed an extraordinary anomaly that a truth for which we are indebted to Scripture alone has become the very watchword of infidelity, and that the enthusiasts of unbelief, its poets, dreamers, and political agitators, should have gone mad upon an idea which is historically the gift of revelation to mankind—the greatness of man as such."[4]

"The sacred representation of man's original relationship to God excels in sublimity, truth, and force. . . . Ancient philosophers have already felt, and in some

[1] Gen ii. 19.

[2] Οἶμαι μὲν ἐγὼ τὸν ἀληθέστατον λόγον περὶ τούτων εἶναι, ὦ Σώκρατες, μεῖζω τινὰ δύναμιν εἶναι ἢ ἀνθρωπείαν τὴν θεμένην τὰ πρῶτα ὀνόματα τοῖς πράγμασιν, ὥστε ἀναγκαῖον εἶναι αὐτὰ ὀρθῶς ἔχειν.—Plato, Cratylus, 438, C.

[3] רוּחַ אֱלֹהִים, Ex. xxxi. 3.

[4] J. B. Mozley, Ruling Ideas in Early Ages, p. 232 (Lond., 1877).

degree expressed this truth; but revelation has been the first to give to that feeling its just expression and its highest meaning. It teaches us to think humbly of ourselves, but loftily of mankind." [1]

Another point of analogy between the divine and the human spirit the Bible finds in *Self-consciousness*. "A candle of the Lord is the spirit of man searching through all the chambers of the heart." [2] The phrase "candle of the Lord" may assert divine origination— the light in man which the Lord has kindled—or divine possession—the light which is His, the true light which lighteth every man—or both; but the characteristic of the human spirit to which it affixes the description is its self-penetrating power, that it searches the innermost regions of the human being. [3] With a very similar figure, moral consciousness or conscience is denoted in the New Testament as "the eye," "the light of the body," "the light within." Still more explicitly is it asserted that the spirit of the man which is in him alone knows the things of the man, and is therefore analogous to the Divine Spirit, which alone knoweth the things of God. [4] This analogy is, in yet another text, strengthened by the idea of correspondence or communication. "The Spirit itself beareth witness with our spirit that we are the children of God." [5] It may be fairly inferred from these passages that the Bible regards self-consciousness in man as an essential feature of the divine similitude.

---

[1] Van Oosterzee, *Christian Dogmatics*, p. 377.

[2] Prov. xx. 27.

[3] חַדְרֵי־בָטֶן, ταμιεῖα κοιλίας.

[4] 1 Cor. ii. 11.

[5] Rom. viii. 16.

From self-consciousness it is a short step to *Personality*. It is a truism that self-conscious free personality is the Bible representation of God. Pervading every line of Scripture, from the first to the last, runs the assumption that God is personal. It is easy enough to call this anthropomorphism. But the Bible, as a revelation from God to man, begins with God. And its own account of its doctrine is not that it gives a God fashioned like unto man, but that God can reveal Himself to man, because man is made in the likeness of God. No wonder on this showing that man should be taught to think of God as Person, Will, Holiness, Love,—ideas of which he finds some copies in his own constitution, since that constitution is framed upon the divine model. It is not in any metaphysical formula that the Bible claims personality in man as the image of something in God, but in its profound principle of the relation between God and man, *i.e.* between God and the individual human being, as well as between God and the human race. This principle is asserted, for example, in Num. xvi. 22, where the relation of God to the spirits of all flesh is pleaded as a reason for His dealing with one man who has sinned, rather than that He should punish a whole people. It is repeated in Num. xxvii. 16 as a reason why God should choose a particular leader for the congregation. The same argument of divine property in man is made the foundation of a splendid declaration by the prophet Ezekiel[1] of God's moral dealing with individuals, as contrasted with the unbroken

[1] Ezek. xviii. 1–4, 19–32.

federalism on which Israel presumed to reckon. The right of God in each soul (where *nephesh* denotes the human being, " all souls are mine," ver. 4) is made the ground of the divine prerogative to exercise in each individual case both punishment and pardon. The other side of this relation is presented in those passages which speak of man as existing for God, even the Father,[1] as sought for His worship,[2] as redeemed to an eternal life which consists in the knowledge of the Father and the Son.[3] Even in his present fallen condition, and under the most unfavourable forms of that condition, St Paul represents man as being the offspring of God, to this effect, " If haply we may feel after Him, and find Him." [4] In this passage the entire inwardness of the resemblance between the offspring and the great Parent is made a reason against the artistic efforts of the Greek paganism to humanise the divine. Since man is the offspring of God, he ought not to think that he can frame an outward image of God,—a far better one lies deep within. The relationship of man with God ought to be thought of not as physical, but as moral. The sentiment that " we are the divine offspring " is quoted to illustrate the fact that mankind has been destined to seek God, who was not far from them, *i.e.* who has made Himself cognisable and conceivable by them. Only personal beings can feel after and find a personal God, and in so doing their likeness to Him is affirmed and confirmed.

We cannot complete the analogy between divine and

---

[1] εἰς αὐτόν, 1 Cor. viii. 6.
[2] John iv. 23.
[3] John xvii. 3.
[4] Acts xvii. 27–29.

human personality without a glance at the Trinity in unity. This doctrine is one of the most prolific and far-reaching among the discoveries of revelation. Fully to receive it, influences most profoundly every part of our theological system and of our practical religion. It is that which sets the theism of the Bible on a ground of vantage far above all the partial systems of the philosophers. It is the consummation and the only perfect protection of Theism. It alone clears the relation of God to the world from all the defects of Deism, Polytheism, and Pantheism respectively. It alone furnishes the connecting link between God and man in the person of the Incarnate Logos. It alone provides for the absolute truth of that entirely biblical definition, "God is Love." The God of the Bible is a totally different being from the solitary God of the deist. How the God of Deism can be a loving God it is hard to conceive; that he should ever be declared to be Love in his very essence is inconceivable. For in this philosophic figment which has too oft usurped the place of God even in Christian theology, knowledge and power are in a sense superior to love. In the God of the Bible, on the other hand, absolute being, unbeginning and self-sufficing existence, are united in the most marvellous way to essential relativity and unbeginning love. And it is the Trinity in unity which gives us this grand conception. The intertrinitarian relations are coeval with Godhead. God is not first solitary existence, then power in creation, then love to the created, then pity for the fallen,— these latter being secondary effluences from a God who is in the first place self-centred. On the contrary,

God is essential and eternal Love.   Love in exercise
from eternity has laid the foundations of all that God
is to His creatures, and especially to man.   Hence
the bearing of the doctrine of the Trinity upon that of
the divine image.   "We are apt to take the word
'Father' as metaphorical in its application to God, a
metaphor derived from human parentage."[1]   The
doctrine of the Trinity implies the converse.   If there
be an Eternal Son, there must have been an Eternal
Father,—an absolute and essential Fatherhood must
belong to Godhead.   The most sacred human relationships, therefore, are copies of realities eternally existing
in God.   The relations of man to God and to his
fellow-man have their archetype in relations which lie
within the essence of the Godhead.   For the divine
original, after which man is made, is thus presented
not as mere sovereign will, but as eternal love ; not as
exclusive life in the absolute and infinite, but as that
fulness of life which cannot be without a perfect union
of distinct personalities.

Let us note that exactly here some light arises on
that subtle element of personality in man.   Instead of
saying that personality is not strictly, but only by way
of accommodation, ascribed to the persons of the Godhead,—as if person were more properly used when
applied to man,—ought we not, on the analogy just
suggested, to say the reverse ?   Ought we not to say that
personality in its proper and archetypal sense, as inherent

---

[1] R. H. Hutton, *Essays*, vol. i. p. 235, in a characteristic passage
contrasting the Unitarian with the Catholic and Evangelical conception
of God.

in God, is discovered to us through the Trinity in unity, and that herein is revealed at once the personality of God and the image of that personality in man ? The absolutely solitary God of natural religion is not one whose personality receives any illumination to our minds from our own, for no such absolute, self-centred, self-sufficing personality is conceivable among men. If this be personality at all (for can person be realised without another in whom it shall be reflected ?), it is such as has no shadow of a copy among us. There has never been any Adam made in the image of the God of Deism. Every human being has a consciousness of freedom and personality, given only along with a sense of relation and inter-dependence, which finds its prototype not in the God of the philosophers, but in the God of the Bible. The God who is essentially Three-in-one, an inter-linked personality—this God alone furnishes the mould on which our personality could be formed.

Thus we seem to get a full meaning for those words : "Let US make man in OUR image after OUR likeness." The emphasis on plurality in the Maker is very poorly accounted for by those who would exclude a trinitarian interpretation, either by reading it as the sovereign "we" on the one hand, or "we, the divine order," meaning God and angels, on the other. In the light of the entire biblical delineation of God, the words have no strain put upon them, but are only seen to be divinely pregnant, if we hold them as now indicating to us that man was created an image of *something inter-trinitarian*. If we reject, as we must do, the patristic scholasticism of finding that something in the individual constitution,

—in the " three souls " of the Platonists, or in the three elements of the trichotomy,—we are fully borne out by Scripture when we put it that the inter-trinitarian relations of God find a copy in man's personality, as related to God on the one hand and to his fellow-men on the other.

The question here suggests itself, What relation, then, does the image of God in man bear to the Second Person in the Trinity,—to Him who is the image of the invisible God ?

What Scripture clearly teaches as to the Christological relations of the divine image can be very briefly stated. It has two lines of statement connecting the Son of God with the formation or constitution of mankind,—the one referring to creation, the other to redemption. Man is represented in Scripture as the crown or goal of that earthly creation of which the Eternal Word is the Author. The Eternal Word,—Image of the Invisible God, is also declared to be the first-born of the whole creation—the Absolute Heir and Sovereign Lord of all. There is thus a propriety in holding man to be in this sense a copy of the Logos, to be created after the image of the Image. But there is no express Scripture assertion of this resemblance of man, as at first created, to the Eternal Son. On the contrary, it is always the image or likeness of God that is spoken of in this connection. That the Logos is He through whom, and in whom, and for whom man is created, is, of course, implicitly asserted in Scripture. But, as Delitzsch says, it would be a mistake to affirm that man was created after the image of the Son, and not of the Father or of the Holy Spirit. Everywhere Scripture says that man was created after the image of the Elohim, or of the Godhead.   Man is called the Image and Glory, not of Christ, but of God.[1]

On the other hand, when we come to the new creation, the language of Scripture is explicit in asserting that the Son is the prototype of redeemed or renewed humanity.   The divine image is restored in those who are predestinated " to be conformed to the image of His Son ";[2] we are renewed in the spirit of our mind only as we " put on the new man, which is renewed in knowledge after the image of Him that created him ";[3] and in this new creation Christ is all in all.   Our likeness to His image is only to be completed when in the final manifestation of the Redeemer and of the redeemed as sons of God, we shall see Him as He is.[4]   Then the resemblance shall extend even to the outward form our humanity is to wear, for " He shall transform the body of our humiliation that it may be made conformable to the body of His own glory."   " As we have borne the image of the earthy, we shall also bear the image of the heavenly," that is, of " the second Man, the Lord from heaven."[5]

All this is clear.   But when we attempt any more detailed connection between these two lines of statement, we find little in Scripture to support us.   When we endeavour to connect in thought the relation of the Logos to humanity in the first creation with the relation of the incarnate Redeemer to renewed humanity, we

[1] 1 Cor. xi. 7. See, however, for the theory of the Christ-Image, Grinfield's booklet, named on p. 141.

[2] Rom. viii. 29.   [3] Col. iii. 10, 11.

[4] Cf. Rom. viii. 19, 1 John iii. 2.

[5] Phil. iii. 21 ; 1 Cor. xv. 49, 47.

enter upon a somewhat "dim and perilous way." It looks very tempting to say that man must have been created at first in the image of Him who was afterwards to be incarnate for man's redemption; that there must have been a special relation of the pre-existent Logos to mankind, preparatory to that near relation which He was afterwards to assume when He became flesh. But it leads directly to the theory of an incarnation apart from the necessity of redemption. And the evangelical Church has always been jealous of speculations leading that way. Some of them are pre-Christian. Philo characteristically holds man an image of the Logos, whom, indeed, he calls the Archetypal Man. The Jerusalem Targum makes the Logos say, "The Adam whom I created is the only-begotten Son in the world, as I am the only-begotten Son in the high heavens." The theory appears in Christian theology as early as Irenæus,[1] and stray hints of it can be found in Tertullian, Clement (Alex.), and Eusebius. It was a favourite speculation of the Schoolmen, such as Hales, Aquinas, Occam, and Bonaventura. It was mooted by Osiander, a kind of Schoolman among the Reformers. But Reformation theology distinctly disowned it, consequently the proposition on which it was based has also been looked upon with disfavour.[2] S. Schmidt, alluding to opinions held by disciples of Origen, and in the Middle Ages by Peter Lombard, represents the view that Christ only was the prototype of Adam's creation as one rejected by the Church, and rejected because of the terms of the

---

[1] See *Contra Omnes Hæreticos*, V. xvi. § 2.
[2] See Calvin, *Instit.* II. xii. 4–7 ; Mastricht, *Theologia*, i. 441.

original edict of man's formation in the image of God.[1]

Earnest thinkers in theology have often sighed for some pathway that would lead direct from an original relation of the eternal Logos with the human race to the actual incarnation of the Redeemer. Some have even said that the theory of expiation cannot " retain its place in the thoughts of the Church unless it can be shown that the death of Christ as a propitiation and a sacrifice for the sins of men is the highest expression of an eternal relation between Christ and the human race." [2] Doubtless there is something more in the great texts (Col. i. 15–17; Eph. i. 10–22; Rom. viii. 18–23, etc.) which combine the relation of the Son to the universe with that of the glorified Redeemer to the " restitution of all things," than the Church has ever formulated. In that direction there is theological territory to be possessed. But it would serve no end of conquest to open toward it mere hypothetical gateways. For to affirm that man was at first created an image of the Logos is but a hypothesis, and one at best but slenderly supported.

Note to Chapter VIII

RECENT VIEWS OF THE DIVINE IMAGE

The following sentences present a brief summary of the considerably divergent opinions put forth by the five modern Continental theologians named in the chapter.

---

[1] *Tractatus de Imagine Dei*, p. 339.
[2] Dale on *The Atonement*, p. 405.

SCHLEIERMACHER notes its emphasis in Gen. i. 26, 27, as expressing the type of man; not referring to the first man in his individuality, but rather as he is the first copy of the human species; for him it sets forth the nature of man in its supereminence above that of all other creatures. As for any direct information to be further derived from the expression, he is inclined to hold that little or nothing can be made of it, because of the untenable consequences in which one is landed by every attempt to reason from man the copy to God the original,—reasonings which leave only an alternative of gross pantheism on the one hand, or still more gross anthropomorphism on the other, or at least an impure mixing up of the divine and human, which leads either to the ascription of properties to God not to be conceived as divine, or to man of such as are not conceivably human.   This (says he) is an example how little biblical expressions, especially in connections not expressly didactic, are to be transferred *brevi manu* to the language of dogmatics.   He does not therefore wonder that many theologians, seeing these consequences of a rigid interpretation of that divine declaration (about the image), incline with the Socinians to refer it rather to the plastic and governing (*bildende und beherrschende*) relation of man to outward nature than to man's inner being.   Gathering so little from the sacred narrative, it is to him matter of indifference whether it be intended to be historical or not. He does not expect to be able to evolve from it any information how the first man was educated or came to the knowledge of God.   He is content with the position demanded by his own scheme of Christian belief, namely, that since piety or religion is a common element of all human life, it must be as old as the human race itself; and the first human beings must have been in a position to effect the development of the God-consciousness in those who immediately succeeded them.   This constitutes for him " the original perfection of the human being," and is quite consistent in his view with an incapacity long to resist temptation.   Of this theory of man's original state it may be not unfairly said, that it represents him as created in a condition of unstable moral equilibrium.   It is not much, if at all, higher than the Pelagian view. [*Der christliche Glaube*, i. 337, 338. For Schleiermacher's view of original righteousness, see Chapter ix. *infra*.]

HOFMANN maintains that the scriptural doctrine of the image was never meant to express what kind of being man is, but only in what relation to God he was created.[1] So he values his own definition of the "image," because it says nothing about the constitution of human nature, but only sets forth the double relationship of that nature to God. In discussing Gen. i. 26, he defines wherein, according to him, the divine image in man consists. That it refers to similarity of form, falls with the assumption that God appeared to man in a bodily shape. The connection will not suffer us to think of a similarity in holy moral being, for the thing described is not the formation of Adam as distinguished from his now sinful posterity, but of mankind in contradistinction from the animal world. Neither is it the dominion alone. This is a consequence of the divine likeness, but not the content of it. Man rules over the earth and the animal world as a personal being. The divine image therefore consists in that which makes him capable of ruling over the world around him. He is created to be a free, conscious ego ; and in virtue of this, he, a created and corporeal being, is related to his environment, as the Godhead, which is a Spirit, is related to the universe at large. The divine image therefore denotes not a moral condition, but a moral relation. Hence it is propagated even by the first man after his fall (Gen. v. 1), and is predicated of man not as holy, but of man as he is man (Gen. ix. 6 ; Jas. iii. 9 ; 1 Cor. xi. 7). We say, then, in accordance with Scripture, that the image consists in the personality of man the corporeal being, and we have also Scripture with us if we go farther and express the double relationship of man to the divine. Since, on the one side, man is a conscious, free personality, on the other side a nature or being serving himself by means of himself (*sich zum Mittel seine selbstdienende Natur*), he thus becomes the image of God in a twofold manner. There is

It is at this point that he makes objections to the possibility of biblical psychology, in a passage already quoted, Note to Chap. I.

posited on the one hand a relation of man to God, which is a copy of the inner relations of the Godhead. On the other hand, man becomes a created copy of God, as He is the archetypal purpose of the universe. We can only draw our proof of this, says Hofmann, from the New Testament doctrine of Christ, not from the Old Testament account of man's creation. And he argues against Delitzsch, who will have man to be an image of the Trinity, that both positions are true; just as of Christ it may be said all fulness of the Godhead dwells in Him (Col. ii. 9), and yet that in the sense of John xiv. 9 He is the image of the invisible God, *i.e.* of the Father (Col. i. 15; Heb. i. 3). Thus we may quite consistently affirm that man's relation to his environment is an image of the relation of the Godhead in general to the world, and also that humanity has a more defined relation to the Father in the Son; so that as the divine likeness in the Son is more accurately expressed by saying that he is the image of the Father, the divine likeness in man is more fully defined by saying that he is the image of the Son, or rather that the relation of man to God is a relation to the Father in the Son; that humanity is δόξα Χριστοῦ, as the woman is δόξα ἀνδρός, 1 Cor. xi. 3, 7 (*Schriftbeweis*, i. 283–291).

JULIUS MUELLER is more consistent in working out a similar line of thought. He does not start with saying that the expression tells only of man's relations, and not of his being or nature. He holds that צֶלֶם and דְּמוּת denote a resemblance in character between the image and its original, rather than in the relation which each bears to something else (*Christian Doctrine of Sin*, ii. 351); that not only is there no positive proof in Scripture that the image wherein man was created was lost in the Fall, but that there are statements proving the presence in man of God's image still; that the distinction of theologians between a wider and a stricter sense of the image is a makeshift, to bring the texts into harmony with their doctrine concerning the forfeiture of the divine image (ii. 353). The way in which the divine image is introduced in Genesis suggests, he says, that it is "something in man which specially distinguishes him from all other existences in nature." He holds, therefore, that it consists manifestly in man's personality. Other beings show forth His power and Godhead, but beings in His image are a revelation of God, not for others only, but for themselves; who not only are, but know that they are: who are conscious of themselves, and therefore of God also. That IN GOD man lives, etc. (Acts xvii. 28, 29), implies that man must be a self-conscious *ego*, a person, for he can be in God so far only as he is, in the highest sense, in himself; and for this very reason he is the "offspring" of God (τοῦ γένος ἐσμέν), God and man,—absolute and relative personality, —being a γένος distinct from all impersonal existence. The truth that IN HIM we live, that we are of His kind, is stated as a guarantee that "we can feel after Him and find Him" in His world. Man should not let himself be hindered from knowing and loving God, as like to himself, by any deistic or pantheistic abstractions which would deny him this fellowship. God, in creating man, made him in His image. There is therefore no anthropomorphism when man conceives of God as a being like himself, a Spirit who knows and wills. "If then, the divine image in man is spiritual personality, it cannot be a merely transitory gift, but is an essential part of his constitution, still possessed by him, though in a state of sin, leading to his dominion over the creatures, and fully realised in the image of Christ wrought out in him by redemption" (ii. pp. 354, 355, 2nd ed. Clark, Edin. 1868).

OEHLER holds that Gen. i, 26 expresses the very idea of man, that this divine image is propagated (Gen. v. 1, 3), and that it is clear from Gen. ix. 6 that the divine image lies inalienably in man's being. In answer to the question what is to be understood by it, he posits the *whole dignity of man* (כָּבוֹד וְהָדָר, Ps. viii. 6), in virtue of which (1) human nature is sharply distinguished from that of the beasts, as proved by the unique divine act of human origination, by the fact that there was no mate for man among the animals, and by the permission to kill the beasts, but not man; and (2) man is set over nature as a free personality, designed for communion with God, and fitted to take God's place on earth (*Old Testament Theology*, i. 211, 212).

DELITZSCH holds that the image of God in man refers primarily to his *invisible nature*, founding this remark upon his exegesis of Ps. viii. " Thou hast made him fall a little short of the nature of the Elohim, *i.e.* of the divine and angelic," which must be incorporeal and purely spiritual. Then, as distinguished from the angels, it is peculiar to man that God created him, the earthly one, after His image. He thinks it not erroneous to regard the spiritual nature of man as the image, in so far as that is something common to men and angels. However, this view of the Fathers, which seems to satisfy a later theology, that the divine image subsists in the νοερὸν καὶ αὐτεξούσιον, or, as we say, in personality, he holds to be quite insufficient, for fallen man is also a person. But he rejects the distinction of a broader or physical and a narrower or ethical aspect of the image, the first of which cannot be lost, and the second of which has been lost, as subject to the charge of an unreconciled dualism, felt even by the dogmatists who have invented it. Scripture, he says, only knows of one likeness of God in man, which is at once moral and physical, and which cannot be lost morally without being at the same time physically ruined. Scripture nowhere says that fallen man possesses the *imago Dei* still in living reality : it places the dignity of man now only in the fact that he has been created after the image of God. This strikes us as exceedingly correct and acceptable, provided it be not bound up with any theory as to the πνεῦμα in man, which would commit us to view the image as physically constituted in creation and physically destroyed by the Fall. What he goes on to add in his latest edition as to the image in man being a creaturely copy of the entire absolute life of the Triune God, and not merely of the Logos, belongs to the dreamy theosophy which is the least valuable feature in the productions of Dr. Delitzsch. [See *System of Biblical Psychology*, pp. 78--87. Edin. 1867.]

CHAPTER IX

MAN'S PRIMITIVE STATE

HAVING traced the divine similitude in which man was formed on its natural side, we should now pass on to its moral aspect. It is plain that the former belongs to what is permanent in the image, in the modified sense in which that distinction can be accepted.[1] Man's self-conscious, free personality, illustrated as it is by his place in creation, is that God-likeness which belongs to him as such, and is inalienable. When we come to speak of what is supremely divine, namely, that God is Holy Love, we can no more say that man as he is will be found to bear the likeness of God. But we have still to take note of the Bible doctrine that man was created in uprightness.[2] This doctrine sufficiently asserts the capacity of man's nature, even though now fallen, for receiving the moral image of God; the possibility of the restoration of that image, nay, of its renewal by grace in a degree higher than that of its original creation. At present, however, we are discussing the image as the Bible declares it to have been originally bestowed, and accordingly we must next inquire — To what extent the primitive state, as described in Scripture,

[1] See *ante*, p. 156. [2] Eccl. vii. 29.

reveals in the first human beings the *moral likeness* of God.

The primitive state of man is represented in Scripture as perfect in its natural and moral conditions—a being created in the divine image could begin no otherwise than as holy and happy. Yet it will appear, upon examination, that Scripture ascribes to primitive man the conditions of attaining perfection, rather than the actual attainment of it.

I. Take first the *natural* conditions,—the physical and intellectual elements. The idea of man conveyed to us in the biblical narrative of his creation, is, as we have seen, one that connects him with earth and the creatures on one side, and with God on the other. It sets him before us as God's representative here below. In keeping with this original idea of man is the primitive state which the narrative goes on to depict. It is one of happiness,—of undisturbed alliance with physical nature ; a state in which work was without toil, in which life was bright and joyous in the consciousness of security and strength, when mastery over the world was a natural inheritance conveyed by the divine benediction. In this delicious picture there is presented to us a human family, consisting of the first pair, living in a relation to the vegetable world of sustenance from it without pain or labour ; in a relation to the animal world of artless familiarity. Over all this arose a relation to God of filial dependence, implicit obedience, and of fearless intercourse. The natural and intellectual elements of this picture present the entirely original conception of a state neither cultured nor savage, neither civilised nor barbaric, yet of that childlike and paradisaic sort which man's creation in the divine image would lead us to expect.[1]

That this primeval state was real and not merely ideal, is confirmed by the consideration that in all literature, secular and sacred alike, the conception of man's beginning takes the form of a happy reminiscence, a golden age which was once. This argument is gracefully expanded in a chapter by the late Isaac Taylor, entitled, "The Tradition of Paradise the Germ of Poetry."[2] Ewald, in his papers on The Bible View of the Origin of Man, says : "Peace, as God meant it, is the primitive state of humanity, a state after which, though it has long fled, humanity still yearns, the hope of which forms the rosy fringe of the future, and to restore which is the effort and aim of all true religion."[3] What it concerns us chiefly to maintain is that this Scripture view of the beginning in Eden,—not as a fable, but as a fact, —is presupposed by the whole system of revealed truth.

II. The *moral* conditions,—the ethical and religious elements of man's primitive state. Here the ruling theological expression is that which speaks of man as possessing *Original Righteousness*.

We are to interpret this phrase as descriptive, not merely of the moral type, after which man was made, but also of the actual state of holy character, in which, for however short a time, he must have existed. It is

[1] See *ante*, p. 43.
[2] *Spirit of the Hebrew Poetry*, p. 98 (Lond., 1861).
[3] See the place cited, *ante*, p. 26.

to this we now direct our attention. Its actuality requires to be defended from *dilution* of it into mere moral indifference, and from *exaggeration* of it into fully attained moral perfection.

1. It has suffered *dilution* at the hands of Pelagians, Socinians, and Rationalists generally. According to Pelagian doctrine man was created a rational, free agent, but without moral character. His character was to depend on the use he made of his natural endowments. He was made neither righteous nor unrighteous, neither holy nor unholy. He had simply the capacity for becoming either. There can be no such thing as concreated moral character. It will be observed that the underlying postulate here begs the whole question. That postulate is, that acts of will alone constitute character. There can, on this hypothesis, be no such thing as a holy nature,—man must start with moral indifference. This postulate precludes the possibility of " original righteousness," but also of " original sin " (as we call it) *i.e.* an inherited evil nature ; nay, even of a regeneration of nature, and even of permanent moral character in any form. But thus put, it is a postulate contrary to human experience, and to the Scripture which confirms it. Our Lord's doctrine is, " Either make the tree good and his fruit good, or else make the tree corrupt and his fruit corrupt." That is to say, the fruit reveals the nature of the tree, but does not form or constitute that nature. So must all man's willing and working start from a nature which has moral quality to begin with. It cannot start from indifference.

As to the sense in which the first man could be said to possess "original righteousness," the criticisms of Schleiermacher are worth recalling, though his own view leans to the rationalising side. The phrase itself, as an expression for man's primitive moral condition, he thinks inconvenient, "not only because *righteousness* requires for its development a social state, but chiefly because the proper conception of *righteousness* as a virtue is that of something arising or acquired in the course of the development of a personal life, not that of a fundamental state or condition from which the development is to take its rise. So that a most undesirable conventional or technical meaning must attach to the expression *righteousness* when applied to the original condition of man, such as it never has in any other connection." He goes on to contrast the two views thus: "If nothing more be meant by representing the first man's actual condition as one of original righteousness, than simply to oppose the Pelagian position by maintaining that it could not have been one of sin, it may be unconditionally accepted. But if it be meant to imply an actual power which has elevated the higher faculties over the lower, then it would be impossible to conceive of anything else than a continual progression of this power to higher and further degrees, *i.e.* it would be impossible on this hypothesis to conceive of the Fall as ever actually taking place. This is probably the reason why the Romish Church has conceived of the original state as caused and maintained by an extraordinary divine influence, which, of course, commits the holders of it to a Pelagian view of human nature. It may not be so detrimental in its consequences, but it is just as perplexing to the true conception of the 'original perfection,' when some of our Protestant expounders of the faith affirm that our first parents were in their original condition partakers of the Holy Spirit." [1]

" Pelagians, on their supposition, have a twofold advantage,—that they assume no original perfection which was lost, and that from the point of commencement which they do assume, a continuous development can find place. But their disadvantage is also twofold, namely, that goodness with them is not the original state, and that in the development of goodness the Redeemer appears only as a single member. The Catholic doctrine, on the other hand, secures two things: that goodness is represented as something immediately drawn from God; and that when, after the loss of this original condition, the development is broken off, and a new point of commencement rendered necessary, the Redeemer can step forward as the turning-point. It has the double disadvantage: that the goodness, which in appearance was already attained by our first parents, could be lost despite of the upholding divine omnipotence; and that the only purpose for which we can be tempted to imagine to ourselves the original condition of the first man, namely, to have a point of commencement for the genetic presentation of all that follows, cannot be reached, *i.e.* we cannot picture to ourselves how that original moral state was realised. Consequently it is more to the point to hold it purely ideal, having or its real ground the fact that our religious consciousnes still contains this notion of primitive rectitude, though it was not actual in the first man.

[1] Cf. the view, *e.g.* of Bp. George Bull.

But would we see in one single human appearance all displayed that can be evolved out of such original perfection, this must not be sought for in Adam, in whom it must again have been lost, but in Christ, in whom it has brought gain to all." [1]

Whether intentionally or not, Schleiermacher has clearly admitted the superiority over all others of the evangelical view of man's original moral standing. That we are unable to construe in our own minds its mode and habit, which is his main difficulty, is no valid objection to its actuality. It is confessedly the only point of commencement which is consistent with the entire history of human sin and redemption as given in the Bible. Schleiermacher's own view is really no better than that of the Pelagians, for through a confounding of possibility with potential existence, he posits a "germ of evil" in primitive man. That man's original moral position was one of being and doing right, which the Creator Himself had originated, is the only view which will carry us consistently through the Bible scheme of man's moral history. So much for undue *depreciation* of the primitive righteousness.

2. It must be remembered, on the other hand, that under the pressure of dogmatic necessity, there has been some departure from the simplicity and modesty of Scripture statement. The whole conception of the primitive man has been *overcharged*. This is, of course, the case with the romancing descriptions to be found in the Fathers, and in some mediæval writers. Bishop South's famous sermon on Gen. i. 27 is a comparatively modern example

[1] *Der christliche Glaube*, i. 341, 342.

of these.[1]   All such rhetoric, with reference to the
splendours of the first man's natural and intellectual
powers, is based upon an unwarrantable view of his
spiritual position.   And this is to be found in writers
who avoid these other absurdities.   The temptation to
exaggerate the details of the unfallen state is obviously
that thus the ruin of the Fall can be more forcibly
brought out.   Indeed, the general disposition of orthodox
theology has been to suggest for the head of the human
race a moral and spiritual giant, who is as much a myth
as the physically gigantic Adam of the Rabbinic and
Mussulman tales.   More particularly, it has been the
habit to ascribe to man in Eden a degree, if not a kind
of perfection, which has no basis in Scripture.   " It is to
be observed that Genesis simply gives us, in historic form,
the fact of a primeval sinlessness. . . . Yet it must be
admitted that, beyond the fact of a yet unfallen state,
Scripture does not give us much material bearing directly
on the primitive condition of man." [2]   These familiar
exaggerations not merely create a recoil to which we
may partly trace the modern disposition to distrust the
theory of original righteousness ; they also encumber
theology with an unworkable hypothesis,—an ideal Adam,
of whom his creators find it difficult afterwards to dispose.

---

[1] "Discourse was then almost as quick as intuition.   It could sooner
determine than now it can dispute.   There is as much difference between
the clear representations of the understanding then, and the obscure
discoveries that it makes now, as there is between the prospect of a
casement and a keyhole.   We may guess at the stateliness of the building
by the magnificence of the ruins.   An Aristotle was but the rubbish of an
Adam, and Athens but the rudiments of Paradise."—*South's Works*,
vol. i. p. 26 (Oxford Edition, 1842).

[2] Principal Rainy, *Delivery and Development of Doctrine*, pp. 328, 329.

If we take the Romanist view, which is one form of exaggeration, that this high state was maintained by a supernatural endowment, or even the Lutheran one of a direct influence of the Holy Spirit, we are at a loss to understand how the Fall was possible, except through a capricious or causeless withdrawal of the divine help. Even on the usual supposition that goodness was con-created, that Adam was so made as naturally to love and serve God, we have no means of understanding how he had arrived at a spiritual condition so high as theologians are wont to ascribe to him, except upon the supposition of a time and progress nowhere granted in the narrative. If we assume that man's personality and free will are essential to him, an initial state of perfected holiness is inconceivable, or, if insisted on, would simply render it inconceivable how he should have fallen. In that case, moreover, "original righteousness," which is not a Scripture expression, would have to be read with a sense nowhere else given to the word "righteousness"; namely, not of a character formed and acquired, not of a habit of confirmed and faultless rectitude, but of some sudden preternatural endowment. At the same time, we must do theology the justice to remember that by "righteousness," in all its applications to man, is meant that which forms a ground of acceptance, or of non-condemnation before God. It does not necessarily imply in every case an acquired personal rectitude. The entire neglect of this meaning by modern writers, and their constant use of "righteousness" in the subjective sense of holy character, explains their inability to understand the doctrinal position.

The modest statement of Scripture, that "God made man upright," supplies us with a theory of original uprightness, which is what most evangelical divines really mean by *justitia originalis*. This much, however, be it remembered, is essential to the whole Bible view of man. It cannot be given up without " transforming the scheme of man's relations and obligations from end to end." [1] Not only so ; the Scripture account has on its side an inward sentence which predisposes us to embrace it. Conscience requires and approves of the position that man's primitive condition was sinless, for we instinctively feel that to be sinful is not a natural but a fallen state. But the Bible account carries us farther. It represents the state of the first man as more than innocence, certainly more than that of balance between good and evil. The theories of equilibrium are plainly unscriptural, whether the unstable equilibrium of Socinus and Schleiermacher, or the equilibrium, stable by miracle, of the Roman Church. They are based upon the assumption of a concreated strife in man between his higher and his lower powers. The Bible starts man, not with a schism at the root of his being of which the Fall would be an almost necessary consequence, but with a positive rightness, a living commencement of being right and doing good. This leaves room for trial, and all theologians admit that man in Eden was on his probation ; was *viator*, and not *comprehensor* ; was on the way to a confirmed moral and spiritual condition, but had not attained the goal.

If, in addition to the fact that man was made upright,

[1] Dr. Rainy, *op. cit.* p. 230.

the phrase "original righteousness" be meant to include the divine approval of man in the state of his creation, we have Scripture ground for it. The Creator, pronouncing all that He had made to be "very good," approves man as good, *i.e.* as fulfilling the end of his creation so far as a beginning and growing moral creature could be said to fulfil it. We thus obtain an account of man's creation in the divine image on its ethical side. Knowledge, righteousness, and true holiness were in germ essential to man's nature, but they had to be freely developed. "He was in principle perfect, . . . potentially, Adam was everything which he must primarily have been, but actually he had still to become all of which the germs had been implanted in him."[1] Moral capacity and actual conformity being both implied in this likeness to his Creator, the latter is that in which he received power to fashion himself. The only full realisation of the likeness would have been his continuous appropriation of the divine will as his own. He has lost it through the fall, in the sense that he has sinned and come short of its attainment. And this has entailed further consequences. For though he has not lost capacity for the likeness, he has lost the ability of himself to recover it, and for this is now wholly dependent upon a Redeemer in his own nature.

One last word regarding dogmatic exaggeration. Tempted to draw their view of the first Adam from the description of man as renewed in the Second Adam, theologians seem to make the outcome of redemption

---

[1] Van Oosterzee, *Christian Dogmatics*, p. 381 (Hodder & Stoughton, Lond., 1874).

merely the recovery of what was lost by the Fall. But, as Müller says, " It cannot be proved that the new creation in Christ is nothing more than the restoration of the state wherein Adam was at first created. There is, indeed, a relationship between the two ; the divine image wrought by Christ's redemption is the only true realisation of the image .wherein man was at first created. Man was originally given the one in order that he might attain the other, if not directly, by continuing faithful in obedience and fellowship with God, yet indirectly after his fall by means of redemption. But it is evident from the very nature of this relationship that the two are not identical." [1] To make them so is a strained interpretation. It puts a strain upon Scripture to imply that Adam had actually attained that to which Christ brings us by His grace. It detracts from the greatness of redemption, as if it required all the energy of divine wisdom, love, and power to bring back what sin and Satan took away. It is inconsistent with that gradual rise and march in the divine dealings towards man of which the Bible is full. To make the entire history of redemption a mere eddy in the stream of divine developments, to place redeemed humanity in Christ only after all where Adam began, is a view that falls short of the breadth and grandeur of the Scripture representation. Scripture conveys not obscurely the idea that the type of redeemed man is higher than that of man unfallen ; that the second creation, when completed, shall excel what the first had been even had it remained unsullied by sin ; that " as we have borne the image of the earthy,

[1] *Christian Doctrine of Sin*, ii. 352, 353 (Clark, 2nd Edition).

13

we shall also bear the image of the heavenly "[1]; and that when earth and heavens are dissolved, "we look for new heavens and a new earth wherein dwelleth righteousness."[2]

We take leave of this whole topic of man's original type and primitive state by recalling the value of the great Bible definition of his nature,—that he was made in the image of God.

This definition is of vital moment, in face of modern anthropological theories, as answering to the fact that while man is on one side of him earthly, animal, and mortal, he takes rank on the other by his essence as *spiritual being and free personality* above physical causation and succession. In relation to mere physical nature, man is supernatural, and so bears the likeness of the Supreme Supernatural or of God.

That this image of God, in which man was made, had for one of its essential elements *uprightness*, or *moral conformity* to his Maker, is also a position of inestimable worth in its bearing on the origin and nature of moral evil. That the constitution of man, like everything else in creation, was from the first very good, is essential to the monotheism of the Bible, as contrasted with the dualism of the ethnic religions and of much modern speculation.

These two biblical positions present the "Image" in twofold aspect as natural and ethical, potential and actual, or however else we may choose to express what is after all a "double-faced unity"—a thing inalienable from man even as fallen, yet so affected by sin that only

[1] 1 Cor. xv. 49.   [2] 2 Pet. iii. 13.

a supernatural redemption can restore it. How worthy of being the religious book of the human race is that which on its opening page foretells man's mental and practical progress by declaring that he was made to replenish the earth and subdue it; which vouches for the possibility of his moral renovation in the still more profound doctrine that he was constituted after the similitude of God !

MAN FALLEN : HIS NATURE UNDER SIN AND DEATH

"Il y a deux vérités de foi également constantes : l'une, que l'homme dans l'état de la création ou dans celui de la grâce, est élevé au-dessus de toute la nature, rendu semblable à Dieu, et participant de la divinité ; l'autre, qu'en l'état de corruption et du péché, il est déchu de cet état et rendu semblable aux bêtes."

"Ainsi tout l'univers apprend à l'homme ou qu'il est corrompu ou qu'il est racheté ; tout lui apprend sa grandeur ou sa misère. . . . Les hommes sont tout ensemble indignes de Dieu et capables de Dieu—indignes par leur corruption, capables par leur première nature."—PASCAL, *Pensées*, pp. 292, 294, 295 (Molinier), Paris, 1877.

> " The candid incline to surmise of late
> That the Christian faith may be false, I find ;
> . . . .
> I still to suppose it true, for my part,
> See reasons on reasons ; this, to begin :
> 'Tis the faith that launched point-blank her dart
> At the head of a lie—taught Original Sin,
> The Corruption of Man's Heart."
>
> ROBERT BROWNING,
> *A Legend of Pornic.*

ECCLES. vii. 29.—"Lo, this only have I found that God hath made man upright; but they have sought out many inventions."

GEN. vi. 5.—"And God saw that the wickedness of man *was* great in the earth, and *that* every imagination of the thoughts of his heart *was* only evil continually."

GEN. viii. 21.—"The imagination of man's heart *is* evil from his youth."

JER. xvii. 9.—"The heart is deceitful above all *things*, and desperately wicked : who can know it?"

MATT xv. 19.—"For out of the heart proceed evil thoughts," etc.

JOHN iii. 6.—"That which is born of the flesh is flesh; and that which is born of the Spirit is spirit."

ROM. v. 12.—"Wherefore, as by one man sin entered into the world, and death by sin; and so death passed upon all men, for that all have sinned."

CHAPTER X

BIBLE DOCTRINE OF THE FALL

[LITERATURE.—On the Fall. Holden, *Dissertation on the Fall of Man* (Lond., Rivington, 1823); Macdonald, *Creation and the Fall* (Edin., 1856); cf. Cave, *Inspiration of the Old Testament*, Lect. ii. (Lond., 1888); Davis, *Genesis and Semitic Tradition* (Lond., Nutt, 1894); Lenormant, *Les Origines de l'Histoire* (Transl. 1882).

On Sin. Owen's various treatises, e.g. *Indwelling Sin, Mortification of Sin, Dominion of Sin and Grace*; Jonathan Edwards, " On Original Sin " (in vol. i. of *Collected Works*); G. Payne, *Doctrine of Original Sin* (2nd Edition, 1854); Pascal, *Pensées* (Edition, Molinier, Paris, 1877); Wiggers, *Augustinianism and Pelagianism* (Transl. 1840); Principal W. Cunningham, *Historical Theology*, vol. i. (Edin., T. & T. Clark, 1863); Tholuck, *Die Lehre von der Sünde und vom Versöhner* (9th Aufl. 1871); G. Heinrici, *Die Sünde nach Wesen und Ursprung* (1878); Julius Müller, *The Christian Doctrine of Sin* (2nd Edition of Transl., Edin., T. & T. Clark, 1868); Principal Tulloch, Croall Lecture (with same title, Edin., Blackwood, 1876).

On Death. Krabbe, *Die Lehre von der Sünde und vom Tode* (1836); Mau, *Vom Tode, dem Solde der Sünde* (1841); F. Weber, *Vom Zorn Gottes* (1862).]

WE go on now to consider what light the Scripture account of the Fall throws upon its view of man's constitution, and, conversely, how far the simple psychology of the Bible may help us to ascertain the significance of the Scripture doctrine concerning sin and death. It is but a few hints we can supply on each topic. The doctrines of the Fall and sin are exclusively biblical ideas; or at least they are only fully conceived and applied in the biblical scheme of religious thought. These doctrines are solvents, not sources of difficulty. Into the problem of evil, Scripture introduces elements of explanation. It accounts for man's present moral and physical condition, for the broad phenomena of life and death, in a way that is thinkable and intelligible. Pascal has said that the Christian faith has mainly two things to establish,—the corruption of human nature, and its redemption by Jesus Christ.[1] The first of these has been most thoroughly brought out in connection with the second. The evil which is in man has been most entirely probed and sounded in connection with that power above man which the gospel brings to his help. This is a principle at once profound and beneficent. Knowledge is not given to man for its own mere sake; it is when an end of use and benefit is to be served that knowledge comes. Men first learned the structure of their own bodies not from the pure love of knowing, but because the necessities of human disease made such knowledge the indispensable handmaid of the healing art. We may be asked, Why go to a book so simple and practical as the Bible for the solution of the mysterious problems of moral evil, or for any theory of the being of man? We answer that we do so relying upon the surest analogy.

---

[1] "La foi chrétienne ne va principalement qu'à établir ces deux choses, la corruption de la nature et la Redemption de Jésus-Christ."—Pascal, *Pensées*, Preface générale, p. 10 (Faugère).

It is because revelation has proved such an instrument for man's renovation and recovery to God, because it has achieved the only success in the remedy of man's evil, that we aie entitled to expect in it profounder views than anywhere else as to what man and his evils are.

I. Nothing is more characteristic of the Bible than the manner in which it accounts for the ORIGIN of man's evil. It differs from those ethnic religions, which sought the root of evil in the elements of the world, as if good and ill were alike of its essence ; from those ancient and modern philosophies which find it in the make of the creature man ; from those recent theories which place it in the tendency of a being, typically lower than now appears, to revert to his original savage or bestial condition. The origin of evil within the human sphere is, according to Scripture, a Fall— *an unnatural movement.* And this is a practically hopeful, as well as a speculatively high view of man's nature, even as fallen. On the other views, just named, it is hard to see how evil could be aught but inevitable, how it ever could be removed or even remedied. The Bible represents the ills in which man is involved not as the necessary faults of a being low, earthly, and animal by his constitution, but as effects from the fall of a being made in the image of God. Our religion can deal hopefully with ignorance, barbarism, vice, and crime, because it views these not as the nature of man into which he tends to relapse, but as degradations of a nature still bearing the stamp of God, and from which, therefore, it can be redeemed.

Let us keep our eye, then, on the speculative significance of this Bible doctrine of a fall, when we are considering the nature of man as now under sin. The Bible descriptions of fallen human nature are drawn in very dark lines. But let us not forget that what is so described is " not pravity but depravity ";[1] that it is not nature, but un-nature; that when Scripture speaks of the nature of fallen man, it does not mean the nature in which, nor the nature in the midst of which God created him. All flesh has now corrupted his way upon the earth; that which is born of the flesh is flesh. It is in this sense that, according to Scripture, man is now a child of wrath by nature. " Very many pious people do not rise high enough in their anthropology. They ascend to the fall, and forget the higher fact that we fell from a height where we were fitted to dwell, and where we were intended to remain. And Jesus Christ has come that He might raise us even higher than to that height, and make us sit in the ' super-celestial ' with Himself."[2]

It is necessary at this point to say something about the narrative (Gen. iii.) of the Temptation and Fall, both as to form and content; first, as to its character as a record, and then as to the teaching conveyed by it, as that is countersigned throughout the whole of Scripture.

I. *The character of the narrative.*—The real question is an alternative one. Are we to read it as myth, allegory, or the like, on one hand ? Or, on the other, as a traditional account of something actual and historic ? It may be said, at once, that no one takes it in exact literality. Evangelical teaching has always held that quite another agent is at work than the serpent which alone

---

[1] Dr. John Duncan, in *Colloquia Peripatetica.*
[2] *Op. cit.* pp. 120, 121.

is mentioned in the story. Indeed, such features as the " subtil " animal endowed with speech, and the two emblematic trees, fairly warn us that there is here a symbolic element not soluble in literal everyday speech. Yet to treat the story as a *mythus* or " didactic fable deliberately composed by some one," [1] is inadmissible. Such a thing would require a much later date for its production than is consistent with the simple and archaic style of the actual writing. Much the same argument disposes of the still more untenable view that it is an allegory or parable. " It can be no mere representation," says Dorner, " of the fall which comes to pass in every individual at all times and in all places. The passage has to do with the first human pair and their historical fall, so that in the narrative there is accordingly given actual history, though in a mask of symbolism." [2] " It is a figurative representation," says Martensen, " of an actual event." [3] The remarks of the elder Nitzsch, in accounting for the figurative form, is also suggestive. " It is a true history, though not a literal one, because of the prehistoric character of the event itself. The fall of David or of Peter is capable of actual narration ; that of Adam is not so. Only the truth of it could be given, and that only through the word of God." [4] The best way of accounting for the peculiar form is to regard the narrative as the figurative or symbolic version of a fact which that form served to hand on from generation to generation. " The coincidence in certain important features

[1] Müller ii. 347, *note*, defining this view and rejecting it.

[2] Dorner, *System of Christian Doctrine*, iii. p. 13 (Clark's Transl.).

[3] Martensen, *Christian Dogmatics*, p. 155 (Clark's Transl.).

[4] C. I. Nitzsch, *System der christlichen Lehre*, p. 228 (Bonn, 1851).

between the Mosaic narrative and other Oriental traditions concerning the origin of evil also points to a
common historical basis." [1] The way in which it is inter-
woven with the annals of the whole human race given in
those first eleven chapters of the Book renders the notion
that it was meant by the writer to be taken either as
myth or allegory quite incompetent. To this much we
must certainly hold fast, that as the whole teaching of
Scripture is bound up with a historical commencement
of the race, an actual primitive state in which they were
originally planted by their Creator, so the account of
their fall is substantially that of an historical event.

Thus far, of the impression which the narrative makes
when regarded in and by itself. But this impression of
its being a real history,—though conveyed in a form
necessarily veiled and traditional, is confirmed when we
look at the external evidence, *i.e.* the concurrent testimony of other literature, both within and beyond the
Bible. There are (1) The allusions to it in other parts
of Scripture. Those in the Old Testament (*e.g.* Job
xxxi. 33, Eccl. vii. 29, Hos. vi. 7, Ezek. xxviii. 13, 15,
16) are comparatively few and slight, because, as Dorner
says, from the days of Abraham the glance is concentrated pre-eminently upon the chosen people and its sin
(cf. Isa. xliii. 27). As for the New Testament, the references in the Johannine writings to the part of Satan in
the origin of human evil (John viii. 44, 1 John iii. 8,
12) are unmistakable. And Paul not only expressly
alludes to the narrative (2 Cor. xi. 3, 1 Tim. ii. 14), but
recognises in his religious consciousness the fall of Adam

[1] Müller, ii. 348.

as a primal historic fact (Rom. v. 12–19, 1 Cor. xv. 21, 22). (2) Then, we must note, the clearly historic impression which is made by it on the Jews, the early Christian writers, and, in fact, on all unsophisticated minds. The evidence of some non-biblical Jewish authors may be easily gathered by noting the references to man's primitive state and his fall, contained in Old Testament apocryphal works, *e.g.* Wisdom i. 13, 16, ii. 23, 24; Ecclus. xxv. 29. No doubt the allusions in such literature are often of an allegorising sort. The tendency so to use the primitive facts in human history was strong, *e.g.* in the Jewish Alexandrian schools, in the Rabbinic, and in the early Christian. Yet even such spiritualising upon primitive material assumes the actuality of the transactions to which it gives a secondary import.

(3) Still another and quite distinct confirmation arises from researches which are being vigorously pushed at the present hour. The comparison of the biblical narrative with Oriental and other ethnic traditions about the primal facts of human history is now yielding important results. The whole body of early events, such as the Creation, the Flood, recorded in these *Origines* of Genesis, are to be found clothed in various garb among the religious traditions of mankind. Of late, these have been undergoing special observation in the archaic remains on the Tigris, the Euphrates, and the Nile.[1] For some time after these discoveries began, no such clear and un-

---

[1] For the fullest account of these, see *Les Origins, etc.*, Lenormant (1882); The Assyrian and Chaldæan researches of Rawlinson, George Smith, and Layard; Dr. A. Cave's *Inspiration of the Old Testament* (1888); and Professor Sayce, *The Higher Criticism and the Monuments* (1894).

mistakable reference to the Fall-narrative was found, though certain pictorial and sculptured representations of the trees, the woman, and the serpent had been long familiar to archæologists. Now, however, this gap begins to be filled up. A Babylonian fragment, forming part of the third tablet in the creation series, describes in tolerably plain terms the fall of man, and has other resemblances to the third chapter of Genesis.[1] What is common to these ethnic sources with the Scripture narrative is the framework of primeval events, and the argument from this coincidence in the records of diverse nations is that these are original recollections of the race conveyed along the stream of historic religions. Euhemerism, as applied to the stories and poetic remains of classic antiquity, is a method now thoroughly exploded. Instead of being literary constructions, or deliberately composed fables, enshrining nature-worship or other abstract ideas, scholars now hold the true key in regarding them as veiled and fanciful forms of handing down primeval facts and events. Similarly, one of the best fruits of recent biblical research is to have set aside the old rationalistic interpretation of these narratives. With a firm step and growing hope of future light, biblical science advances in its own proper line of archæological discovery, to restore the historical interpretation of the primeval facts in human history, sacred as well as secular.

The strong point in contrast, however, should be stated along with the analogy. It is that while the

---

[1] Sayce, *ut supra*, p. 104, and Boscawen, in *Expository Times*, vol. iv. p. 440. Cf. also, however, Davis, in the work named on p. 199.

narratives of the "Inscriptions are full of extravagant detail, mixing their nucleus of facts with stories of the gods and heroes of Polytheism, divine inspiration has filled the sacred narrative with a totally different spirit. The difference has never been better expressed than by Lenormant: "The essential features in the form of the traditions have been preserved, and yet between the Bible and the sacred books of the Chaldæans there is all the distance of one of the most tremendous revolutions which have ever been effected in human beliefs. . . . Others may seek to explain this by the simple, natural progress of the conscience of humanity. For myself, I do not hesitate to find in it the effect of a supernatural intervention of Divine Providence, and I bow before the God who inspired the Law and the Prophets." [1]

II. This brings us to consider the *teaching of the narrative,*—the moral and religious positions which it is intended to maintain. The doctrinal results, so far as we may venture to express them in definite propositions, are these : (*a*) that the first sin was an act of free-will, a transgression of law, or breach of commandment ; and (*b*) that it was followed by consequences which prove it to have been a real fall and loss to man and the race. With these findings the whole strain of Scripture agrees.

(*a*) Fall into sin is represented, not only in this story, but constantly through the Bible, as a moral crisis, taking place within the sphere of man's free-will. Physical evil is always viewed in Scripture as a consequence of moral evil. The whole creation was very good. There is no physical necessity of sinning suggested by anything

[1] *The Beginnings of History, etc.*, Pref. p. xvii.

in the Bible from beginning to end. Sin is consistently
represented as a free movement in the creature. "God
made man upright, but they have sought out many inventions."[1] "They are all gone aside."[2] Though sin
makes its first appearance in connection with the physical world, and as a bodily act, yet it is no mere natural
result of the presentation of the forbidden fruit to the
senses. A clear and full view of the temptation narrative leads one to look upon the first sin not as a sensual
slip, but as a moral revolt. "Its point of departure," as
Delitzsch says, "was in the spirit."[3] It arose with an
external suggestion, and upon an external occasion; but
it was an inward crisis. The motives most efficient in
bringing it about were ambitious desire of a short road
to divine knowledge, and doubt of the divine love.
When these had conceived, the sin which they brought
forth was disregard of the limit which divine love had
imposed, or "transgression of law."[4] Sin, therefore, is
constantly represented in Scripture as arising, not out of
nature, not out of anything in man's own constitution,
far less out of the constitution of things around him, but
from an act beyond nature—an act of the human spirit
freely departing from God by traversing His law. In so

---

[1] Eccles. vii. 29. "'They seek many arts' (*Künste*, Luther), properly
calculations, inventions, devices, namely, of means and ways by which
they go astray from the normal natural development into abnormities.
In other words, invented refined degeneracy has come into the place of
moral simplicity."—Delitzsch, *in loc.*, Clark's Transl. p. 335.

[2] Ps. xiv. 3. "Gone out of the way," ἐξέκλιναν, LXX. Note the
absolute sense in which the verb סוּר is used in other places, as *e.g.* Deut.
xi. 16 ; Jer. v. 23 ; Dan. ix. 11. A kind of *vox signata* for the initial
movement of sin. It is the revolt, the departing, the turning aside.

[3] *Bibl. Psychologie*, p. 124.   [4] 1 John iii. 4.

far as the narrative alludes to the ultimate origin of evil,
it refers the first human sin to the suggestion of an alien
will, to the influence of a higher spirit previously fallen,
thereby indicating that the possibility of sinning belongs
to spiritual creatures.   But the chief result of the Scripture teaching here as to origins is, that it traces all
human evils to a source beneath the scientific level,
deeper than all observed sequence, to a preternatural
root in the revolt of the human will against God; as it
also reveals for this root-evil a supernatural remedy in a
divine-human Redeemer.   It is usual to say that the
Bible does not solve the problem of the origin of evil, but
profound thinkers find that insolubility belongs to the
essence of the question.   It lies in the idea of evil to be
an utterly inexplicable thing.   The attempt to explain
or account for it assumes its rationality, or some other
element of rightness in that which is essentially wrong.
This is an additional confirmation of the position that it
rises in an act of free-will, for in vain do we seek a cause
beyond the will itself.   It is in this connection that
Augustine concludes that the question of its origin can
have no solution.   " Who asks the efficient cause of an
evil will ?   There is no efficient in the case, only a de-
ficient.   Who would ask to see darkness, or to hear
silence, let him ask the reason of the unreasonable, that
is, of sin." [1]

We are to note, then, that the Fall, so far as man is
concerned, was an act of his spirit, of his free will, and

[1] *De Civitate Dei*, lib. xii. capp. vi. vii.   So also Pascal, *Pensées*, i. pp.
293, 294 (Molinier) ; Neander, *Planting and Training, etc.*, i. 423 (Bohn) ;
Tholuck, *Guido and Julius*, p. 19 ; F. D. Maurice, *Life and Letters*,
vol. ii. ; Professor J. Duncan, *Colloquia Peripatetica*, pp. 3-6.

was above all things sin, because it was transgression of the divine law and departure from God. It was possible to man because of his possession of free spiritual personality. To any nature lower in the scale of being than man, sin was impossible. But it is mere perversion of thought and language, on this account, to represent man's experience of moral evil as not a fall but a rise. That sin was possible to man belongs, indeed, to the height on which his nature was originated; yet that it became actual was loss and ruin. The greatness of the ruin, the gravity of the shock, Scripture consistently represents as the correlate of his original dignity. The Bible account of the Fall and sin, instead of vilifying human nature, implies the highest view of man and his constitution. The present degradation of the edifice consists largely in the fact that it no longer serves the purpose of its erection,—to be a temple of the living God. The music of man's life is no longer in harmony with the divine order and glory to which it was set, therefore are " the sweet bells " so " jangled and out of tune."

The first sin, although suggested by an alien evil spirit, marked itself as a voluntary act of departure from God. The deliberateness of the act on Adam's part is specially asserted : " And Adam was not deceived." [1] Accordingly, this representation is the one which is central for the whole Bible view of sin and its effects. It is the main element in its description of universal sinfulness : " There is none that seeketh after God." [2] If we maintain clearly these two positions, that the fall of

---

[1] 1 Tim. ii. 14.   [2] Rom. iii. 11.

man was an act of his free will, and that the act was
sin because it was transgression of divine law and revolt
from personal divine authority, all the other elements of
Bible truth on the subject will take their proper places.
From this view of the Fall, as primarily a spiritual and
religious catastrophe, all the rest of the scriptural teaching about man's evil depends.

(b) The account in Gen. iii. of the immediate consequences of the first sin represents it as rending in a
moment the veil of ideal glory in which man, as a self-
conscious, free, yet holy being, had moved in his primal
state. The spiritual animal, having spiritually fallen,
becomes at once rudely conscious of the mere flesh:
"The eyes of them both were opened, and they knew
that they were naked." [1] The friend and fellow of the
Most High flees from His voice and hides himself from
His presence: "Adam and his wife hid themselves from
the presence of the Lord God amongst the trees of the
garden." [2] Sensual shame and superstitious fear are the
prompt first tokens of the Fall of a being who is created
eminently spiritual and religious. The whole position of
man towards God is changed. He has parted from His
fellowship, and must therefore be driven out of Paradise.
And his relation to nature and to the world is altered, as
well as his relation to God. In the divine sentence immediately following on the first sin,—a sentence of
degradation and final destruction for the serpent, of sorrow in conception for woman, of painful toil and ultimate
return to dust for mankind,—we recognise, as we should
expect, the effects of the Fall upon nature and man to-

---

[1] Gen. iii. 7.   [2] Gen. iii. 8.

gether.   The revolt of the being made in God's
image, with dominion over the creatures, was a
cosmic event, and has a disturbing effect upon the
cosmos, " as when a kingdom falls with its king." [1]
Upon this hint in the sacred narrative is founded St.
Paul's doctrine of nature's sympathetic suffering with
fallen man.

The further description given in Genesis of the effects
of the Fall upon the first man and his successors, confirms the same general principles, namely, that sin is no
mere weakening, but an active and energetic perversion
of our moral nature ; that it originates in the revolt of a
spiritual personality against God and His law, and that
this revolt carries in it the seeds of its own punishment.
It is not followed in Adam's case by an instantaneous
and literal death on the day of his transgression.   It is
not followed by the eclipse of his intellectual powers.
There is a sense in which his spiritual fall is an advance
in knowledge : but it is followed by the immediate cessation of that divine fellowship and paradisaic felicity in
which he was created.   So with his offspring.   There is
not at first any marked degradation of their constitution
as creatures.   Instead of physical degradation, there is
in the immediate descendants of the first man great
physical splendour.   Instead of intellectual extinction,
there springs up a brilliant civilisation.   In the line of
the first murderer we have the early rise and growth of
agriculture, cattle-breeding, city-building, music, and other
arts.   Instead of decay, feebleness, and early death, the
narrative suggests gigantic strength and marvellous long-

[1] Baader, quoted by Van Oosterzee.

evity.   Upon that further step in the development of the
race, which is enigmatically described as the inter-marri-
age of the sons of God with the daughters of men, evil
became more rampant.[1]   The power and prevalence of
sin was manifested in monstrous crimes, high-handed
and clamant vices—the iniquities, therefore, of a race
physically strong and mentally active.   " The earth also
was corrupt before God, and the earth was filled with
violence.   And God looked upon the earth, and,
behold, it was corrupt; for all flesh (*i.e.* the whole
human race) had corrupted his way upon the earth." [2]
This description is eminently consistent with that view of
sin's origin which represents it as a religious fall.
The physical force, the longevity, the rapid progress of
the first men in the sacred narrative, is quite inconsistent
with any theory of man's evil as arising out of weakness
or want of balance in his original constitution ; as coming
into human nature entirely by the animal side ; as the
prevalence of the flesh over the spirit.   But it is perfectly consistent with the view that sin began as a
spiritual revolt in a creature made in God's image, the
consequences of which should slowly broaden down
among his descendants, to shorten life, to break up and
disperse the race, to produce physical degradation, savage
ignorance, and at last brutality.   These final results,
however, were only partial.   The loss of the preserving
salt of spirituality would no doubt have made these
effects universal had it not been counter-checked by a
redemptive process centred in one chosen people, sustained in a providential *economy of preparation* among all

[1] Gen. vi. 2.   [2] Gen. vi. 11, 12.

nations, and now spreading itself among the foremost and governing races of mankind.

In connection with the words (Gen. iii. 22): " Behold, the man is become as one of us, to know good and evil," more special note may be taken of the question whether the Fall was an advance of any sort. The only thing about that view which has reason is that self-determination must be a moral movement. We have already decided that moral indifference or equilibrium is not, according to Scripture, a thinkable view of man's original state, that a human being without moral quality is no such being as God could create. Yet though we cannot start man with moral indifference, though he must begin as originally upright (*yashar*, straight, *rectus*), the Scripture makes it sufficiently plain that there lay before him in his primitive state such a self-determining act or series of acts as would have led him out of moral childhood or pupilage into moral perfection and holy manhood. From this state of pupilage he would have emerged by self-denial and obedience. But it is true that he did emerge from it the wrong way, by his act of self-assertion and transgression of law in the Fall. There was a portion of truth in the tempter's plea that there should be a gain of knowledge by disobedience. The idea of moral progress in Adam's case implied a self-determining act in the matter of the commandment. And the Fall was such an act: it brought him at once out of the child-like *naïveté* of the paradisaic state. But so far is this from supporting the theory that evil enters as a necessary factor into human development, that it only rightly states the truth of which that theory is a perversion.

CHAPTER XI

SIN IN THE RACE AND IN THE INDIVIDUAL

FROM the first sin and its effects we pass now to consider
(1) the Scriptural account of the UNIVERSAL PREVALENCE
of sin in the race. As to the fact, Scripture and
experience agree. The absolute universality of sin is so
frequently and emphatically affirmed in the Bible that
detailed proof is unnecessary. The testimony of human
experience is vividly presented even by ancient non-
Christian writers. On two points their evidence is
overcharged, and has to be corrected by revelation.
The one is that which leads them to throw the burden
of evil on nature, or on the Author of nature. "Some
of the ethnic philosophers," to use the language of Howe,
"have been so far from denying a corruption and
depravation of nature in man, that they have overstrained
the matter, and thought vicious inclination more deeply
natural than indeed it is."[1] The other is, that their
account of the universality and increase of evil leads to
a fatalistic despair of humanity, and is at variance with
fact. If Horace's maxim were true, that each generation
of men is worse than the preceding, the race ought long
ago to have become extinct. The fact not present to the

[1] *The Living Temple*, Pt. II. c. iv.

mind of the pagan world is, that humanity is under a remedial economy which has its centre in revealed religion. But the truth with which we have to do now is that which Scripture posits to account for the universal prevalence of sin. It exactly coincides with observation, and falls in with the known laws of nature, namely, that moral evil is hereditary, *vitium originis.* It is a proof of the inner unity of Scripture thought, that its teaching as to the presence of sin throughout the world is so thoroughly in accordance with its teaching as to man's origin and nature. ⌊Evil, according to the Bible, is no inherent part of man's nature as created; yet its actual prevalence among mankind is explained in perfect consistency with this initial truth.⌋ The universality of sin is a corrollary and consequent from the unity of the race. The fact of that unity has a most direct theological interest. The ethnic doctrine of Autochthones, "men sprung of the soil," the theory, recently favoured but now abandoned, of several starting-points for the human race, taken in connection with the fact of universal sinfulness, would go to make moral evil something original in man's constitution—a characteristic of the whole *genus homo.* "Only on the supposition of first parents can evil be regarded as something which was introduced afterwards, and which has penetrated through to all." [1] Evil is not necessary, eternal, and irremediable. Hence the emphasis of the Scripture position, that "by one man sin entered into the world." [2] ⌊Men are sinners by birth, by generation, not by constitution.⌊

[1] Martensen, *Christian Dogmatics*, p 150 (Clark, Edin., 1866).
[2] Rom. v. 12.

How this hereditary depravity connects itself with the consciousness of personal guilt is a problem of much psychological interest. That conscience charges sin upon each individual, although each has become a sinner through his connection with the race; that a truly awakened soul charges itself not only with its own conscious sin, but with a sinful disposition; and that the inherited sin is not a palliation but an aggravation of the evil,—these are facts which have occupied the most profound and serious thinkers from the dawn of Christian theology. We note the views of those only who admit the facts. There is no means of testing the proposed explanations directly by Scripture proof, but we may judge them by their bearing upon doctrines otherwise established by Scripture. They may be divided, as Julius Müller suggests, into the organic or substantial theory on the one side, and that which is atomic or subjective on the other. The former, which from the time of Augustine to the present day has been held in various forms, amounts in brief to this, that all human beings are contained in the first man. We are not at present discussing the Scriptural position that Adam represented his posterity in covenant. We leave this federal unity or identity out of account for the moment. It has no direct bearing on the subjective question, which alone we are considering, how hereditary depravity involves personal guilt. The theory we are describing asserts that the unity of the human race involves community of essence, or at least such identity as belongs to a tree or other complex organism. Consequently, each individual is not only a member of the race, but the beginning of the race is his beginning. And since the beginner of the race has sinned, his sin is the sin of all who descend from him. This view of each having sinned in Adam because of an essential or numerical oneness in the race, is a mere philosophical theory,— sometimes the product of Realism, sometimes of this combined with Traducianism, sometimes held upon a peculiar and independent position.[1] But it is quite unnecessary for the support of the great Protestant doctrine of imputation, which rests securely enough upon the fact of a representative unity. The theory of numerical unity exposes itself to the absurd conclusion that men acted personally thousands of years before they were born, or otherwise entails materialistic views of the soul. And in most of its forms it renders inconceivable the entrance into the race of a truly human and yet sinless Redeemer.

As an example of the opposite, namely, the atomic view, may be cited the theory of Julius Müller himself. It is that we must hold each sinful human being to have exercised a personal self-decision in that extra-temporal existence which he assumes to belong to created personality, and thus to have served himself heir to the sin of the first man. In his own words, that " each one who in this life is tainted by sin has in a life

---

[1] Neander thinks that Augustine's view of Adam, as bearing in himself germinally the entire human race, was determined by his Platonico-Aris-totelian Realism [see *Church History*, Bohn's Edition, iv. 350]. Jonathan Edwards held that the oneness or identity of the posterity of Adam with their progenitor was simply a oneness established by the divine constitution. It is from Hofmann that we have cited the modern realistic theory as above described. See *Schriftbeweis*, i. 540.

beyond the bounds of time wilfully turned away from the divine light to the darkness of self-absorbed selfishness."[1]   Not to speak of its fantastic and startling appearance, it is plain that this view derives no support either from consciousness or from Scripture.   But what is still more conclusive against this and all other attempts to account for the first consciousness of sin on the lines of individualism, is the inadequate theory of guilt which they involve, namely, that in order to render man justly responsible for acts determined by an internal state or character, that state must be self-produced.   This theory is contrary to common judgment, to conscience, and to the analogy of the leading doctrines of Scripture.   According to all known human and divine modes of reckoning, a being is reckoned good or bad because he is so, however he may have come into the state or constitution which produces such moral character.

The Augustinian or Protestant doctrine of imputation must not be identified with either or any of these theories.   Its basis is the federal unity of the race—a fact supported by independent Scripture proof, and which tends to explain the existence of corruption in all as a just consequence of the sin of their covenant head.   How depravity becomes guilt in each, the doctrine of imputation does not profess to explain.   Most of its adherents have leaned to the organic or substantial view of the human race.   It was long put in a form sanctioned by Anselm Aquinas, and others: "In Adam a person made nature sinful; in his posterity nature made persons sin-

[1] *The Christian Doctrine of Sin*, ii. 359 (Clark, 2d Edition).

ful." [1] This suggests the idea of humanity as an essence or species standing by itself, so that in the first man's sin the individual ruled the nature, but ever since the nature rules the individual. In this way there can be penalty where there is no guilt in the sense of moral culpability, and there can be guilt in the sense of legal exposure to penalty where there is no personal sin. This view is not philosophically complete. But Augustine long ago perceived that we must distinguish the fact from all explanations offered. He knew how to distinguish the conviction that sin and guilt had spread from the first man to all, from his own realistic speculations regarding the propagation of guilt and penalty. In like manner, he saw how easily the question concerning the propagation of a sinful nature would connect itself with another philosophical question respecting the origin of individual souls. But he declined to allow a vital point of Scripture doctrine to be confused with mere speculations which were indifferent to faith. He refused to decide for Creationism or Traducianism on scriptural grounds, for he could find none such. He perceived the strength of the former on philosophical grounds, however much the latter might seem to favour his own theological system. In the same way, Protestant divines of both the great communions agree in maintaining the doctrines of depravity and of imputation ; yet, for the most part, Lutherans favour Traducianism, while the Reformed prefer Creationism. These facts remove the question out of the region of opinions having any theological value. Nor

---

[1] Hence the formula, "Natura a primis personis corrupta, corrumpit cæteras personas."—Quoted by Müller, *op. cit.* ii. 312.

will biblical psychology enable us to decide for the one or the other of these theories as to the origin of the soul. The whole mode of conception out of which the strife arose, involving a sharp distinction between material and immaterial substance, is other and later than the biblical. The Bible account of man includes both. Its dualism is precisely that of the earthly and the heavenly—that which man derives from his race, and that which he is at the hands of God. At first formed of the dust, yet God-inbreathed, so now he is begotten of human parents, but formed in the womb by the Almighty, and the spirit within him is a divine product.[1] Yet, though Scripture thus favours the ascription of the higher elements in men to an immediate divine act at their origination, it will not enable us to gather from the account of their formation how evil arises within each.[2]

Scripture, however, is an unmistakable witness to the fact that each of us, as he is quickened to discern himself and his nature, appropriates a sense of guilt derived from the sinfulness of the race. Thus the writer of the 51st Psalm, having stated as the head and front of his offending that it was sin against God, goes on in the next clause to adduce his birth-sin as an aggravation of the case. "Not only have I done such things, but I am the inheritor of a nature which produces them." A

---

[1] Comp. Ps. li. 5, cxxxix. 13–16 ; Isa. xlii. 5 ; Zech. xii. 1.

[2] "Nous ne concevons ni l'état glorieux d'Adam, ni la nature de son péché, ni la transmission qui s'en est faite en nous. Ce sont choses qui se sont passées dans l'état d'une nature toute différente de la nôtre, et qui passent l'état de notre capacité présente."—Pascal, *Pensées*, p. 295 (Molinier).

self-ignorant man might have said : " It is true that I
have done these wrongs and come by these slips, but I
have a good heart.   These doings are not the exponents
of my real self."   A man untaught in the mystery of
human evil would have said : " I have sinned, but my
inherited sinfulness is some excuse for me."   This peni-
tent taught of God says : " I have sinned, but what is
worse, I am by nature a sinner, and in sin did my
mother conceive me.   If such deeds be the streams, how
foul must be the source of them !"   Thus he clears God,
accuses himself, and does truth in the inward part.   Now
this is substantially a doctrinal testimony.   If the depravity which we bring with us into the world were
not sinful, it would to some extent excuse our actual
sins.   But it is never adduced in the Scripture as a
palliation, rather as an enhancement of our evil.   The
same thing is implied in saying that we are " the
children of wrath by nature."   Guiltiness in the
" nature " is the necessary correlative of " wrath," which
is God's righteous displeasure.   The doctrinal expression
of such Bible statements is nothing else than that profound, apparently paradoxical, and much maligned position of the Protestant Evangelical Church,—that original
sin is no mere disease nor flaw in our origin, but is really
sinful ; that inborn depravity is not only an evil and a
sickness, but entails guilt.

From the origin of sin and the propagation of it in
the race, we pass (2) to the SEAT AND DOMINION of it in
the individual.   In regard to the latter, the Old Testament keeps very much to facts and instances instead of
laying down dogmatic positions.   The early narrative

details special instances of its prevalence in particular men and races; and throughout the whole history its hold on man appears "not more from the dominion it exerts over evil men, than from the energy with which it rises up in men who are, on the whole, servants of God."[1] The characteristic candour of Scripture in relating the faults and sins of the patriarchs and saints must not, however, be denuded of doctrinal intention to teach historically the great lines of sin and grace. Although it is only when we come to the New Testament that the opposition of flesh and spirit in human experience is crystallised into a doctrine, yet passages in the Old Testament lay a foundation for it, beginning with that immediately following the fall, when the Lord says, " My Spirit shall not always strive with man, for that he also is flesh."[2] To trace the progressive import of the expressions "flesh" and "spirit" would confirm the view already advanced, that "flesh" in its ethical meaning denotes not the animal character of sin, nor its carnal seat, but the inherited or birth-condition of our nature.[3] The "flesh," in this its higher or secondary import, is human nature as generated in the race—a view confirmed by the Bible account of the progress of corruption in man's early history, and by the experience of the rise of sin in every individual life. The further consideration of the sense in which "flesh" seems to be identified with indwelling sin, especially in Pauline phraseology, we postpone till it can be looked at in its relation to grace.[4]

[1] Rainy, *Delivery and Development of Doctrine*, p. 334.
[2] Gen. vi. 3.　　　　　　　　[3] *Supra*, pp. 119, 120.
[4] See *infra*, Chap. XIV.

When we ask what is the doctrine of Scripture regarding the seat of sin in man's constitution, and the degree in which it has affected that constitution, we have to consider the ascription all through the Bible of sin and its corruption to the human *Heart*. A well-known and much quoted chain of such passages runs across the whole breadth of Scripture. Some of its main links are to be found in the assertion of universal and hereditary corruption at Gen. vi. 5, viii. 21 : "The imagination (*Yetzer*, including all inward product, desires, and purposes) of man's heart is evil from his youth"; in the words of the Preacher: "The heart of the sons of men is full of evil";[1] in those of the prophet: "The heart is treacherous above all things, and malignant; who can know it?"[2] and in the saying of our Lord: "Out of the heart proceed evil thoughts," etc.[3] These Scriptures present a view of man's sin full of inward penetration. They speak of the evil as "being from within, not from without—a part of the self-life, and not of the accidental or external life."[4] It is a view at once broad and deep. It asserts the universality of the evil and its radical character in one single formula. Individual differences and degrees in wrong are fully admitted in the Bible utterances, but the leading assertion is common and universal wrongness at the heart. Now what is "the heart" . Scripture language? The proper appreciation of the

---

[1] Eccles. ix. 3.

[2] Jer. xvii. 9. אָנֻשׁ, "malignant," in the sense used when speaking of a disease or a wound, and rendered "incurable" in Jer. xv. 18, Job xxxiv. 6, Micah i. 9.

[3] Matt. xv. 19.

[4] Tulloch, *Croall Lectures*, p. 123.

phrase will help us to state correctly the Bible doctrine of human corruption. Deriving its import from its physical analogue, " heart " in the language of biblical psychology means the focus of the personal and moral life. It never denotes the personal subject, always the personal organ. All the soul's motions of life proceed from it, and re-act upon it. The Bible term " heart " might be read as it is used in the popular speech of men, were only this peculiarity kept well in view, that in biblical usage it includes the intellectual as well as all others movements of the soul. No doubt, however, while regarded as the home of every inward phenomenon, mental, emotional, moral, it more particularly denotes that which constitutes character. It is that which determines the whole moral being: " Out of it are the issues of life." [1]

Plainly, therefore, when the heart is spoken of as the seat of sin, this indicates the radical nature of human corruption. It consists not in words, acts, appearances. These merely show it, for it reigns within. It has tainted the roots of life, the formative sources of character. " This goes far beyond the superficial doctrine which makes man a morally indifferent being, in whose choice it lies at each moment to be either good or bad. The Bible understands sin as a principle which has penetrated to the centre, and from thence corrupts the whole circuit of life." [2] Thus is explained its influence on all the powers and faculties, its blinding effect upon self-

---

[1] Prov. iv. 23. On the term " heart," see *supra*, Chap. VI. pp. 121, 122.

[2] Oehler, *Theology of the Old Testament*, i. 223 (Clark).

consciousness,—for "who can understand his errors?" the radical nature of the change needed to remove it, the energy of that whole divine process which constitutes redemption; for the sin, from which God is risen up to redeem us, sits where God alone ought to dwell, at the source of our moral and spiritual being.

This language, however, while confirming the evangelical doctrine of human corruption, corrects some mistakes and exaggerations. It is of interest to find that the very words of Scripture, when thus carefully observed, exclude, for example, the exaggerated dogma of Flacius, that sin is a corruption of the nature of the soul.[1] For heart never means the being or constitution of the soul, always only its sources and principles of action. This language is also clear in affirming that sin is not seated in any special faculty or part of our nature, but at the centre of the whole. Heart, no doubt, is emphatically *to praktikon*, as the Greeks say,— the practical principle of the soul's operations. But we shall at once introduce confusion into the Bible doctrine of sin, and, indeed, into its whole doctrine of man, if we use "heart" as excluding the rational or intellectual element. It is usual to say that "the Scriptures do not make the broad distinction between the understanding and the heart which is common in our philosophy."[2] It would be better to say that "mind" and "heart," as these terms are used through the Bible generally, never do imply that distinction between the intellectual and the emotional nature which we denote

[1] Of which see more, *infra*, pp. 251, 252.
[2] Hodge, *Systematic Theology*, ii. 255.

by them even in popular language, much less the stricter division of man's faculties into the understanding and the will, or into the intellectual and the active powers. The Scripture doctrine of corruption, therefore, in accordance with its own simple psychology, is this, that the heart, *i.e.* the fountain of man's being, is corrupt, and therefore all its actings, or, as we should say, the whole soul in all its powers and faculties, perverted. A proper application of this principle will deliver us from the question whether the power of depravity lies mainly in the evil affections or in the darkened understanding; as also from the correlative question, whether saving faith is an emotion of the heart or an assent of the understanding. Much more will it keep us from the error of supposing that man's corruption is only a practical bias, leaving the judgment pure and uncontaminatèd by evil. Scripture gives no countenance to such distinctions, both because it recognises the whole soul under the name "heart" as the seat of depravity, and because it proceeds upon a different psychology from those which afford play for such controversies. "The heart in the Scripture is variously used; sometimes for the mind and understanding, sometimes for the will, sometimes for the affections, sometimes for the conscience, sometimes for the whole soul. Generally it denotes the whole soul of man and all the faculties of it, not absolutely, but as they are all one principle of moral operations, as they all concur in our doing good or evil. . . . And in this sense it is that we say the seat and subject of this law of sin is the heart of man."[1] Edwards, speaking not of sin,

---

[1] Owen, *On Indwelling Sin.* Works (Goold's Edition), vi. 170.

but of grace, uses "heart" in its scriptural inclusiveness, thus: "Spiritual understanding consists primarily in a cordial sense, or *a sense of heart, of that spiritual beauty.* I say *a sense of heart,* for it is not speculation merely that is concerned in this kind of understanding; nor can there be a clear distinction made between the two faculties of understanding and will, as acting distinctly and separately, in this matter."[1]

Once more, let us observe that while the Scripture statement is so strong in asserting a corruption of man's whole nature, and in assigning that corruption to the centre and fountain of his moral life, and while the force of that statement is vainly sought to be evaded or softened down, yet the Scripture asserts no corruption, depravation, or destruction of his natures, faculties, or powers as such. It recognises a constitution which, in relation to the end for which man was made, is wholly gone wrong, and has no power to right itself. But this just strength of statement is entirely misapplied when the Scripture language is transferred literally to the wholly different region of human psychology, and the powers of the soul are held to be corrupted as powers and faculties. The great Protestant theologians have always perceived this, and have accordingly repressed as unscriptural all such extremes. They have usually repelled the error by saying that, while man since the Fall can do no good in any divine relation, his natural and civil actions may be correct and virtuous.[2] Not only so, but maintaining the

---

[1] *On Religious Affections*, Works, i. 283 (Lond., 1840).
[2] Commenting on Mark x. 21, "*Intuitus eum Jesus dilexit,*" Calvin

validity of man's natural faculties and of their operation on natural things,—the denial of which would be
a universal pyrrhonism,—it has been an essential of
the evangelical theology to maintain, further, that
there is possible to fallen man a natural knowledge
of God, and even a natural acquaintance with truth
supernaturally revealed, as contrasted with a spiritual
and saving knowledge of God and things divine. This
position was strongly contended for by the orthodox
theologians of the seventeenth century in opposition to
the Socinians, who denied it. Its value consists in its
forming the proper foundation of natural theology, as
well as in its being an essential part of the Scripture
doctrine of the divine image.[1]

The Scripture view of the Fall, as we have seen, is
that it was radical and fatal as regards man's relation
to God. The consistency of this with the maintenance
of validity in fallen man's natural faculties, and of the
goodness of his actions in a natural sense, is sometimes
stated in this form, namely, that it is the constitutional working of man in his moral and religious life
that is vitiated by sin, but not his parts and faculties.
As if we should note that a timepiece may cease to
give accurate time and yet be unimpaired in its wheels,

says : "Interdum vero Deus, quos non probat, nec justificat, amare
dicitur : nam quia illi grata est humani generis conservatio (quæ justitia,
æquitate, moderatione, prudentia, fide, temperantia constat) politicas
virtutes amare dicitur, non quod salutis vel gratiæ meritoriæ sint, sed quia
ad finem spectant illi probatum."

[1] See the pamphlet of the late Prof. James Macgregor, entitled, *A
Vindication of Natural Theology*, (Elliot, Edin., 1859), the surviving
monument of a now forgotten controversy in the Glasgow F.C. College
case.

plates, jewels, and other constituent portions. The analogy has only to be carried out, however, to suggest the complete statement. If a watch or other timepiece fail of its chief end, and be laid aside from its proper use of keeping time, it is certain that its wheels, plates, and jewels will not long remain untarnished. So the Fall affects indirectly the natural powers of man, as it directly affects his spiritual condition. It is most evident that the working of sin, and especially of vice, darkens the understanding and blunts the judgment even in common things; that it not only sears the conscience, but deadens the natural affections; in short, that the failure of human nature to attain the chief end of its constitution carries with it consequences which affect even its constituent parts.

Very fully have evangelical divines brought out the breadth and harmony of Scripture statement as to the two positions, covered in this and the preceding chapter, namely, that man though fallen is still in a natural sense constituted in the image of God, but that in a spiritual sense that constitution is through sin totally ruined; and hence, that though the natural powers and faculties have still the stamp of God, and are not in themselves sinful, they are all indirectly under sin's power, and suffer from its effects. The eloquent passage in Howe's *Living Temple* is well remembered, but it is not always observed with what exquisite balance it keeps both these lines of truth in view. "That God hath withdrawn Himself and left this His temple desolate, we have many sad and plain proofs before us. The stately ruins are visible to every eye that bear in their front (yet extant) this doleful inscription, '*Here God once dwelt.*' Enough appears of the admirable frame and structure of the soul of man to show the Divine Presence did some-time reside in it; more than enough of vicious deformity to proclaim He is now retired and gone. The lamps are extinct, the altar overturned; the light and love are now vanished, which did the one shine with so heavenly brightness, the other burn with so pious fervour; the golden candlestick is displaced, and thrown away as a useless thing, to make room for the throne of the prince of darkness; the sacred incense, which sent rolling up in clouds its rich perfume, is exchanged for a poisonous, hellish vapour, and here is, 'instead of a sweet savour, a stench.' . . . Look upon the fragments of that curious sculpture which once adorned the palace of that great King: the relics of common notions; the lively prints of some undefaced truth; the fair ideas of things; the yet legible precepts that relate to practice. Behold with what accuracy the broken pieces show these to have been engraven by the finger of God; and how they now lie torn and scattered, one in this dark corner, another in that, buried in heaps of dirt and rubbish! There is not now a system, an entire table of coherent truths to be found, or a frame of holiness, but some shivered parcels; and if any, with great toil and labour, apply themselves to draw out here one piece and there another, and set them together, they serve rather to show how exquisite the divine workmanship was in the original composition, than for present use to the excellent purposes for which the whole was first designed. . . . You come, amidst all this confusion, as into the ruined palace of some great prince, in which you see here the fragments of a noble pillar, there the shattered pieces of some curious imagery, and all lying neglected and useless among heaps of dirt. He that invites you to take a view of the soul of man gives you but such another prospect, and doth but say to you, 'Behold the desolation!' all things rude and waste. So that should there be any pretence to the Divine Presence, it might be said, If God be here, why is it thus? The faded glory, the darkness, the disorder, the impurity, the decayed state in all respects of this temple, too plainly show the Great Inhabitant is gone." [1]

[1] John Howe, *The Living Temple*, Pt. II. chap. iv. sec. 9.

CHAPTER XII

DEATH THE PENALTY OF SIN

THE preceding pages have been carrying us into our concluding topic in this department, namely, the RESULTS OR CONSEQUENCES which sin has entailed on *the nature of man.* The substance of what Scripture teaches on this subject may be held as condensed in the sentence, " The wages of sin is death." Like the terms " Sin," " Flesh," " Heart," the term " Death " is one of the pivot words of Bible anthropology. To examine how much it means would require a treatise of itself. But we assume for our present purpose that it has three meanings, a legal, a moral, and a physical.

1. " In the day that thou eatest thereof thou shalt surely die," clearly means, " in that day thou art dead,— legally dead, as under condemnation, sentence being pronounced; spiritually dead, as fallen from righteousness and separated from God." The literal or physical death is a consequence which flows from these; liability to it dated from the moment of the transgression, yet this liability does not surcease with that deliverance which is effected in redemption, for even in the redeemed " the body is dead because of sin," though " the spirit is

life because of righteousness." [1]   The two latter meanings of the term "Death," namely, the moral and the physical, cover the ground of our present question as to the direct consequences of the fall upon man's own nature.   Spiritual inability and physical dissolution are those results of sin which may in a sense be called constitutional changes.   In what sense they can be so regarded it is for us to inquire.

2. *Spiritual inability*, or the loss of "all ability of will to any spiritual good accompanying salvation," is only part of what is generally called spiritual death; but it is an essential part of it, and is, moreover, that part which alone properly belongs to this place, as a result of the Fall affecting man's moral constitution.   Our interest in it, however, is chiefly negative; that is to say, we are concerned to show that what is called in the Bible death in trespasses and sins, is not such a derangement of man's original constitution as implies either (*a*) a destruction of his free agency, or (*b*) the loss of any essential element or attribute of his nature.   Under (*a*) it is of some moment to note, that those who have been most strenuous in maintaining the Scripture position that fallen man cannot of himself return to God, cannot repent unto life, cannot believe unto salvation, in his natural mind receiveth not the things of God, in his carnal state cannot please God, have nevertheless uniformly and consistently held that man under sin has not ceased to be a free and responsible agent.   This " natural bondage "—that is, servitude to sin in a fallen nature—is perfectly consistent with " that natural

[1] Rom. viii. 10.

liberty " wherewith " God hath endued the will of man, that it is neither forced, nor by any absolute necessity of nature determined, to good or evil." [1] Even in times when a controversy such as that between Luther and Erasmus was possible, when men might be said to be tilting from opposite sides of the field, the Augustinians at least did not mistake the real issue. In the second age of Reformed theology the two positions were seen to be both practically and speculatively consistent, as the clear and well-balanced lines of the Westminster Confession show. This is now so well understood, that even those who theologically differ from the Augustinian or Calvinistic view, and maintain the Arminian position, do not impute to their opponents any real inconsistency in holding the natural liberty of the will. That fallen man should be spiritually bound, yet metaphysically free, is now seen to be a position consistent with Scripture, with sound theology, and with common sense.[2] (b) In refuting the unscriptural position that man's death in sin means that by the Fall some element of his constitution was lost or fell into abeyance, we have to glance at some

---

[1] Westminster Confession of Faith, chap. ix. 1.

[2] For an interesting incidental commentary on the ninth chapter of the Confession, see the late Principal W. Cunningham's article on " Calvinism and the Doctrine of Philosophical Necessity," in the course of which he points out the theological confusions of the philosophers Stewart, Mackintosh, and Hamilton, as well as the converse oversights of the divines Edwards and Chalmers. He shows that the positions of all the Reformers—the Lutherans, when cleared of their earlier exaggeration, as well as the Calvinists—was, like that of Augustine himself, one which entirely conserved the natural freedom of the human spirit, and which did not involve the question of man's bondage under sin and deliverance by grace with any philosophical theory whatever. See Dr. Cunningham's *Reformers and the Theology of the Reformation*, pp. 471-524.

forms of error recently revived. Modern trichotomists undertake to deliver us from a controversy of fourteen centuries' standing regarding the will, its natural liberty and its bondage under sin, by substituting the simple-looking formula that the *pneuma* in fallen man being dead or dormant, regeneration consists in the quickening or awakening of that *pneuma*, the absence or inaction of which was enough to explain man's spiritual death. This pretension is very poorly supported. Indeed, there is no point where the attempt to construct a scheme of Christian doctrine in terms of the so-called "tripartite nature of man" more entirely fails than this. In the first place, it is impossible to ascertain whether the writers of this school mean to maintain that this sovereign power in man's constitution, the spirit, is since the Fall dead, or disabled, or defective, or dormant, or wholly absent.[1] Further, the theory that this defect or absence of the *pneuma* in fallen man accounts for his spiritual bondage under sin errs in precisely the opposite direction from that in which its supporters seem to think they are moving. Instead of being a cautious or moderate statement of the consequences of the Fall, it is implicitly a very serious exaggeration. One of these writers contrasts the orthodox view with his own by calling the

---

[1] For an instance of this confusion see Delitzsch, *System der bibl. Psychologie*, pp. 337, 338 (Clark's Transl. pp. 397, 398). Mr. J. B. Heard is still more self-contradictory. Almost every page of his chapter on "The State of the *Pneuma* in Man since the Fall," contains the conflicting epithets "dead," "defective," "dormant," as applied to that "faculty" of which he also says : "When God withdrew from Adam the presence of His Holy Spirit, the *pneuma* fell back into a dim and depraved state of conscience toward God." (!)—*The Tripartite Nature of Man*, 5th Edition, pp. 175-197, (Edin., 1882).

former the dogma that original sin was something positive, and the latter the negative or privative idea of birth-sin, which he holds to be sufficient to explain the facts of the case.[1] Now the theory of these writers is, that the *pneuma* in fallen man is a dead organ; that there is a " defect of that special religious faculty in man which is called the spirit "; that by the eating of the forbidden fruit " the spark of the divine image in man was quenched." And all this is put forward as " only saying that birth-sin is privative and not positive," and as " enough to account for the condition of man as we see him to this day." Enough, certainly! Almost as much more than enough as was that famous *dictum* of Flacius, that original sin was a corruption of the substance of the soul. For according to this theory man's natural subjection to sin depends upon a physical defect, the defect of an organ, the dead or disabled state of the sovereign power of the regulative *pneuma*—a " fatal defect," as the upholders of the theory rightly name it, for it makes man's recovery inconceivable. It is the more needful to advert to this, since the tripartite psychology has been largely adopted by the holders of what is called " conditional immortality." The writer, whose application of it to eschatological speculations has become most noted, speaks according to the same theory even when he touches on man's spiritual state since the Fall. " This moral ruin consists in the paralysis of the *pneuma*, or spiritual faculty, which no longer either *sees* or *wills*, as is necessary for a life in union with God. This is the cause of the sinful life,

---

[1] *The Tripartite Nature of Man*, p. 195.

and 'the wages of sin is death.' "[1]   The whole of this
fallacious train of statement rests on the incorrect
assumption that Scripture warrants a tripartite analysis
of natures or constituent elements in the original constitution of man, such as would enable us to give what
may be called a physical explanation of man's fallen
state, accounting for it by the absence or abeyance of a
special religious or spiritual faculty.

There is, therefore, no course open to us but to state
the effect of the Fall upon the human will in the terms
which have so long exercised the theologians, if we are
to state it philosophically at all.   But the profound
affirmation of Scripture is that man is " dead in trespasses and sins."   No faculty or element is singled out
as that in which this death takes special effect.   It is an
effect upon man's entire moral position.   Hence this
doctrine of human inability in spiritual things presents
the same complex problem as that concerning the sinfulness of concupiscence.   The Bible solution is, that such
inability to good on the one hand, and evil desire on the
other, conditioning the will, are at once sinful and penal.
They are sin in one sense ; they are death or the wages
of sin in the other sense.   They constitute a moral
character at the back of all acts of will.   They characterise man's fallen nature as depraved, corrupt, in a
word sinful, before any actual transgressions.   But they
are themselves the consequences of sin—penal consequences—taking effect in a form conditioned by the
federal unity of mankind.   The peculiarity of the Bible
view here is that the same thing is represented as sin

[1] Edward White, *Life in Christ*, 3rd Edition, p. 280, (Lond., 1878).

and death in one. " O wretched man that I am, who
shall deliver me from the body of this death ? The
principle that in this region sin and its punishment are
practically identical, is one which receives the attestation
of nature, of conscience, and of Scripture alike. Man's
will is spiritually disabled by the Fall, because of that
profound law that sin subjects the sinner to a moral
fatalism, a *misera necessitas mali* expressed by our Lord's
words : " Whosoever committeth sin is the servant
of sin." [1]

3. Whether *physical death* implies a constitutional
change resulting from the Fall, is a question which requires to be answered with more care than is sometimes
given to it. A general acquaintance with physiological
and geological facts has now made the idea familiar to
all educated people, that death is a law of organised
matter. It is not uncommon, however, to represent the
Bible as saying that the sin of man first introduced
physical death into the animated world. It is plain
that the Bible makes no such assertion. Indeed, the
scientific principle that death is a necessary step in
organic processes is expressly affirmed by our Lord and
by St. Paul in application to the vegetable world.[2] And
there are indications by no means obscure in the earlier
chapters of Genesis that the same law is recognised as
applicable to all animal organisms. Observing that the
maxim, " Death by sin," applies to man alone, the best
divines and exegetes have always maintained that the
sentence of death which followed the Fall was not the

---

[1] See Martensen's *Dogmatics*, p. 209 (Clark, Edin., 1866).
[2] John xii. 24 ; 1 Cor. xv. 36.

introduction of any new physical law or constitutional change in regard to the human body. They hold that man's physical nature was by its constitution mortal, though his actual death followed only upon sin. In the light of these interpretations, given some of them centuries before science had propounded its maxims, Scripture is shown to be in no way committed to the absurd position that the Fall introduced into the world the principle of decay in animal organisms.[1] Accordingly, the *locus classicus* on this subject, Rom. v. 12, " By one man sin entered into the world, and death by sin," must be read in the light of the Old Testament narrative on which it is grounded. Now, when we consider what is stated in Gen. ii. and iii. with regard to the constitution of the first man, we see that there is obviously a sense in which he was created mortal. He was Adam from the *adamah*, the ground. Dust was the material of his body. Organised matter has naturally in it the seeds of decay, the certainty of dissolution. That the body of the first man could not be immortal by its constitution is implied, if not expressed, in the narrative. " Dust thou art, and to dust thou shalt return." That is to say, the curse assumes the form of a prediction, that in consequence of sin the law of organised matter should be

---

[1] Augustine, *De Peccatorum Meritis*, etc., Opera (Benedictine Edition), x. 193. Grotius, *De Satisfactione Christi*, Opera, iii. 382. Owen, *Commentary on Hebrews* (Goold's Edition of the whole Works), vol. xxiii. pp. 408, 409. Julius Müller, *Christian Doctrine of Sin*, vol. ii. pp. 290, 295 (Clark's Transl.), who excellently states in what sense death is natural to the body, and in what sense unnatural to the human being, and an effect of sin. So also Dr. A. B. Bruce, *Humiliation of Christ*, pp. 277, 278 (Edin., 1876). Neander, *History of the Planting of Christianity*, vol. i. pp. 426, 427 (Bohn).

allowed to have its way, even in the case of man. On the other hand it is plain that, according to this narrative, man was not made to die, that he was created for incorruption. It bears out what Bishop Bull calls the " foundation of the whole Catholic doctrine concerning the state of man in his integrity, namely, that Adam should not have died if he had not sinned.[1]

Man's constitution, however, even in innocence, implied, to use the language of the theological schools, not an *impossibility of dying*, but only a conditional *potentiality of not dying*. In the event that man had not sinned, there are several conceivable ways in which the "*posse non mori*" might have issued in a confirmed physical immortality. The favourite patristic view was, that after probation Adam would have passed from the earthly to the heavenly paradise by an Elijah-like translation. Others have supposed that, even remaining on earth, his body would have undergone a change analogous to that which Christians are taught to expect at the second coming of Christ. Others, again, have contented themselves with saying that holiness confirmed and established should have effected such a change on man's physical being as to render it impassible and immortal.[2] There is a good deal to be said for the view favoured by Augustine, Luther, J. Müller, and others, that the narrative itself supplies us with a suggestion on the point. " The tree of life, in the midst of the garden," was the divine provision for effecting this transition. The

---

[1] *State of Man before the Fall*, vol. ii. p. 60 of Works (Burton's Edition, Oxford, 1846).

[2] Turretine, *Instit. Theolog. Elench.* Loc. v. Q. xii. 3, 4.

mention of it may be regarded as the way, proper to this transcendental narrative, of stating that the Creator had prepared a process for man's passing into the immortal or undying life, as a being made up of body and spirit, had he continued obedient.   The idea of " the tree of life " is of that original paradisaic sort to which the imagination of mankind in all ages bears witness, when it represents its heroes as seeking to bathe in the fountain of perpetual youth, or toiling in search of some secret " elixir " to counteract the decays of mortality.   If physical death be implied in man's original constitution, in so far as he is of the earth earthy, yet according to Scripture (and the instinct of mankind answers thereto) it was so only as a possibility which could and ought to have been averted.   The provision made for averting it lay symbolically and sacramentally in the use of the tree of life, though really and spiritually in man's being so formed in the image of God that perfect obedience was possible to him.[1]

The chief value of this view is, that it simplifies the connection between the Fall and that part of its effects under consideration.   When man sinned, physical death followed as a natural consequence.   The sentence was carried out by no introduction of constitutional change. It was effected simply by denying to man that " immor-

---

[1] See Julius Müller, *The Christian Doctrine of Sin*, vol. ii. pp. 296, 297.   So also Bishop Bull (*Op. cit.* p. 54).   " Now it is certain the tree of life was so called because it was either a sacrament and divine sign, or else a natural means of immortality ; that is, because he that should have used it would (either by the natural virtue of the tree itself continually repairing the decays of nature, or else by the power of God) have lived for ever, as God Himself plainly assures us, Gen. iii. 22-24."   So also Augustine, *De Genesi ad Litteram*, Opera iii. 343.

talising transition" which would have occurred in his path of progress had he remained holy. This denial was sealed by his expulsion from Paradise and consequent exclusion from the tree of life. The dust of which his body was framed, instead of being transmuted into such a garb for the perfect spirit as it should have become by his feeding on that ambrosial nourishment, is left to the law of its own decay and returns to dust. Man in consequence of sin becomes subject to physical death as an inevitable necessity and the law of his being. Augustine has put this with epigrammatic effect when, commenting on Rom. viii. 10, 11, he says, "'If Christ be in you, the body is dead because of sin.' Paul is most careful to say 'dead,' not 'mortal.' The body was mortal by its nature, yet that mortal did not become dead but on account of sin. . . . And again, 'He that raised up Christ from the dead shall also quicken your mortal bodies.' Paul says not 'your dead bodies,' as before he had said 'the body is dead,' but 'shall quicken,' says he, 'even your mortal bodies, and that in such a way that not only shall they not be dead, but also no longer mortal." [1]

While, therefore, we repel as unscriptural the absurd position that sin introduced the principle of decay and death into the animated world, yet on the other hand

---

[1] *Corpus*, inquit *mortuum* est . . . vigilantissime non ait mortale, sed *mortuum*. . . . Sic et illud corpus jam erat mortale ; . . . sed ipsum mortale, non factum est mortuum nisi propter peccatum. Quia vero illa in resurrectione futura mutatio, . . . non ait *Qui suscitavit Christum Jesum a mortuis vivificabit et* mortua *corpora vestra* ; cum supra dixisset, *corpus mortuum* ; sed *vivificabit*, inquit, *et mortalia corpora vestra* ; ut scilicet jam non solum non sint mortua, sed nec mortalia."—Augustini, Opera (Benedictine Edition), Tome x. p. 193.

Scripture clearly teaches that death in all its meanings
is to man a consequence of sin. No exegesis of texts
such as Rom. v. 12 is tolerable which would exclude
either the spiritual or the physical sense of the term
"death." As Philippi has well said, it lies in the very
nature of such biblical notions ["life," "death," "sin"],
embracing a rich variety of elements, that often several
or even all these elements should appear in combination,
the context of the passage deciding how many and
which are to be conceived as blended in one.[1] The
death which came by sin, the death which is the wages
of sin, is no doubt largely spiritual death, but the
position of physical death under this general statement
is clear. It is a part of the curse. It is a consequence
of sin, in the sense that had man not sinned it would
have been averted. It is an effect of the first sin, of the
race-sin, in such a sense that for sin it has come upon
those who have not personally and consciously sinned.
To say that "death, as a simple physical fact, is unaffected by moral conditions, that its incidence is natural,
and lies in the constitution of things,"[2] is to break up
the whole scriptural view. Mainly and primarily, no
doubt, the death of the soul is death. Sin is the death-
dealing thing, but man is always presented in the Scriptures as a unit, and that which is death to him in one

[1] See his *Commentary on Romans*, *in loc.* vol. i. p. 254 (Clark's Transl.
Edin., 1878).

[2] Prin. Tulloch, *Croall Lecture*, p. 76. This and the similar expression
on p. 189, "The physical death of infants, therefore, does not require
sin to explain it," are statements irreconcilable with the principles which
in the main are followed throughout the book. The author seems to be
influenced by a desire to combine fidelity to Scripture theology with some
homage to views that are entirely the reverse of scriptural.

element of his nature must extend to all. It is germinant in meaning as in power.

No doubt there is a sense in which decay and death are natural—natural in animals, natural to the body of man as animal; but the Bible consistently represents man from the first as more than animal—as a personal, responsible, and God-related creature. For him death means separation, cutting off: primarily, of his spiritual life from God; secondarily, of his soul from his body. Physical death is for him corruption of the body and deprivation of the spirit. By the New Testament revelation, death is for the Christian greatly transformed. But it is not to be treated by Christians after the fashion of philosophy, either ancient or modern. The extinction of corporeal life in man is a real evil, is in the strictest sense part of the wages of sin. How it is met, modified, and even transmuted into blessing is a leading characteristic of the Christian revelation in regard to man's future.

The discussion thus summarised is no mere incidental one. It involves principles essential to the Bible view of man, and which distinguish it from the positive or non-Christian view. That man is a part of nature, that he is rooted in nature, is that portion of the truth about him, on which the Bible and observational science are at one. But the Bible places man in a realm of his own, in which he is also above nature. Science tends to view him exclusively from the nature-side. Justice can only be done to his entire and unique being from a larger standpoint. The question now sketched turns exactly upon this point. According to Scripture teach-

ing "death is an abnormal fact in the history of the
race; and redemption is, among other things, the undo-
ing of this evil, and the restoration of man to his completeness as a personal being." [1]

[1] Professor James Orr, *Christian View of God and the World*, p. 229
(Edin., Elliot, 1893). Cf. Dr. James Denney, *Studies in Theology*, pp.
97–99 (Hodder & Stoughton, Lond., 1894).

V

PSYCHOLOGY OF THE NEW LIFE

" Toute la foi consiste en Jésus-Christ et en Adam ; et toute la morale en la concupiscence et en la grâce."—PASCAL, *Pensées*, p. 296 (Molinier).

" C'est un des grands principes du Christianisme que tout ce qui est arrivé à Jésus-Christ doit se passer dans l'âme et dans le corps de chaque chrétien ; que comme Jésus-Christ a souffert durant sa vie mortelle, est mort à cette vie mortelle, est ressuscité d'une nouvelle vie, est monté au ciel et sied à la droite du Père ; ainsi le corps et l'âme doivent souffrir, mourir, ressusciter, monter au ciel, et seoir à la dextre. Toutes ces choses s'accomplissent en l'âme durant cette vie, mais non pas dans le corps. . . . Aucune de ces choses n'arrive dans le corps durant cette vie ; mais les mêmes choses s'y passent ensuite."—*Ibid.* I. 28, 29 (Faugère).

JOHN iii. 3.—"Except a man be born again, he cannot see the kingdom of God."

EPH. ii. 5.—"Even when we were dead in sins, hath quickened us together with Christ."

EPH. iv. 22-24.—"That ye put off concerning the former conversation the old man, which is corrupt according to the deceitful lusts; and be renewed in the spirit of your mind; and that ye put on the new man, which after God is created in righteousness and true holiness."

2 COR. v. 17.—"Therefore if any man *be* in Christ, *he is* a new creature."

GAL. ii. 20.—"Nevertheless I live; yet not I, but Christ liveth in me."

Also

GAL. v. 16-26 and ROM. vii. 5-viii. 14.

CHAPTER XIII

THE NEW LIFE: ITS ORIGIN

[LITERATURE.—Calvin, *Institutio Christ. Relig.* lib. iii. Owen, *Pneumatologia; or, A Discourse concerning the Holy Spirit.* Stephen Charnock, *Works*, vol. iii. (Nichol's Reprint, Edin., 1860). Jonathan Edwards, *Treatise Concerning Religious Affections.* Marshall, *The Gospel Mystery of Sanctification.* Harless, *System of Christian Ethics.* Martensen, *Christian Ethics* (Clark, Edin., 1868, 1873). For Literature on the Pauline Theology, see Note to next chapter.]

THE rise of the new life in the soul must be considered a central topic in our theme, for it is here that the supernatural scheme of the Bible emerges in human experience. The religion of revelation—a system of supernatural facts—touches at this point the natural scheme of man and his being; for the supernatural, in this form of a personal spiritual change, becomes a fact of consciousness. "The doctrine of grace," it has been said, "can never perish, for it creates defenders of itself."[1] Fresh witness for its truth arises with every additional human being who becomes the subject of divine grace. He has the evidence in his own person of a divine interposition on man's behalf. The kingdom of

---

[1] Pascal.

heaven is within him. The origin of the spiritual supernatural in man, the entrance of the redemptive power into his nature, or his entrance into its domain, is called in Scripture a birth—a being "born again" or "from above,"[1] a quickening and resurrection,[2] a new creation or a new creature.[3] These expressions indicate, of course, the entirely divine origination of the change; that in it God—the Spirit of God—acts upon the human heart in a direct or immediate transaction. It follows that in the regenerative act the subject of the change is passive, and even, it may be, at the time unconscious of the change, as the analogies of Creation, Birth, and Resurrection imply.

There is no theological term which we now use more definitely, and with less risk of mistake, than "Regeneration." It invariably denotes the strictly initial act of grace by which a human being passes from the kingdom of darkness into the kingdom of God. But even so defined, it has two sides. It may mean the act or work of God's Spirit in producing the change; or it may mean the change itself so produced in the subject of it. What we have to do with now is the subjective meaning,—the change effected in the human soul. In what that change consists, and in what not, has been clearly made out in the best schools of evangelical theology, though, as usual, not without controversy.

[1] John iii. 3, 5 : ἐὰν μή τις γεννηθῇ ἄνωθεν.

[2] Eph. ii. 5, 6 : συνεζωοποίησε . . . καὶ συνήγειρε. Comp. Col. iii. 1; Rom. vi. 5, 11.

[3] 2 Cor. v. 17 ; Gal. vi. 15 : καινὴ κτίσις. Comp. Eph. ii. 10, 15: κτισθέντες, κτίσῃ ; iv. 24 : κτισθέντα ; Col. iii. 10 : κτίσαντος. Comp. also παλιγγενεσία in the only two places where it occurs, Tit. iii. 5, in our present sense, and Matt. xix. 28. in a dispensational meaning.

I. What it IS NOT. Here it chiefly concerns us to notice that when we speak according to Scripture we must repudiate all theories of regeneration which make it consist in a change (1) upon the substance of the soul, or (2) upon the constitution of human nature, or even (3) upon any special faculty or element in that nature. The first of these erroneous opinions is commonly connected with the name of Matthias Flacius Illyricus, a name among the most considerable in the second generation of the German Reformers. A man of strong evangelical feeling, but a keen controversialist rather than an exact thinker, he had allowed himself, in dealing with opponents of the scriptural doctrine of depravity, to use some incautious expressions which seemed to make sin the very substance of fallen human nature; and then proceeded, in spite of the remonstrances of his fellow-Reformers, to elevate this exaggeration into a dogma. His favourite texts on the subject are: "I will take away the hard and stony heart"; "Our old man is crucified with Christ"; "Ye were once darkness," etc. Relying upon such Scripture terms as these, and upon certain expressions of Luther, he contended that the substance of human nature was by the Fall changed, corrupted, and depraved. Accordingly he held that in the production of the new spiritual man there is a corresponding substantial change. When charged with Manichæan heresy, he explained that he had never used the phrase quoted against him, "that sin is the substance," but had always asserted that it is the "essential form" of fallen nature. He clung tenaciously, however, to his main position that the corruption of human nature is essential and substantial, not accidental. In the *Formula Concordiæ*, drawn up about two years after the death of Flacius, his opinion is alluded to and condemned, as destroying the distinction between the substance of human nature—or the man himself as created by God—and that original sin which inheres in his nature and corrupts it.[1] The error of this able, laborious, and much afflicted divine has served chiefly as a foil to bring out with greater distinctness the teaching of the evangelical church on the point. It is clear that, according to Scripture, neither the Fall on the one hand nor Regeneration on the other can be regarded as effecting a change in the substance of human nature.

(2) But although the Lutheran symbols are perfectly at one with those of the Reformed Church in repudiating all errors of this kind belonging to the age in which they were written, the doctrine of the regenerate life, as taught by some Lutheran theologians now, does suggest the idea of constitutional or substantial change. This tendency arises in a way quite different from that above described. It is a reflex of the sacramentarian views prevalent in the Lutheran and in some other

---

[1] To bring this out, the authors of the *Formula* allow the expression that sin, even in fallen human nature, belongs to its *accidents*, not its *essence* or *substance*. Though these terms, they say, should not be used in popular teaching, as being liable to misunderstanding, and as not being expressly scriptural, they are to be retained in theological discussion concerning Original Sin. "For by means of these terms, the distinction between the work of God and the work of the devil can be set forth with the greatest clearness. For the devil cannot create any substance, but can only, by way of accident, under the permission of the Lord, deprave a substance created by God."—*Form. Concord.* I. xiii. ; see Schaff, *Creeds of the Evangelical Protestant Churches*, p. 105.

communions. When men teach that our Lord's
humanity is partaken of in the sacraments, it is easy
to see how a general theory might arise to the effect
that the divine humanity of Christ is the basis of the
new life in believers, or that regeneration consists in
the communication of His theanthropic life to the soul.
When this tendency is intensified, as is the case with
some Lutheran divines, by a favour for the trichotomic
partition of human nature, the result may be anticipated.
Delitzsch, in the section of his *Biblical Psychology*
treating of regeneration, has given full expression to
the theory. "Since the mystery of the Incarnation
was realised, divine influences are at work which make
sinful man partaker of the spirit, soul, and body of
Christ; so that he who, according to his connection
with Adam, is earthy, becomes, according to his connection with Christ, spiritual and heavenly." "This,"
he explains, "does not take place through physical
impartation any more than did the entrance of man's
soul at the first through the divine inbreathing, or than
does the derivation of soul or spirit in children from
their parents. Yet influences proceed from Christ
according to His tripartite human constitution which
place men in such communion with the spirit, soul,
and body of Christ as exercises a transforming power
over their threefold nature." "In the work of grace,"
he proceeds, "we are made partakers of the *spirit* of
Christ, whereby is revived and preserved the once extinct image of God in our spirit; of the *soul* of Christ,
that is, of His blood, which divine-human blood becomes
the tincture of our soul to the recovering of its God-like

glory; of the *flesh* of Christ, which enters into us
without mixing with our sin-pervaded, material, animal
flesh, and which becomes a tincture of immortality,
laying hold of the essence of our flesh in order to
assimilate to itself eventually even its outward appearance, in the resurrection." After such a statement, it
is not surprising to find him closing the paragraph in
words which almost echo the Flacian exaggeration :
" Since the natural spiritual-psychical constitution of
man is not merely ethically but substantially affected by
corruption, the restoration of it must be also at once
ethical and substantial." [1]

The opinion that through Christ a constitutional
change is effected upon human nature has been taken
up by a school of writers in this country, who hold it
in a far cruder form than that of the Lutheran
theology, and without any sacramentarian proclivity
which could account for it. With them it originates
in a different interest. In support of his theory of
" conditional immortality," Mr. Edward White, for
instance, sets forth the doctrine that " God unites the
divine essence with man's mortal nature in the regeneration of the individual by the indwelling of the Holy
Spirit, ' the Lord and Giver of life,' whose gracious
inhabitation applies the remedy of redemption by
communicating to good men of every age and generation
God-likeness or immortality, to the soul by spiritual
regeneration, and to the body by resurrection." Like
the Lutheran divines, he holds that " this mighty change

---

[1] *System der bibl. Psychologie*, pp. 338–340. The paragraphs are summarised above, not quoted at full length.

is conveyed to mankind through the channel of the incarnation." But, in stating what the change is, a serious discrepancy occurs. "We hold," he says, "that the Scripture teaches that the very object of redemption is to change our nature, not only from sin to holiness, but from mortality to immortality,—from a constitution whose present structure is perishable in all its parts, to one which is eternal, so that those who are partakers of the blessing 'pass from death unto life,' from a corruptible nature into one which is incorruptible in all its parts, physical and spiritual." [1] And again: "Apart from such renewal in the divine likeness, life, however intelligent, is perishable, for the soul has no union with Eternal Love. It is, then, a moral change in the character of the soul and the discipline of the body, and not an ontological or physical change in substance, which is the condition of salvation and the present result of the indwelling of the Divine Spirit." [2] How these two paragraphs are consistent, or how even the two sentences of the last can be saved from self-contradiction, we leave the reader to consider. Nor do we concern ourselves at present with their bearing on the doctrine of man's natural immortality. Meanwhile, our business with this theory is simply to set its startling and confused view of the change effected in regeneration side by side with that drawn by the consent of centuries of evangelical thinking from the statements of Scripture.

(3) After what has been said in preceding chapters in refutation of theories which restrict to certain elements

---

[1] *Life in Christ*, p. 117, 3rd Edition.   [2] *Ibid.* p. 280.

or faculties in man the chief effect of the Fall, it is not necessary that we should now discuss the corollary from these theories, which would restrict in a similar manner the act of regeneration. We have already dealt with the view which makes the great change in conversion to consist in the re-awakening of a buried or dormant *pneuma.*[1] It is thoroughly untenable. To give any significance to the theory, it is necessary for its defenders to maintain, as Mr. J. B. Heard does, that this dormant *pneuma* is always ethically incorrupt, is only affected by depravity in the sense of being buried before conversion and still weak after it; and that sanctification acts upon it not in the way of making it holy, but simply by enabling it to assert its supremacy. Now to say that " the *pneuma* or God-like in man," which regeneration quickens and sanctification strengthens, " is not prone to evil,—indeed, cannot sin," [2]—is to contradict the whole strain of Scripture, if not even its express language, when it declares that in the regenerate there is defilement both of the *Sarx* and *Pneuma* from which they are to cleanse themselves.[3] But this theory must fall under a broader and more general condemnation. To make regeneration the re-awakening of any such dead or dormant faculty is to contravene the Scripture view that man's whole inward being—his heart—is the seat of sin, and consequently the subject of renewal. This principle, so characteristic of the Bible, namely, the unity of our inward life, confronts, indeed, all theories which would

---

[1] In Chapter XII., at pp. 236, 237.
[2] *Tripartite Nature of Man,* p. 225, 5th Edition.
[3] 2 Cor. vii. 1.

place the seat of regeneration in any one faculty or
department of the soul, as the intellect, the affections, or
the will. It is the whole inner man, as such, that is
spiritually dead. It is the same that is spiritually made
alive. Regeneration is something which affects the whole
man. It is a quickening, *i.e.* the impartation of a new
form of life. It is a second birth, or the entry into a new
spiritual state. It is the gift from God of a new heart,
a new moral self. The inner man, that is, the human
being in the centre and unity of his life, is the seat or
subject of the life-giving power of the Holy Ghost which
produces this new creation; and the new creature is
identified with that abiding or indwelling of God's Holy
Spirit.[1]

II. What it is. It is the infusion of a new principle
under which man exercises all the powers and faculties
he has by nature in a new way. The Puritan writers,
who even among evangelicals carry the palm in their
studies of Christian experience, are at one in so describing the great spiritual crisis. "Regeneration," says
Charnock, "is a mighty and powerful change wrought
in the soul by the efficacious working of the Holy Spirit,
wherein a vital principle, a new habit, the law of God,
and a divine nature are put into and framed in the heart,
enabling it to act holily and pleasingly to God. . . . It
is a certain spiritual and supernatural principle, a permanent form, infused by God, whereby it is made
partaker of the divine nature and enabled to act for

---

[1] See all this fully stated by Dr. Charles Hodge, *Systematic Theology*,
vol. iii. pp. 16, 17, 33–36. In connection with his discussion of the
"Nature of Regeneration," stands another concerning the "Psychology
of Faith," which will be found *ibid.* pp. 42–67.

God." Still more pithily it is expressed by Owen as "an habitual holy principle wrought in us by God and bearing His image." The precision with which such terms as "principle," "habit," "nature," are here used by these writers comes of their intention to repel the persistent misrepresentation, not unheard even yet, that the New Birth claims to be a change in the constitution of the human mind, or in some of the natural laws under which it acts. What is changed is, as Paul has it, "the spirit of the mind," the dominant tendency. The mind itself is not changed in essence or substance, but its bias is altered, the prevailing character is changed, the man has received a "new heart and a right spirit." Jonathan Edwards— the greatest writer on such topics since the Puritans— has asserted the true and rejected the false here, in the nearest approach to a psychological definition of the new nature when he says : " This new spiritual sense and the new dispositions that attend it are no new *faculties*, but new *principles* of nature : I use the word ' principles ' for want of a word of more determinate signification. By a ' principle of nature,' in this place, I mean that foundation which is laid in nature either old or new, for any particular manner or kind of exercise of the faculties of the soul ; or a natural habit or foundation for action, giving a person ability and disposition to exert the faculties in exercises of such a certain kind, so that to exert the faculties in that kind of exercises may be said to be his nature. So this new spiritual sense is not a new faculty of understanding, but it is a new foundation laid in the nature of the soul for a new kind of exercises of the same faculty of understanding. So that the new holy disposition of heart that attends this new sense is not a new faculty of will, but a foundation laid in the nature of the soul for a new kind of exercises of the same faculty of will."[1] This definition expresses quite simply and yet with an approach to philosophical accuracy, the position of the Scriptures upon the nature of the change effected by regeneration. It holds the proper mean between extremes against which the evangelical Church has always contended. It rejects the Flacian extreme. There is no change in the substance of the soul. There is no essential or constitutional transformation of man's nature. There is not even the implantation of a new part or faculty. Yet, on the other hand, there is more than the revival of any existing faculty. There is far more than the origination — even though that were admittedly supernatural—of certain conscious acts or actings of the soul itself. This view, which errs in the opposite direction from that of Flacius, was held by the later Remonstrants, and more recently by adherents of what was called the New School divinity in America.[2] Regeneration lies deeper than consciousness. This is true not only of the act of the Divine Spirit originating it, but in a sense also of the thing originated. Deeper than consciousness and will, the Spirit produces in regeneration that new abiding state, disposition, principle, or habit, which constitutes the regenerated character,

---

[1] Edwards, *Treatise concerning Religious Affections*, Pt. III. sec. 1. Cf. some remarks of Neander in "The Conversion of Natural Talents into Christian Charisms," *Planting and Training*, vol. i. p. 469 (Bohn's Transl.).

[2] See Dr. Hodge, in refutation of the views of Emmons, Finney, and Taylor, *Systematic Theology*, vol. iii. pp. 7–15.

which gives it stability and perseverance, and which makes the renewed man's walk and conversation to be what they are.

Taking our stand, then, on the scriptural definition of the new life as something supernatural in itself and supernaturally introduced, we might now proceed to attempt such psychological questions as these :—1. What ground in human nature though fallen does Scripture indicate as making regeneration possible ? 2. How does the principle of spiritual life, supernaturally introduced,— the subject being passive or even unconscious,—become act or movement consciously realised ?

1. We ask, first, How fallen nature remains capable of regeneration and redemption ? This can be dealt with here only in a few sentences, for the whole question of the natural conscience, and other witness for God in man even as fallen, would lead us too far afield.

It is plain that what Scripture recognises as the thing reserved in man's nature, rendering recovery by divine grace still possible, is not the possession of any dead or buried faculty, such as the so-called *pneuma.* Its view, as we have seen, is much broader and simpler. It is, that notwithstanding the Fall, man continues in an important sense to bear the divine image, to be by his constitution a temple of the Living God, though the Divine Inhabitant may in another sense have ceased to dwell in it. To restore this image to its full glory is the end and aim of the whole redemptive process. Calvin, using the term " regeneration " in the wide sense as equivalent to the entire recovery of man from the Fall and its effects, says that the scope of it is nothing

else than to restore in us that image of God which had
been defiled, and only not obliterated, through the sin
of Adam.[1] The position of Calvin and the reformers
generally, expressed in such phrases as this *tantum non
obliterata*, is wholly overlooked by the hosts of writers
who, like Mr. J. B. Heard, charge evangelical theology
with leaving no *nidus* in human nature now on which
the renewing Spirit of God can descend.

If we desire to be more specific in our answer to this
question, we must go back to the consideration of the
sense in which Scripture affirms the image of God to be
unobliterated by the Fall. The leading peculiarity of the
Bible doctrine of man in his origin and constitution, we
have seen to be its ascription to him of spiritual personality, formed and upheld by the Divine Maker. This
places not the first man only, but all men, in a peculiar
and inalienable relation to God : " In Him we live, and
move, and have our being." And it is because the
human spirit was, and continues to be, a spirit derived
from God that it is possible for it still to approach or feel
after, and in a sense apprehend God. It is the other
side of the relationship, however, which Scripture employs
to throw light upon redemption. Its possibility is secured
in the fact that God continues to stand in His original
relation to all men, " the Father of spirits," " the God of
the spirits of all flesh," " for we are also His offspring."
This, indeed, will not of itself give us a cause or reason
for the undertaking of redemption. That is uniformly

---

[1] " Uno ergo verbo pœnitentiam interpretor regenerationem, cujus non
alius est scopus nisi ut imago Dei, quæ per Adæ transgressionem fœdata,
et tantum non obliterata fuerat, in nobis reformetur."—*Instit.* lib. iii.
cap. iii. 9.

ascribed in Scripture to gracious love, the highest expression of the divine energy and nature. But that lost men are still His, in a sense which specially belongs to man in the universe of being, is the Bible ground of the possibility of redemption. Nay more, it is the basis of that large *præparatio evangelica* which Scripture recognises everywhere. Because men are His, God has never left Himself without witness, nor without avenues of approach to the human spirit under the most unfavourable dispensations of humanity.

There are still more specific Scripture statements, telling of an intellectual and a moral aspect of this universal divine witness, implying a corresponding capability in the nature of man to receive it. It is affirmed that the invisible things of God can be perceived from His works, arguing a certain power in men, as they still are, to perceive or apprehend God.[1] It is declared that the uncodified moral law of nature stirs the consciences of the heathen, and that this shows the effect or practical force of divine law to be written on their hearts.[2] It is not well to press these Scripture statements into rigid scientific form,—to insist, *e.g.*, on the intellectual element alluded to, as a *sensus communis* or organ of revelation, or to speak of " conscience " as a " law within," self-subsistent and self-acting. But these indications that God retains for Himself a way of return to the human spirit and a ground for its recovery are most valuable. That men everywhere grope after God; that the prevalent ungodliness of men is only possible through denial and resistance of evidence which they are

[1] Rom. i. 19–21.   [2] Rom. ii. 14, 15.

capable of receiving; that the human spirit is never
unvisited by a sense of duty and a corresponding sense
of sin, yea, is moved at times by longings for salvation,
—these are the natural preparations for the gospel.   It
is one of the grand credentials of the Bible, as a system
of revealed truth, that it so clearly and fully recognises
these as the heritage of man.   That it meets these pre-
sentiments and carries on these preparations to fulfilment, conclusively proves the religion of the Bible to be
from God,—to be a supernatural provision for man's
redemption.   What pagan religions and human philosophies barely and partially recognise as man's deepest
need, Christianity not only recognises but satisfies.[1]

2. The second of these questions introduces us to the
theology of Conversion.   The current of Scripture usage
distinguishes Conversion as man's act in turning to God,
from the immediate act of the Divine Spirit in regenerat-
ing him or giving him the power to turn.   Scripture
speaks of the *necessity* of Regeneration, " Ye must be born
again."   It speaks of the *duty* of Conversion, " Repent
and be converted."   The connection between them is of
the closest possible kind, but the distinguishing of them
is also real, scriptural, and useful.   The distinction has
been worked out in theology by the same school of
evangelical thought which has accurately defined Regeneration.   This root-grace was in technical language,
named *Conversio habitualis*, or *passiva*, as consisting in
the infusion of a supernatural *habitus* or principle, through
the direct acting of the Holy Spirit.   The closely-connected

---

[1] I need hardly remind the reader under this section of the brief but
most eloquent tract of Tertullian, *De Testimonio Animæ.*

result, to which we now confine the term Conversion, was called *Conversio actualis* or *activa*. It was defined as being " brought about by the exercise of the gracious *habitus* implanted in the foregoing divine acts. In the former the man is renewed and converted by God ; in the latter the man, divinely renewed, turns himself to God ; being acted upon, he acts." [1] In less formal language, but with a precision founded upon these definitions, the Puritan Charnock contrasts and connects the two. After the description of the new birth already quoted [2] he adds : " It differs from conversion. Regeneration is a spiritual change ; conversion is a spiritual motion. In regeneration there is a power conferred ; conversion is the exercise of this power. In regeneration there is given us a principle to turn ; conversion is our actual turning ; that is, the principle whereby we are brought out of a state of nature into a state of grace ; and conversion the actual fixing on God, as the *terminus ad quem*. One gives *posse agere*, the other *actu agere*.

"Conversion is related to regeneration, as the effect to the cause. Life precedes motion, and is the cause of motion. In the covenant, the new heart, the new spirit, and God's putting His Spirit into them, is distinguished from their walking in His statutes (Ezek. xxxvi. 27), from the first step we take in the way of God, and is set down as the cause of our motion : ' I will cause you to walk in My statutes.' In renewing us, God gives us a power ; in converting us, He excites that power. Men are naturally dead, and have a stone upon them ; regeneration

[1] Turret. *Instit. Theologiæ Elencticæ*, Loc. XV. Q. iv. sec. 13
[2] See p. 257, *supra*.

is a rolling away the stone from the heart, and a raising to newness of life; and then conversion is as natural to a regenerate man as motion is to a living body. A principle of activity will produce action. In regeneration, man is wholly passive; in conversion, he is active: as a child, in its first formation in the womb, contributes nothing to the first infusion of life, but after it hath life it is active, and its motions natural. The first reviving of us is wholly the act of God, without any concurrence of the creature; but after we are revived, we do actively and voluntarily live in His sight; Hosea vi. 2 : 'He will revive us, He will raise us up, then shall we follow on to know the Lord.' Regeneration is the motion of God in the creature; conversion is the motion of the creature to God, by virtue of that first principle; from this principle all the acts of believing, repenting, mortifying, quickening, do spring. In all these a man is active; in the other merely passive; all these are the acts of the will, by the assisting grace of God, after the infusion of the first grace. Conversion is a giving ourselves to the Lord (2 Cor. viii. 5); giving our own selves to the Lord is a voluntary act, but the power whereby we are enabled thus to give ourselves is wholly and purely, in every part of it, from the Lord Himself. A renewed man is said to be led by the Spirit (Rom. viii. 14), not dragged, not forced; the putting a bias and aptitude in the will is the work of the Spirit quickening it; but the moving the will to God by the strength of this bias is voluntary, and the act of the creature. The Spirit leads, as a father doth a child by the hand : the father gave him that principle of life, and conducts him and hands him in his motion; but the child hath a principle of motion in himself, and a will to move. The day of regeneration is solely the day of God's power, wherein He makes men willing to turn to Him (Ps. cx. 3); so that, though in actual conversion the creature be active, it is not from the power of man, though it be from a power in man; not growing up from the impotent root in nature, but settled there by the Spirit of God." [1]

The distinction between the passive and the active side of the Great Change is thus Scripturally grounded, logically clear, and consented to by all evangelical thinkers. But beyond this, there is hardly anything pertaining to this topic which they can be said to have solidly deduced from Scripture. Reformed theology presents no reasoned connection between regeneration in the stricter sense and conversion with its fruits. It scripturally affirms, as we have seen, in all cases a divine work deeper than consciousness, before that subjective apprehension of salvation which is the turning-point in the conscious spiritual life. It more than admits the possibility of infant regeneration. But it has no uniform theory of the mode either of production or existence of grace in the unconscious or habitual state. In those Protestant communions where the idea of sacramental grace has retained prominence, there has always been a tendency to relapse from the evangelical to the Romish view of conversion. But those who have examined carefully the opinion of Luther, tell us that his notion of the faith of infants, begged and obtained for them in their baptism by the prayers of the Church, is not so

---

[1] *Works of Stephen Charnock* (Nichol's Edition), iii. pp. 88, 89.

divergent as at first it seems from that which has prevailed in the Calvinistic and Puritan churches. Earnest Christians in all the churches build much of their practical religious life on the correct assumption that grace, habitual and unconscious, must exist in many cases long before actual conversion; and that even what are called sudden conversions may sometimes be the bursting into flower of what was long preparing in the bud. The region, however, to which this question belongs is a difficult one in theology, and it has been the habit of theologians to avoid it. By modern Continental divines it is sometimes treated as belonging to Christian ethics, a study which with us lies as yet almost wholly uncultivated. Harless, for example, thus states what he considers the fundamental problem of that study: " With respect to the principle of Christian life and Christian ethics, in its reality it is just Christ Himself who has taken possession of me; and for ethics, the only question is to find an expression of the consciousness conformable to experience, of the way in which I know myself regulated by Christ as the principle of my moral life, and in what form of my inner life I have Him as such. . . . For the Christian finds not within himself the principle of a sound life, but in an objective power which brings him to restoration. The beginning of this life he wins not by his own struggles after this good, but he obtains it as a gift of grace to be possessed, into whose fulness of life he enters." [1]

---

[1] *System of Christian Ethics*, p. 13 (Clark, 1868). One section of this treatise is entitled, "The Entrance of the Blessing of Salvation into the Spiritual Life of the Individual"; and under it are such paragraphs as "The Appropriation of Regeneration in our Conversion."

CHAPTER XIV

THE NEW LIFE: ITS GROWTH AND VICTORY

[MAINLY AN EXPOSITION OF ROM. VII., VIII.]

THE New Life, as we have seen, begins from a super-natural principle, introduced into human nature by a supernatural act. It is consequently carried on and sustained in a way that is above nature. The Scripture treats of it as really the "life of God in the soul of man." "It is no longer I that live, but Christ liveth in me."[1] We must not, therefore, expect that the life of grace will yield us direct psychological material. Its processes can no more be subjects of strict scientific treatment than its commencement could be accounted for on natural principles. Nevertheless, the kingdom of grace is no exception among the realms of God, in respect of fixed and forecast order. Spiritual life, like all other life, has its laws and processes. Its course is constantly described in Scripture as a process of growth.[2] But there is a peculiarity in that growth which renders the usual analogies, derived from vegetable or animal progress, less applicable. It is not simply the evolution

[1] Gal. ii. 20 (R.V. *m.*).
[2] *E.g.*, Eph. iv. 13–16 ; 2 Pet. i. 5-8, iii. 18.

of the new vital principle implanted in regeneration. This spiritual principle has been introduced into a moral constitution where sin had its seat. Its progress is largely by conflict. Its growth is a growth in the over- coming of evil as well as in the divine life itself. A prominent part of its history, therefore, is that of the opposition between sin and grace, of the struggle between flesh and spirit. The exposition of this con- flict leads into the very heart of the doctrine of sanctifi- cation. The struggle itself has a large place in the spiritual experience of Christians. It needs hardly be said that the great Pauline passages, Gal. v. 16–26, Rom. vii., viii., where it is discussed, are of special moment for biblical psychology.

The pre-requisites for the solution of the teaching of these chapters are (I.) the settlement of the psychological terms, and (II.) the determination of the precise stages of spiritual history delineated.

I. We have already shown that the psychological terms of the New Testament writers generally, and of Paul in particular, were based upon the corresponding Old Testament expressions. Further, that what is new and peculiar in their meaning they have derived from the growth of divine revelation itself, rather than from any philosophical influences. In regard to the very prominent terms "flesh" and "spirit," so charac- teristic of the Pauline passages under consideration, this has been in effect admitted even by Pfleiderer, whose negative attitude as a theologian lends a certain value to what he admits as an exegete. "In brief, then," he says, "the real (ethically intensified) dualism of *sarx* and *pneuma* is not an element of the philosophical anthropology of Paul and a presupposition of his dogmatic, but a somewhat secondary product of his Christian speculation, the psychological reflex of his dogmatic antithesis between sin and grace.   The case is exactly the same with the so-called dualism of John.   This is the reason why here, as there, it is decidedly inadmissible to rank these contrasts under philosophical categories, or to refer them to the metaphysical dualism of philosophical systems.   It produces only confusion and mis-statement." [1]   What is of moment to us here is the virtual admission that the meaning of "flesh" and "spirit" in the writings of St. Paul is one newly charged with evangelical content, not an import of extraneous or even of Jewish philosophy.   That the writer now quoted attempts, after the manner of his school, to rationalise the process by which the apostle arrived at this meaning, does not invalidate his testimony to the fact that the ideas are peculiar to the Pauline system of the gospel.   We prefer the apostle's own account of how he received them.

A consistent view, as we have seen, of the two important terms "flesh" and spirit," [2]   will not allow us to narrow them each to a single meaning.   A double sense at least is indispensable.   There is, first, the simply natural meaning, according to which they respectively denote the lower and higher, or the material and immaterial elements in man's constitution, character-

---

[1] *Der Paulinismus*: " Ein Beitrag zur Geschichte der urchristlichen Theologie," p. 25 (Leipzig, 1873).

[2] See Chapters V. and VI. *supra.*

ised, however, rather by their origin than by their nature
—the one as of the earth, and perishable, the other as
immediately from God. But there is also a sense which
is ethical or religious, the meaning with which the terms
are fully charged in the New Testament, and especially
in the Pauline system. In the passages under consideration, for example, "flesh ˙ becomes identified with
the force or principle of sin in fallen nature, and " spirit "
with the principle of spiritual life in the new creature.
How the primary passes into the secondary meaning
is a question in the answer to which rationalising interpreters betray the characteristic weakness of their
system, unwillingness to admit the supernatural.
Pfleiderer, for instance, holds *pneuma* to be " an original
transcendent physical conception," and admits it to
have acquired "an ethical application under the influence
of Paul's mystic faith." Accordingly, he finds it no
violent transition that a corresponding ethical application
should have been given by the apostle to the physical
conception of *sarx*. This testimony that there are two
such distinct applications in the Pauline writings of both
" flesh " and " spirit," first a physical and then an ethical,
has its value. But when the concession is virtually
retracted by attempting to show how the secondary
meaning was developed by Paul out of the primary, its
value is lessened, and the failure of the " constructing "
becomes conspicuous. We see at once the superior
simplicity and truth of the view that the higher
meaning was poured into the terms by the increasing
volume of divine ideas opened up to such as Paul by the
Holy Spirit. Take first the two meanings of " flesh,"

and note how impossible it is, in a way of mere ratio-
cination, to develop the one out of the other. The
attempt to get the ethical significance which Paul gives
to it out of the elementary Hebrew conception of the
perishable (*i.e.* the bodily) part of man signally fails.[1]
It leaves out the clearly Scriptural position of the change
in human nature caused by the Fall. It is quite
inadequate to account for selfishness, wrath, pride,
and other non-fleshly sins bearing prominently the name
" works of the flesh." To assert that *sarx*, from its
primary meaning, " living material of the body," came by
a natural process of thought and language to mean
" the principle of sin," is to assume human nature to be
subject to sin by its physical constitution—a view
wholly untenable, because at variance with the most
radical conceptions of the Bible from its earliest to its
latest writings.

Then take the correlative term " spirit," and mark the
relation of its two meanings to the psychology of the passages
before us. That there are two meanings we need not
again wait to prove. Recent discussion of the point has
produced fresh and ample evidence of the primary force
of *pneuma* as an element in man's natural constitution;
and of the process through which a secondary and higher
meaning was added.[2] We have already (in Chapter V.)
traced the connection between its early and natural

[1] See Pfleiderer's discussion of *Sarx* in his *Paulinismus*, pp. 47–56.
Note particularly the weakness of the proofs on which he rests the assertion that the Old Testament traces the sinfulness of man to his fleshly
origin and fleshly nature. These proofs are merely references to Ps. li. 7,
ciii. 10, 14 ; Isa. xlviii. 8 ; Job iv. 17, xv. 14, xxv. 4–6.

[2] See, *e.g.*, Prof. Dickson's Baird Lecture, pp. 168, etc. ; Gloël, *Der
heilige Geist in der Heilsverkündigung des Paulus*, ss. 73 u.s.w.

meaning of "life as derived from the Creator," and its fullest spiritual meaning of "the new life implanted in regeneration." We have said that this latter was arrived at, not by a mere process of human thought, but by the clearer discovery of the personal Author of spiritual life, the Holy Spirit, and by the altogether new revelation of Jesus Christ, the quickening Spirit, as the Head of a redeemed humanity. Pfleiderer's mode of accounting for the peculiar Pauline use of *pneuma* to denote the new life in believers is, that " a transcendent physical, or transcendent eschatological idea became of necessity," according to a process which he undertakes to describe, "an immanent ethical one." Or again, "that the eschatological participation of life with Christ is to the apostle imperceptibly transformed into the ethical new life of the Christian present."[1] Here, as before, we have a testimony to the correctness of the evangelical rendering of Pauline ideas. *Pneuma* with the apostle acquires the special meaning of "the new life," and that because he regarded believers as supernaturally united to Christ, and partakers of the *pneuma Christou*. We are content to use the testimony on that point of a critic so little biassed in the evangelical direction. We do not encumber ourselves with his construction of what he calls "the genesis of this whole mode of representation." The Scriptures themselves give us a better account of it, namely, that Paul and the other apostles had the "mind of Christ."

In its natural meaning, however, "spirit" ranges from the mere physical sense of wind or breath,[2] and from

[1] *Paulinismus*, pp. 18, 196. [2] Ezek. xxxvii. 8 ; Hab. ii. 9 : John iii. 8.

18

denoting life in general, up to the indication of man's innermost mental and moral being. In the New Testament, and even within the Pauline epistles, *pneuma* is freely used in this natural sense. sometimes as the simple psychological correlate of the flesh or the body;[1] at other times as the seat of self-consciousness;[2] or again, as the inner essence of the man, which, as well as the flesh, is defiled by sin,[3] and the salvation of which is the aim of all gospel work.[4] But it is worthy of our exact attention that in the great passage, Rom. vii. and viii., where the new life is to be designated by the term *pneuma* in its intensified spiritual force, *flesh* and *spirit* are not introduced antithetically earlier than the beginning of chap. viii., when the dominion of the new principle has been asserted. The higher elements of the human being himself to which the law makes its appeal are denoted in chap. vii., not by *pneuma*, but by "mind" and "inward man";[5] so that confusion between the two senses of *pneuma* is avoided, and that term reserved in this connection to denote the new life introduced by regeneration.[6]

A word or two still falls to be said concerning the *voces signatæ* last mentioned,—"mind," and "inward man." *Nous* throughout the Pauline writings is not substance like *pneuma*, but conscious faculty, and knowledge

---

[1] For the use in this sense of "body" and "spirit," see 1 Cor. v. 3, vii. 34, Jas. ii. 26; of "flesh" and "spirit," as exactly equivalent to the other pair, see Col. ii. 5. 1 Cor vi. 20 might be added, but the reading καὶ ἐν τῷ πνεύματι, κ.τ.λ. is now given up.

[2] 1 Cor. ii. 11.   [3] 2 Cor. vii. 1.   [4] 1 Cor. v. 5.

[5] νοῦς; ὁ ἔσω ἄνθρωπος.

[6] Compare what was said on the relation between *pneuma* and *nous* at p. 125, *supra*.

both of God and duty.[1] Even in the heathen it manifests itself as knowledge of God and law of conscience.[2]
It may become so blinded and blunted as to be "the
mind of the flesh," [3] or " reprobate mind." [4] On the other
hand, it may be educated and enlightened by the law
till the law of God so dwells in it as to be appropriately
called " the law of my mind." [5] There is therefore an
evident propriety in *nous* being set over against *sarx* in
Rom. vii., because the field of the struggle there described
is man and his principles of nature under the law of God.
Now it is to the *nous* that the law of God appeals. It
is the *nous* in which it dwells, and through which it
testifies for God against sin. Here, then, we have the
whole field of human nature divided into two camps.
The law of God and the law of sin are the combatants.
But from their encampment or environment respectively,
they are also designated as " the law of the mind," and
" the law in the members."

Finally, we have the important expression, " the inward man," [6] which occurs beside only in Eph. iii. 16,
and with a slight variation, in 2 Cor. iv. 16,[7] with
which also we may connect as synonymous Peter's
" hidden man of the heart." [8] The primary idea of this
expression is evidently one purely natural. It is contrasted with " the outward man," [9] which perishes by

---

[1] 1 Cor. xiv. 19 : "I had rather speak five words with my understanding," etc.

[2] Rom. i. 20, ii. 14.   [3] νοῦς τῆς σαρκός, Col. ii. 18.

[4] ἀδόκιμος νοῦς, Rom. i. 28.   [5] νόμος τοῦ νοός μου, Rom. vii. 23.

[6] ὁ ἔσω ἄνθρωπος, Rom. vii. 22.

[7] ὁ ἔσωθεν, or, according to the better reading, ὁ ἔσω ἡμῶν.

[8] ὁ κρυπτὸς τῆς καρδίας ἄνθρωπος, 1 Pet. iii. 4.

[9] ὁ ἔξω ἡμῶν ἄνθρωπος, 2 Cor. iv. 16.

material decay or by the vicissitudes of time.   It is the
inner and spiritual nature of man as contrasted with the
outward and fleshly.   The use of it is another guarantee,
if any were needed, for the essentially bipartite character of the Pauline psychology.   It may be taken as the
most general expression for the inner or spiritual factor
in the human being.   Under this general expression may
be held as included *pneuma* (spirit), when used to denote
the nature of that factor; *nous* (mind), as its intellectual
or rational aspect; and *kardia* (heart), when it is regarded as the practical centre or fountain of man's life.
But a secondary or ethical meaning of the phrase, " inner
man " evidently lies behind.   Without saying that in its
primary sense it is morally indifferent, it is plain that in
its secondary or ethical sense, where it enters, as in
Rom. vii., into a psychological delineation of spiritual
experience, it has the sense of " morally higher nature."
It points to that inward nature which is capable of
regeneration, which is fitted to become the seat of the
new life, the true field for the operation of spiritual
processes.[1]

Thus we see that the terms " flesh," " spirit," " mind,"
" inward man," as used in these epistles, admit of a consistent explanation, dependent upon the view of human
nature underlying the Apostle's course of thought.[2]

II. The main thing for us, however, is to make out
the spiritual history which this analysis is intended to
trace.   The proper position of the passage, Rom. vii.

[1] Cf. what was said at pp. 261, 262, etc., as to the natural basis or
ground on which spiritual life could be superinduced.

[2] On "The Pauline Anthropology," see Appendix to this chapter.

14–25, in that history may be said to be the knot of
the question.   There are almost equal difficulties in
affirming the experience described in these verses to be
that either of a wholly unregenerate or of a fully regenerate man.   Plainly it cannot refer to that struggle
of the natural conscience with the desires and passions
which belongs to all moral life.   This conflict is a broad
commonplace in the history of the soul, as familiar to
the readers of Plato and Epictetus as to the students of
the Christian Scriptures.   It is not to be thought that
St. Paul, in a treatise professedly tracing the progress of
a soul brought into contact with the truth of God, if not
regenerated by it, should at this stage introduce the
mention of a struggle which was common to the virtuous
heathen, the Stoic philosopher, and the Jewish proselyte.
It is not altogether incorrect to say that " the whole
picture conveys the idea of the essential war there is in
every conscious moral life betwixt the higher and lower
principles at work within it." [1]   But after all, this is
only the frame of the picture.   For the chief question
we have to answer is, What are the contending principles at work within the soul here described ?   Now it
is expressly said that the holy law of God is one of
them, and that law indeed brought home or become " the
law of the mind."   It is certain, therefore, that if this
delineation present a state previous to conversion, that
state is not previous to the entrance of the divine
element into the strife.   If it is pre-regenerate, it is not
pre-spiritual.   It is not a conflict between man's own
higher and lower powers alone, for a spiritual visitation

- Principal Tulloch, *Croall Lecture*, p. 155.

of the man by the divine commandment has already taken place. Further, it is said the man here described "wills to do good," is distressed because of his own evil; and that not merely because of evil deeds, but of motions and desires toward evil. His subjection to sin, therefore, is not that described in a former chapter, " yielding your members instruments of unrighteousness unto sin, servants to uncleanness and to iniquity."[1]   It is rather that of being sold as a slave against his will,[2] of being brought into captivity by the violence of war.[3]   He delights in the law of God after the inward man.   That law is the law of his mind, and with the mind he himself is subject to that law even when with the flesh he serves the law of sin.   It is impossible that this can be a man unvisited by that divine working which precedes salvation.   Instead of enmity against God, which is " the carnal mind," there have entered into the inmost heart of the man consent to the divine law and aversion from sin.   Such a position of true willingness toward the good, and absolute unwillingness toward the evil, could not be occupied by any but a spiritually quickened soul.   It is a state brought about neither by the aspirations of natural virtue, nor by the unsupported appeals of the moral law, but only by the grace of God.

On the other hand, considerable injustice has been done, not only to the interpretation of an important passage of Scripture, but, what is more serious, to the entire doctrine of sanctification, by some of those who

---

[1] Rom. vi. 13, 19.

[2] πεπραμένος ὑπὸ τὴν ἁμαρτίαν, Rom. vii. 14.

[3] ἀντιστρατευόμενον, ver. 23.

are bent on maintaining that the latter half of the seventh chapter of Romans describes the experience of a converted man. It has been too often read as if it described the ordinary and normal state of a child of God; as if nature and grace were so exactly balanced in believers that "they cannot do the things that they would"; as if the sum and substance of sanctification were this death in life, or this living death expressed by the perpetual cry, "O wretched man that I am!" Now it has been well said, that if this were all that grace did for its votaries, St. Paul would only have proved that it was as futile and insufficient as the law. If all that regeneration could accomplish were only to awaken a sense of inward discord without being able to take it away, this "would certainly destroy the influence of spiritual Christianity and disgrace its character."[1] But the mistake lies in not perceiving that chap. vii. gives us only one side of the picture. The delineation is progressive, and the full account of the conflict is not before us till we pass on to chap. viii., and see how the victory is secured for believers.

Note what are the contending principles. "The law" or principle "of sin," the "law in my members," is on the one side; the divine law, the "law of my mind," is on the other. The former law has its seat, not in me, my now awakened self, but in "my flesh"; that is, in my inherited nature, in my members as constituted through the agency of the flesh.[2] The divine law, on

---

[1] See this hinted *Letters of Thomas Erskine of Linlathen*, p. 248, 2d edition (Edin., 1878).

[2] See in Chap. VI. at p. 119, *supra*.

the contrary, makes its appeal to "my mind"; it has secured the affection or "delight" of my "inward man." That "mind" or "inward man" belongs to the divine image, by which their Maker retains His hold of human souls even when fallen, and which it is the function of grace so to restore that it may be fully possessed and adorned by the life from on high. Speaking roundly and generally therefore, the two camps in this war might he named "the Flesh" and "the Spirit." They are so named in the less elaborate account to be found in Gal. v. 17, where the result of the conflict at this stage is given in the same terms of moral failure as at the corresponding point in Rom. vii.: "The flesh lusteth against the Spirit, and the Spirit against the flesh: and these are contrary the one to the other; so that ye cannot do the things that ye would." But in the fuller and more detailed delineation of the Epistle to the Romans, the term "spirit" (*pneuma*), as we have already remarked, is not used in chap. vii., but reserved for chap. viii., as the word denoting the new life in its proper seat and power. The man who is in the "Spirit" and walks after the "Spirit" is in the main delivered from the body of this death. His own spirit is life because of righteousness. The righteousness of the law is fulfilled in him. The law of the Spirit of life in Christ Jesus hath made him free from the law of sin and death. Thus, in the complete account of the struggle, full justice is done to the results of Christian sanctification.

But now arises the question concerning the relation to one another of the two parts in this whole delineation,

—the description of the conflict ending with the groan,
" O wretched man that I am ! " and the description of
the triumph beginning with the shout, " I thank God
through Jesus Christ our Lord." What is described in
the former is a strife not merely of higher and lower
elements in man's own nature, but of contrasted moral
forces that have entered into him. The power of sin in
his flesh strives with the testimony of law in his mind,
the result of which strife is a sort of moral impotence,—
he cannot do the things that he would. What is described in the latter chapter is grace resolving the strife.
Moral impotence, divided service, is not the real result
of the new principle of regeneration. The new life is
that which is delivered from it, when we walk not after
the flesh, but after the Spirit. Shall we say, then, that
the two parts of the description succeed each other in
time ? that they are spiritual portraits of the same
person drawn at two successive stages of his religious
history ? On this understanding, Rom. vii. 14–25 gives
us the portrait of an awakened Pharisee or of a legal
Christian ; Rom. viii. 1–14, that of a fully regenerate
man, a free child of God. The transition from the one
to the other takes place when the Pharisaic Hebrew is
converted, and trusts not to the law but to Christ, both
for acceptance with God and for the Spirit of holiness : or
when the legal Christian comes to his second conversion
(if the phrase be allowed), and enters on the higher life
of sanctification.; when he ceases to think that he can
subdue sin and attain to holiness under the law and
through his own efforts ; when he accepts the whole
salvation as a free gift of righteousness and of the Spirit ;

in short, when by God's grace he breaks out of bondage
into the liberty wherewith Christ hath made His people
free. Should this historical succession and connection
be insisted on, all reasonable comment must agree that
the man described in the latter half of chap. vii. is
neither, on the one extreme, unregenerate, nor on the
other a regenerate man in his proper and normal state.
He must be in some such intermediate condition as we
have now endeavoured to express, by holding him either
to be an awakened legalist or an unemancipated Christian.

It must be confessed, however, that this rendering of
the description is not entirely satisfactory. There is
another which suggests itself, as more in keeping both
with this particular passage and with the whole strain of
the epistle. It requires, indeed, that we shall not
insist on making the two passages describe two different
types of persons, or even two successive stages in the
experience of the same person. For has not the determination to find historical sequence and contrast in the
two, tended to perplex the meaning? There are such
mixed elements in both delineations, that no application
of them to distinct stages in conversion and spiritual life
is quite satisfactory. It is clear that the two things
really contrasted in the successive passages are the
bondage of law and the reign of grace. How the contrast
comes in here is apparent upon a glance at the broad
argument of this epistle, the scope of which is to establish the superiority of grace to the law. In the early
chapters of it the apostle has demonstrated that by the
law no flesh shall be justified, that justification can come
only by grace in the form of faith. Having finished

this part of his argument in chapter v., he goes on in chapter vi. to lay the Christian foundation of holiness, and in chapter vii. to show that by the law no man, legalist or Christian, can be sanctified; completing the demonstration in chapter viii. by showing that sanctification is of grace—grace in the form of spiritual life and liberty. Now on this interpretation there is no need to suppose that the apostle in the two contrasted passages is describing any other experience than his own, or that of any other regenerate person. Neither is it necessary to suppose that he is contrasting two states, stages, or successive experiences even of the regenerate. Rather is he presenting two ideal conceptions of the relation to law and grace respectively of a man in Christ aiming at the attainment of holiness. In the first, as given in chap. vii., he looks simply at himself and the law. Let us remember, as we read, that he is not merely describing an experience. He is conducting an argument. He is engaged in proving from facts the weakness of the law, its inefficiency at any stage to produce holiness. The experience of the sinner proves it; by the law is only the knowledge of sin. The experience of the awakened proves it; the law in him only reveals and stirs up more sin. The experience of the regenerate proves it; for even in him, though the renewed will be present to do good, though the awakened mind delight in the law of God, there is still that other law in his members warring against the law of his mind, and causing him after all to serve the law of sin. "This is all that the law of God can do," says he, "even for me, a converted man. Not, indeed, that this is the fault of

the law. God forbid! In an important sense it is to
the honour of the law. This is one great service
rendered by it in the process of redemption, that it
reveals the strength and evil of my sin; yea, that it
helps to discern, to divide between me and the sin that
dwelleth in me. Yet, while it discovers this terrible
inward dissension, it cannot heal, but rather intensifies it.
Wretched man that I am! How much more wretched
had I nothing else! What would become of me if I had
only the law to enable me to attain holiness?" "Thank
God!" he cries, passing on to the second and complete
conception of chap. viii.,—"thank God, in Christ Jesus
I have something else! I have the Spirit of Christ.
Through the law of the Spirit of life in Christ Jesus I
am delivered from both the other laws in the sense in
which deliverance from them is salvation. The good
and holy law no more condemns me, for there is now no
condemnation to them which are in Christ Jesus. The
base and evil law of sin no more enthralls me, for the
law of the Spirit of Life has made me free from it. The
Spirit of Christ has taken possession of our spirit, that
we might be free to fulfil all righteousness, to mortify
all sin, and to press forward to the blessed perfection, in
body and spirit, of the life to come."

In this way it will be seen that, though we do not
insist on historic contrast or sequence in the two
passages, we still preserve the progressive character of
the delineation. The two contrasted ideal conceptions
are realised more or less in every true child of God.
The first depicts what he too often is. The second
describes what he ought and what he strives by God's

grace to be. The experience described is that of a double life—the saint's paradox, the believer's riddle. And this rendering of the description has been counter-signed by all the great commentators on a passage which supremely illustrates the maxim that "the heart makes the theologian." No interpretation will satisfy the spiritual mind which does not include in the normal experience of a Christian what is described both in the seventh and in the eighth chapter of Romans. Only it should never be forgotten that the Christian life really moves from the lower experience to the higher; that every living Christian is progressing out of the one into the other until he comes to dwell in the latter, or rather to dwell habitually in Christ, and to have the Spirit of Christ dwelling victoriously in him.

One other point of importance must be noticed before we pass from this great passage, namely, the position assigned in it to the responsible personality, or the relations of the Ego throughout the struggle. On this point the thought of the apostle is very clear. The person is never divided. The Ego is never in two contrasted states or in two hostile camps at the same time. That is as impossible as that a man can serve two masters. He may have within him two contending principles; and in the shifting war of the principles for supremacy, the Ego—I myself—will undoubtedly undergo a change,—will be seen, in fact, as we narrowly mark the tide of battle, to pass over from the one camp to the other. When the flesh bears unbroken sway, and the natural life is undisturbed, the Ego is alive in that fleshly, worldly life, *totus in illis*. When the law comes with spiritual force the Ego dies: its natural hopes of being right with God are crushed; its own fancied power to do well utterly departs; the man exclaims, "It is plain that I am carnal, sold under sin; in ME, that is, in my flesh, dwelleth no good thing." But at this point the inward man asserts itself, wills right, consents unto the law. "Then," says he, "I am no more myself the slave of evil. It is no more I that do the things which I would not." As the moment of liberation draws on, it is "with the mind I myself serve the law of God." And as liberty is realised through the Spirit, "the law of the Spirit of life in Christ Jesus hath made ME free from the law of sin and death."

It is impossible to construe the passage without admitting that the apostle expresses his personality as identified with two contending elements alternately. But it is no less true that the passing of the Ego, on the whole, from being dead in sin, or "alive without the law," through the intermediate experience of being visited by "the commandment," to the final condition of being under grace and walking after the Spirit, is traceable throughout. The sense and thought of the whole passage admit no doubling or confusion of personality, no perplexing of responsibility. Thus much it seems necessary to say, because Paul's vivid phraseology here and elsewhere has been perverted to the support of certain extreme forms of quasi-evangelical statement. What Flacius found in Romans vii., "Two men set in the skin of one man," is not unfrequently the finding of incautious expounders of this great passage on Christian sanctification. We are told by them of two Adams, two

natures, if not almost of two persons in the regenerate,
—the old and evil, who will never be sanctified, and
with whom the child of God has nothing to do, or in
other words, for whom he is not responsible; the new,
born from above, who is always right and accepted with
God.   It need hardly be said that such teaching is at
once mistaken and dangerous.   The "two men in one
skin" has a correct meaning, if we read it according to
the Scripture.   The "old man" and the "new man"
mean two kinds of power, two laws, two principles of
nature.   But whenever these are represented as existing
and contending in one regenerate responsible person, the
"new" is life and living, the "old" is dying and in effect
dead.   The Ego is not divided.   "Every man hath an
edge.   He cuts one way or another.   And as a man's
edge is set, that way is he." [1]   The renewed man has his
edge set towards eternal life.   He lives after the Spirit.
He is crucifying the flesh.   He is mortifying the deeds
of the body.   He is putting off the old man with his
deeds, and putting on the new.   He is, in short, at
one with the Spirit of Christ who now dwells within
him.

' How much is really contained in the new birth?
Why is there so little of the new man in the regenerate?
Why are the spontaneous products of his heart so corrupt and evil after all?   Why deeper than will am I
left so bad?   Should not the new birth have done much
more for me than it has done; and especially in those
deep places within to which I cannot reach to do it for

[1] Dr. John Owen.

myself?' Most Christians will concur in the propriety
of putting such questions, though there be no exhaustive
answer to them.

In regard to the first, it is scarcely necessary to
repeat, that we do not find in the psychology of grace
anything like the introduction of a new element of
being, or the creation of a new faculty, or the implantation in man's constitution of any power, physical, mental,
or moral, which it did not contain before. What we
find in the new birth is the supernatural gift of a new
principle of nature—using "nature" in the sense in
which we say popularly that "habit is a second nature."
By the special act of divine grace, which we call regeneration, a foundation is laid in the nature of the man for an
entirely new exercise of all his faculties in a renewed
life. The natural *nidus* or constitutional seat of this
new beginning is the inward man,[1] which may be viewed
in respect of substance as the spirit or natural *pneuma*,
or in respect of intelligence and conscience as the mind
(*nous*), in respect of life and action as the heart[2] (*kardia*),
so that regeneration is said to be a permanent transformation of the spirit of our mind, and that which is
formed by it dwells in the heart, is the hidden man of
the heart. This new principle of spiritual life is called
"the new man,"[3] and the man under its influence is "a
new creature" or "a new creation."[4] But if we attempt
any further question in what it really or metaphysically
consists, we get the answer, simply, that it is "the law"
(*i.e.* the principle) of the Spirit of Life in Christ Jesus.

[1] ὁ ἔσω ἄνθρωπος.   [2] See p. 276, *supra*.
[3] ὁ νέος or καινὸς ἄνθρωπος.   [4] καινὴ κτίσις.

According to the doctrine of grace, this means that through the mediation or ministry of the Holy Ghost, Christ Himself, the new Head, the second Adam, becomes to each member of His body "a quickening Spirit," and dwells in the heart of His own.   The difficulty we have in such passages as Rom. viii. 1–16, and Gal. v. 16–26, to determine whether "spirit," in certain clauses, means the renewed spirit of the man or the renewing Spirit of God within Him, may be taken as itself an evidence that it is the divine indwelling which constitutes the new life.   Yet it is clear that *pneuma* in these passages has on the human side its enlarged significance—that, naturally signifying the inner man, which is fitted to be the seat of the Holy Ghost, it now signifies the whole life, in its principles and actions, as the result of that indwelling.

How much of actual sanctification this entitles us to expect or enables us to realise, the great Pauline passage we have been considering indicates in a way verified by the experience of most Christians.   It is plain that some of the questions suggested above can receive no answer. They are in their utterance but the reflection of Paul's " O wretched man that I am ! "   The burden and the mystery of sanctification can never be more powerfully stated than in this famous passage where the " unresolved antinomy " stands as a mirror, in which every spiritually exercised man sees the presentment of his own experience.   You may prefer to think the features in Rom. vii. specially those of an awakened Pharisee, as in Gal. v. they are those of an unenlightened or legal Christian.   It is better, as we have seen, to abstract the delineation altogether from time, succession, and special circumstances in the life of the awakened soul. The apostle is not speaking of himself as regenerate; at least he is not describing the effect of regeneration. The antinomy cannot be the right and normal state of a converted man. But he may be fairly held as describing what is experienced in spite of regeneration, a conflict which even for the regenerate has not passed away. That it may describe the special position of a legal or carnal Christian we have admitted, but what is more of importance, it is a permanent description of the difficulty or struggle of sanctification, and reveals some of its causes. "The man who is in Christ—just this very man—is divided into a man actually living in Christ, and a man who, though surrounded by the new life, is not yet actually pervaded by it. . . . In other words, there is even in the regenerate life a region pervaded by grace, and a region, so to speak, only shone upon by grace. . . . Over this latter, a mournful powerlessness of good purposes unaccomplished throws its long dark shadow."[1] We must note, however, that the transition marked by the words, "I thank God through Jesus Christ our Lord" (Rom. vii. 25), if not one in time from an unripe to a riper Christian stage, is at least one in idea from what a Christian too often is to what he can and ought by grace to be. Since the "spirit," in the sense of the indwelling of Christ within him, is that from which nothing but good can proceed, the Christian

---

[1] Delitzsch, *System der biblischen Psychologie*, p. 388, near the close of the section on "Regeneration," headed, "Die unaufgehobene Antinomie," one of the most interesting and able passages in the whole treatise.

has only to "give himself up to this spirit which dwells in him, to walk after it, in order to do good. . . . Again, as the sinful 'flesh' was only the principle of the old man, who died with Christ, it has no further claim on the new man, who lives with the living Christ; it cannot and must not have the mastery over him; he cannot and must not any longer be under an obligation to compliance with it. Thus evil is for the Christian as such that which is contrary to his nature; for him the power and domination of sin are radically abrogated along with the law that was its provocation. The requirement, therefore, to keep from evil and do good, is for the Christian the self-evident consequence of his new nature; he has only to show himself in practice that which he already is in fact—a spiritual man." [1] This is not mere abstract statement. It is a habit of the inspired writers to pass constantly from reasoning to exhortation, and here it is very marked. Plainly, an ideal and an actual are being placed side by side. " This is what you ought to be, what you must be: then be it. The spirit of Christ dwells in you, and has made you free: be free. You are in the Spirit: walk after the Spirit !"

We cannot close without sketching in a few words the doctrine developed in the Epistle to the Romans, as the ground of the experience which we have just been endeavouring to trace. It must always be observed, in order to understand Rom. vii. and viii., that chap. vi. has laid the foundation for what follows. The experience of

[1] Pfleiderer, *Paulinismus*, pp. 21, 22.

"dying unto sin" and "living unto righteousness" is supported by the doctrine of dying with Christ on the cross and rising with Him to newness of life.

It will be noticed that in Rom. vi., parallel to the expressions, "dead to sin," "freed from sin," there runs another set of expressions, "dead with Christ," "baptized into His death," "buried with Him," "planted together in the likeness of His death," "our old man is crucified with Him, that the body of sin might be destroyed." The purport of all this plainly is, that by the death of Christ, a death-blow has been given to the power of sin in believers- -so given as if it had been actually inflicted when the Lord was crucified. The earlier part of the argument in chaps. iv. and v. had gone to show how the cross of Christ is the ground of pardon, peace, and acceptance with God: "He was delivered for our offences." The object now is to show that the cross is also the ground of our sanctification, particularly of our deliverance from the power of sin as well as from its guilt and punishment. In a like manner, the objective historical fact of the resurrection of Christ is made the ground of our rising to newness of life; and this not simply as a type or model after which our moral quickening takes place, nor merely as an expression of allegorical or mystical resurrection, but in the sense that believers participate for their new moral life in the supernatural power of the resurrection, in that supernatural gift of the Spirit which the risen Christ received to bestow upon His people. It is the law of the Spirit of life in Christ Jesus that makes them free from the law of sin and death. Taking it in both branches,

as death to sin and life to God, the whole is thus
expressed by Paul in a later epistle : " That I may know
Him and the power of His resurrection, and the fellowship of His sufferings, being made conformable unto His
death." [1]

The significance of thus connecting the believer's
dying to sin and living to righteousness with the dying
and rising again of His Lord can hardly be overrated.
Practically it is all-important as the support of the
apostolic exhortations.   What comfort could be imparted to Christians by telling them, that since Christ
has died and risen, they also are dead to sin and done
with it, when they feel every day that this is anything
but true ?   They should be overwhelmed in despair
were there nothing more in the saying than a moral
appeal to crucify the old nature,—were they left to
struggle with what it seems a kind of irony to call the
'remains of corruption within them,' aided only by
the consideration that they owe it to so loving a
Saviour to live a life of freedom from sin.   No ! but
the doctrine of these chapters is, that the death of
Christ, besides being an expiatory death for cancelling
guilt and bringing in everlasting righteousness, was
implicitly the destruction of the principle of sin in those
that are His.   It is therefore a most important part of
the apostolic doctrine of Christ's redeeming death, **that**
it secures moral renovation as well as justifying grace.
It is the supreme glory of the gospel to lay the foundations of practical holiness upon the same sure corner-
stone on which are laid those of peace with God.   **No**

[1] Phil. iii. 10.

doubt, its importance is distorted if it be made the chief
thing in the apostolic system, and exalted at the expense
of the doctrine of reconciliation which is really the basis
of it.[1]   No doubt, also, it can be stiffened and formalised
in a dangerously antinomian manner, if it be cut off
from its proper doctrinal correlatives—if the fact of
Christ's death be represented boldly and by itself as the
emancipation of the soul from actual sin.   The principle
of living union with Christ,—by the entrance of His
Spirit into the heart on the one hand, and by the
exercise of our faith on the other, — underlies the
doctrines both of justification and of sanctification.
This principle also secures that holiness must grow out
of reconciliation.   It vitally connects the roots of
sanctification with the grounds of justification.   In the
act which unites him to a crucified Redeemer, the
Christian dies with Christ in a sense which no doctrinal
explanations can ever exhaust, and that because of
the mystic union then formed between the Redeemer
and the redeemed.   His Spirit, taking possession of
their hearts, in that gracious moment deals the being
of sin within them a mortal blow, which is the earnest
and the ground of their final deliverance from its every
motion, and of their appearing in the presence of God
without spot or wrinkle or any such thing.   Their sin
died with Christ on the tree, not only as to its guilt,
but as to its power; and in this sense, they, being
dead with Christ, are dead indeed unto sin.   Like all
the doctrines of grace, this death of the soul to sin

---

[1] See, for example, the paradoxical statements of Matthew Arnold in
his *St. Paul and Protestantism.*

runs back into the mystery of a relationship between the redeemed soul and Christ its living Head. Each of us apprehends it only as this union with Christ is realised and becomes the true ground of hopeful and successful struggle against indwelling sin in the heart. This identification of himself in idea with Christ is the key to Paul's whole doctrine of the new life. The practical realisation of it is the new life itself.

Nor let us fail to remark, that in order to attain holiness, the Spirit of Christ in believers connects them vitally with their Lord's future as well as with His past. To unfold the fulness of sanctification, we must fix our faith, like Paul, on two grand events in the history of our blessed Head and Lord. Between these two facts, as the two great pivots of redemption, Paul's faith travels, and as it goes, weaves out in thought and puts on in practice the garment wrought in gold of a complete salvation. These two are: first, the fact accomplished, "He was crucified and rose again; in Him, with Him, therefore, am I also dead and risen"; then, the future advent, "He comes in glory, comes the second time without sin unto salvation. In Him I also anticipate the glory. For this, even we who have received the first-fruits of the Spirit wait and yearn,— the manifestation of the sons of God,—the adoption, to wit, the redemption of our body."

Thus we arrive at our concluding topic: the light which the Bible view of man's nature, and especially of that nature as redeemed, sheds on the future life and on the resurrection.

NOTE TO CHAPTER XIV

THE PAULINE ANTHROPOLOGY

[LITERATURE.—L. Usteri, *Entwickelung des paulinischen Lehrbegriffes* (Zürich, 1851). Ernesti, *Vom Ursprunge der Sünde nach paul. Lehrgehalte* (1855, 1862). Holsten, *Zum Evangelium des Paulus und des Petrus* (Rostock, 1868). Lüdemann, *Die Anthropologie des Apostels Paulus* (Kiel, 1872). Pfleiderer, *Der Paulinismus* (Leipzig, 1873; Eng. Trans., latest edition, 1891); see also his Hibbert Lecture, 1885. Gloël, *Der h. Geist in der Heilsverkündigung des Paulus.* (Halle, 1888). A. Sabatier, *The Apostle Paul* (1891). G. B. Stevens, *The Pauline Theology*, 1892. Cf. also the more general works in New Testament Theology of F. C. Baur (1874), Reuss (1872), Bernh. Weiss (1882), Hausrath, *Neutestamentliche Zeitgeschichte* (1880), together with the special treatises of Wendt and Professor Dickson, named on p. 51).]

FROM the mass of treatises on Paul and his doctrines, those above named may be singled out as giving prominence to his psychology, and, if one may so speak, to his philosophy. These writers are of various ways of thinking. Holsten is the most distinctly rationalistic in his construction. Writers of this leaning almost invariably sharpen the distinction between Pauline thought and that of the New Testament generally. This tendency belongs to their exaggerated view of the influence of individual genius within the sacred literature. There can be no doubt, however, that both the individuality and the training of St. Paul must be reckoned with, in all endeavours to expound the form of doctrine which Christendom has received through him. And there can be as little doubt that to understand the psychology of this most analytic and introspective of all Scripture writers is an essential aid to the apprehension of New Testament theology.

The most radical subject of discussion within the range of Pauline anthropology is that which concerns his so-called *Dualism*. By several of the authors named above it has been considered as a question to what extent his antithesis of flesh and spirit, so vital to his religious system, is the outcome of an underlying dualism, philosophical and metaphysical.

HOLSTEN has taken up the position that, according to Paul, σάρξ, or the living material substance of man, is evil, so that man stands on that account, in the Pauline system, in an absolute opposition to God (see at pp. 396, 398 of the treatise named). He goes the length (p. 387) of gravely disputing the genuineness of 2 Cor. vii. 1. Its expressions are for him *unpaulinisch, i.e.* they will not square with his view; for if σάρξ is the principle and fountain of all defilement, the phrases are inconsequent.

USTERI maintains what amounts to the same thing in placing the root of all sin in "die Sinnlichkeit des Menschen" (" ἡ σάρξ ist der Reiz der Sinnlichkeit," p. 30), a view sufficiently refuted by the strong emphasis laid on non-fleshly sins as "works of the flesh." The acme of sin, according to Paul, 2 Thess. ii. 4, is something very different from sensuality.

PFLEIDERER, as we have seen, thinks the metaphysical dualism of philosophical systems inapplicable to the apostle's views. He holds that Holsten has erred in identifying σάρξ with the whole man, and thus making the substantial essence of humanity to be ἁμαρτία, "which is quite un-Pauline and Manichæan." Yet he himself interprets σάρξ and πνεῦμα as two substances in their very nature antagonistic. Thus, he holds, from the opposition of physically different substances results the Pauline dualism of antagonistic moral principles. Out of σάρξ, as merely spiritless substance, grows a causality opposed to the Spirit (Rom. vii. 5, viii. 6). He claims Lüdemann as with him here (pp. 53, 54). The struggle of Pfleiderer to show how σάρξ, on his interpretation, can include non-fleshly sins is notable (pp. 54, 55). He has to admit that his view makes sin necessary to man (p. 57).

HAUSRATH (pp. 75–80) ascribes to Paul what he calls an anthropological dualism, resting, he alleges, upon the native Jewish dualism which in the later Hebrew Scriptures (*zumal in den späteren Büchern*) divides the All into two regions, earth and heaven. This is the postulate of the Pauline theology (*die Voraussetzung der paulinischen Theologie*). The distinction of flesh and spirit, and of the outer and inner man, are instances of this dualism, which at last culminates in an ethical dualism, behind which the metaphysical may be looked for; so that it was not to be wondered at that thoroughgoing disciples like Marcion should have completed the circle of thinking in that direction, and that thoroughgoing opponents should have made St. Paul, under the name of Simon Magus, answerable for the entire Gnostic system. Like Pfleiderer, however, Hausrath acknowledges that, after all, such metaphysical dualism could have no place in the mind of the apostle; that his Jewish idea of God was so powerful as to exclude entirely self-existent matter or self-existent evil; that his anthropological dualism was, in short, the outcome of the deep spiritual feeling of his own sinfulness and of God's grace, arrived at as a result of his own conversion.

The most complete discussion is that of LÜDEMANN, who combats Holsten at great length. Like most of his school, he identifies σάρξ with the living material of the body. But his defence of the originality of Paul's philosophy is worth quoting. As his work is not now easily accessible, I give a pretty full digest of his remarks:

The signification attached to σάρξ by some is, that it is identical with the essence of human nature in general. In this case the meaning of the antithesis between σάρξ and πνεῦμα corresponds to that between man and God. Holsten finds it consequently intelligible "that the religious relation should be represented as the relation of the πνεῦμα, the non-material, spiritual substance, to the σάρξ, the material, sensuous substance"; and he arrives in this way at the result already alluded to. If this relation be in its abstract generality that of the finite and infinite, we can understand how for Paul the notion of σάρξ is the expression for the notion of the finite. Holsten reaches this conclusion by working out consequently the absolute transcendence of the πνεῦμα over human nature (*Menschenwesen*) as such, by means of the notions ψυχή, νοῦς, πνεῦμα. If we ask under what historical canon this antithetical foundation of the Pauline view of the universe (*Weltanschauung*) falls, Holsten thus formulates his answer : " That the new feeling of life involved in faith in the Messiah, Paul in his theology has apprehended and raised to consciousness in the *religious* categories of the Jewish *Weltanschauung*, in the *speculative* categories of the Hellenistic.

To settle the legitimacy of this position of Holsten, we require to ask, Can the speculative categories of Hellenism be applied off-hand and without modification to the religious categories of the Jewish consciousness, and yet express a homogeneous system of thought ? To answer this question satisfactorily we must start two others : (1) What is dualism ? (2) How does the religious consciousness of Judaism relate itself to it ? As to the first, we may say generally that to constitute a dualistic antithesis it is necessary to have two notions which are co-ordinate, inconsistent with one another, and contrary opposites. We see that this is the character of dualism in Plato's philosophy. He lays the full stress of being on the side of spirit, of idea. This is the only real. All non-spiritual is unreal, non-existent, mere appearance. But this carried him too far; and so, to explain phenomena as they stood, he had to accept the non-spiritual as antithesis of the ideal, the principle of separateness and multiplicity,—of evil in short. Philo, too, wavers, but in his anthropology clings to Plato's first view, thus bringing out a characteristic of dualism,—that you can never have a harmonious synthesis of the two principles; the one, in so far as it is at all asserted, is asserted inevitably at the expense of the other. Philo's anthropology is : In man there meet two spheres of the universe, the ideal and the material. Properly he belongs to one of them, the ideal. The natural history of the nexus of these two principles is wrought out on the basis of Plato's speculations anent the pre-existence, the fall, the return of souls. Such is a general definition, with historical illustrations, of what is meant by dualism.

(2) We ask, What is the relation of the Jewish religious

consciousness to this ? First of all you have the unity of
an almighty will dominating the universe; there is no
power or principle thought of in the Jewish religious consciousness of the Old Testament which is co-ordinate with
the Creator Jehovah. On the other hand, you find undoubtedly an antithesis between the transcendent majesty
and worth of the Infinite Being, and the comparative
insignificance of the finite. But this antithesis cannot be
regarded as a dualism. It is with contradictory opposites,
not contraries, we are here brought into contact. The
finite is purely privative; this attitude of thought corresponds to Plato's first and non-dualistic standpoint. The
finite must become positive, active, co-ordinate as against
the infinite before you have a real dualism. The less
exact form being the only duality of principles in the Old
Testament, we may expect that there will be as little
evidence of a really dualistic anthropology. Man's earthly
constitution is not inconsistent with the indwelling of the
divine (Gen. vi. 3), and in a religious reference he is
regarded as in his own nature capable of appreciating a
revelation from God. Nay, in this reference we find the
material part of man itself taken as the representative of
his ego. We find precisely the בָּשָׂר placed in religious
connection with God; and mankind in general represented
precisely under the designation כָּל־בָּשָׂר as recipients of
divine revelation (Ps. xvi. 9, lxiii. 2, lxv. 3, lxxxiv. 3; Isa.
xl. 5, lxvi. 23, 24; Joel iii. 1, *orig.*). On the other hand,
in virtue of his finitude, man can occupy the position of
antithesis to God. In this case he apprehends himself
from his sensuous material side, and once again it is the
term בָּשָׂר which becomes the designation of his absolute
frailty and nothingness (Jer. xvii 5; Deut. v. 23; Ps.
lxxviii. 39, lvi. 5—cf. 12; Isa. xl. 6, xlix. 26, lxvi. 16).
Frequently it is also human nature in its totality which
in this way becomes conscious of its great alienation from
the divine infinity (Gen. xviii. 27; Job. iv. 19, xxxiii. 6).
It is the אֱנוֹשׁ as such who has to acknowledge his
inferiority (Ps. ix. 21, x. 18, lvi. 12). Let us now sum up
the state of the case. In the Old Testament we have the

contradictory antithesis of infinite and finite; in Hellenism, the dualistically contrary antithesis of spirit and matter. In the Old Testament we have man as a unity of spirit and body (*eine geist-leibliche Einheit*) standing in the region of the finite under the designation בָּשָׂר, at times in communion with the divine infinite, at times with the emphatic application of this term to his entire being, in a relation to God of the humblest subjection. In Hellenism we have man consisting of a material element and a spiritual which is akin to the divine; these two being dualistically kept apart, and capable of consisting only at the expense of one of them. These two systems of thought being so radically different, it is clear the one cannot be expressed in terms of the other.

As a matter of fact, the sense attached by Holsten to σάρξ is neither Jewish nor Hellenistic. It is not Jewish for the Old Testament בָּשָׂר can never be taken so strictly as to characterise man as a purely material unity, and thus furnish a pretext for placing him as finite being in genuinely dualistic antithesis to the divine. It is not Hellenistic, for the Hellenistic category of σάρξ was never meant to characterise human nature as forming in its totality the dualistic antithesis of the spiritual-divine (*zum geistig-göttlichen*). The Hellenistic category σάρξ restricts itself exclusively to the body as the material constituent of man. Hence it follows that (1) σάρξ as the representative of בָּשָׂר cannot form one term of a dualism. (2) If we start with a metaphysical dualism, this must reproduce itself in our anthropology, and in that case σάρξ will just have the Hellenistic signification of the material of the human body. The religious categories of the Jewish consciousness are therefore incompatible with, disparate from, the speculative categories of Hellenism.

Our investigation may have put us on the way, however, to discover Paul's real position. Though the identification of Jewish and Hellenic categories has demonstrated itself in the concrete to be impossible, yet alongside of a Judaism just grazed by Hellenism on the surface, a third relation of the two spheres of consciousness is at least conceivable, in terms of which the Hellenic dualism so permeates an originally purely Jewish consciousness, that within the forms of intuition of the Jewish world of thought there evolves itself a really *contrary* antithesis, the religious antithesis of the finite and infinite remodels and hardens itself into a dualism in consequence of which there must simultaneously appear a dualistic moment within the anthropology also. In such modified consciousness the Hellenistic categories would never indeed occur in entire purity, but partly alongside of purely Jewish standpoints, partly mixed up with the Jewish categories; perhaps bent on a contest with these latter, and in their consequences gradually sublating and interpenetrating that foundation of the Jewish consciousness which was so pure at its first appearance. Does not the Paulinism of the four great Epistles exhibit precisely such a form of consciousness? In that signification of σάρξ accepted by us at the outset as equivalent to "man" and "finitude," we recognised in Paul a moment of the Old Testament mode of thought and expression. The fact is, he really does at times give expression to the feeling of the inferiority of all that is human by the antithesis of σάρξ and πνεῦμα (Gal. i. 11, 16, ii. 17; Rom. iii. 20; 1 Cor. i. 29, where note, the peculiarly Old Testament ἐνώπιον αὐτοῦ). Reverting to the proper meaning of σάρξ, we find it opposed to πνεῦμα in Rom. i. 3, 4, ii. 28, 29; also Rom. ix. 27; 1 Cor. ix. 11; 2 Cor. x. 4; Gal. iv. 23, 29. No doubt the Old Testament antithesis of finite and infinite lies at the root of such passages as 1 Cor. xv. 34 ff. But clearly there is something more than this conveyed in the uniform character of the predicates, which are almost exclusively privative and passive, and seem intended to designate the essence of the ἄνθρωπος χοϊκός, of the ψυχὴ ζῶσα in its totality. Still we do not get out of these predicates a real dualism; the antithetical principles are not co-ordinate. Over against the absolutely transcendent glory and absolute reality of the πνεῦμα, the σάρξ as φθορά, ἀτιμία, ἀσθένεια, never comes to life at all, never lifts itself above the horizon of genuine reality. That Paul does not occupy the pure Old Testament position appears from the intentional and carefully elaborated antithesis which is exhibited in this passage, opposing attributes being piled on, pair after pair. And when we note that the expression σὰρξ καὶ αἷμα, which Paul himself employs for human nature generally, *e.g.* Gal. i. 16, is applied here (1 Cor. xv. 50) to the purely material side of man's nature, the question suggests itself, whether the purely physical use which we claimed for σάρξ at the outset, and in terms of which we saw σάρξ recur in the signification of matter, and as we believe also in the phrase ἔξω ἄνθρωπος (with διαφθείρεται, 2 Cor. iv. 16),—whether this use of the word be not better fitted to bring the Pauline notion of σάρξ into analogy with the Hellenistic-speculative, dualistic category of matter, than that other would be which, after the manner of the Old Testament, unmistakably embraces the whole of human nature, and with which Holsten makes the attempt.

Holsten would explain certain passages by saying Paul shared the view of his time concerning a purely external relation of the spirit to body. But this is not a proper explanation. In what sense was it the belief of his time? It was different from the two most prevalent theories of his time. 1. From the Platonism of Philo. Philo has two distinct views, though he avoids making them glaringly inconsistent. (*a*) A pure dualism, spirit and matter having nothing in common. (*b*) Into his κόσμος γεγονώς and σωματικός he imports the Jewish distinction of φθαρτόν and ἄφθαρτον, earthly and heavenly. Paul, on the other hand, never attains the Hellenistic dualism of spirit and matter. There is wanting to him—and in this he is and remains a Hebraistic Jew—the abstract conception of pure spiritual being. 2. He differs from the contemporary Jewish views. They had not the dualism of ideal and real, spirit and matter, as Hellenists. Their antithesis was the heavenly and the earthly. But though wide apart and variously distinguished, they are but parts of a whole. Man, notwithstanding his material body, is capable of having revelations made to him, and of converse with God. They are very far indeed from speaking of the flesh in the way Paul does, or from treating it like him as not really a constituent element of true human nature. The Jew cannot think of man apart from his body. And it is characteristic of the genuine national standpoint, that Judas Maccabeus (2 Macc. xiv. 46) expresses a hope that he will receive at the resurrection, in the complete identity, even the bowels he himself has torn out. Compare and contrast Paul in 1 Cor. vi. 13: τὰ βρώματα τῇ κοιλίᾳ, καὶ ἡ κοιλία τοῖς βρώμασιν· ὁ δὲ Θεὸς καὶ ταύτην καὶ ταῦτα καταργήσει. Paul therefore held not what may be stated roughly as the view of his time, but more accurately that modified view indicated above (*Die Anthropologie des Ap. Paulus*, pp. 22–38).

For the ethical and religious view of σάρξ and πνεῦμα, the reader must be referred to Ernesti and Weiss, as well as to the longer-known writers on that side, such as J. Müller, Neander, and Tholuck.

VI

MAN'S NATURE AND A FUTURE STATE

" Thine are these orbs of light and shade :
Thou madest life in man and brute ;
Thou madest death ; and lo, Thy foot
Is on the skull which Thou hast made.

" Thou wilt not leave us in the dust :
Thou madest man, he knows not why—
He thinks he was not made to die ;
And Thou hast made him : Thou art just."
—TENNYSON.

LUKE xx. 35-38.—"They which shall be accounted worthy to obtain that world, and the resurrection from the dead, neither marry, nor are given in marriage ; neither can they die any more: for they are equal unto the angels ; and are the children of God, being the children of the resurrection. Now that the dead are raised, even Moses showed at the bush, when he calleth the Lord the God of Abraham, and the God of Isaac, and the God of Jacob. For He is not a God of the dead, but of the living : for all live unto Him."

JOHN xi. 24-26.—"Martha saith unto Him, I know that he shall rise again in the resurrection at the last day. Jesus said unto her, I am the resurrection, and the life : he that believeth in Me, though he were dead, yet shall he live : and whosoever liveth and believeth in Me shall never die."

PHIL. iii. 11, 12, 21.—"If by any means I might attain unto the resurrection of the dead. Not as though I had already attained, either were already perfect: but I follow after, if that I may apprehend that for which also I am apprehended of Christ Jesus . . Who shall change our vile body, that it may be fashioned like unto His glorious body, according to the working whereby He is able even to subdue all things unto Himself."

Also,

The Fifteenth Chapter of FIRST CORINTHIANS.

CHAPTER XV

THE FUTURE LIFE IN GENERAL

[LITERATURE.—G. F. Oehler, *Ve.... ....nti sententia de rebus post mortem* (1846). H. Schultz, *Die Voraussetzungen der christlichen Lehre der Unsterblichkeit* (Göttingen, 1861). Whately, *Scripture Revelations concerning a Future State* (1830). Bishop Perowne, *Immortality*, the Hulsean Lecture for 1868 (Cambridge, 1869). Prof. C. M. Mead, *The Soul Here and Hereafter: a Biblical Study* (Boston, 1879). Prof. Salmond, *The Christian Doctrine of Immortality* (Edin., 1895). Cf. also the treatises of J. B. Heard and E. White already cited.]

THE last things, life after death, the resurrection, the general judgment, the final destiny of men, are not treated of in Scripture under abstract propositions. What the Bible says on these subjects is said mainly in connection with the revelation of redemption. Moreover, there are two distinct lines on which even these disclosures are set forth. The first is that which we may call " personal," for in it the future is spoken of as part of the development of an individual human being—the after-life and ultimate salvation or destruction of the man. The other is that which we may call " dispensational," when these last events are spoken of on the public scale, as moments in the development of the kingdom of heaven, or of the dispensation of redemption in the hand of the Lord

Jesus Christ. Thoroughly to connect these two in a complete system of eschatology, is a task for which our theology is confessedly incompetent. Nor need this be wondered at. The Scripture itself does not give us a complete view of these connections. Even inspired writers declare that here they "know in part and prophesy in part."

The questions of eschatology with which we have to deal are chiefly those arising in the line of personal redemption. They are those directly related to the view which Scripture takes of man's own being. We have to ask, What is the bearing of the Bible psychology upon its doctrine of the future life? Does the human being carry in himself the credentials of an existence beyond the grave? Does revelation acknowledge or confirm these? What foundation does it lay in its anthropology for a belief and knowledge of the life to come? In connection with the details of revelation concerning a future life, arise many interesting questions as to the separate or intermediate state, the resurrection, and the resurrection body. We must restrict our inquiries to the two topics of the future state in general, and the resurrection in particular. The essential unity of the Scripture doctrine on these two topics, and its close connection with the Scripture view of man's origin and nature, will come out as we proceed.

BIBLE VIEW OF THE FUTURE LIFE.—The relation of Scripture thought on this subject to the religion of the ancient Egyptians, with its vivid but elaborately material views of the future world, to Oriental and Greek beliefs

concerning the soul, or even to the current of Christian
speculation, would open up too wide a field.   We must
confine ourselves mainly to the most simple and central
propositions of Scripture.   But *the bearing of revelation
on man's natural and instinctive belief that he shall live
after death* cannot be passed over.   During most of the
Christian centuries, the Scripture doctrine concerning
the life to come has been held as bound up with and
based upon that of the indestructibility of the human
soul.   Man is a being who must live after death, must
live for ever.   Conscience declares that present conduct
and character are to influence an eternal hereafter.   Nay,
the very make of the soul tells of the timeless and
changeless sphere to which it belongs.   This doctrine of
the natural and necessary immortality of the human soul
has been religiously cherished as of the very essence of
the scriptural or Christian belief in a life to come.   Not,
indeed, that it has escaped question or cavil, even among
Christian thinkers.   The Greek Fathers had a contention
of their own against certain modes of affirming the soul's
indestructibility.   Then there were early heretics, refuted
by Origen, who held that the soul totally dies with the body,
and will be restored to life with it in the general resurrection at the end of the world.[1]   During the Middle
Ages, the philosophical notion of the soul as the " form "
or essence of the man, and therefore that which necessarily survives death, seems to have reigned almost un-
contested in Christian theology.   The Reformers, however,
amid their many controversies, were soon involved in one
upon this subject also.   Calvin's tract in refutation of it

---

[1] Eusebius, *Hist. Eccles.* lib. vi. c. 37

keeps alive the memory of the *Psycho-pannychian* heresy, which was, that the soul dies or sleeps from death till the day of judgment. Luther is charged with having himself given some countenance to the opinion.

The natural mortality of the soul, which is properly the position of materialists and unbelievers, has been repeatedly during recent centuries adopted by Christian thinkers, and combined by them, in ways more or less fantastic, with the Scripture revelation of ? future life. The names of Coward, Dodwell, and Priestley will call up to those familiar with the history, forms of this belief maintained at successive periods in the eighteenth century, —a century of which, however, it has been pithily said, that "the immortality of man was *par excellence* its dogma."[1]   Some English divines in the first part of last century joined the materialists Coward and Anthony Collins, in maintaining the natural mortality of the soul as a positive tenet of Scripture no less than a truth of psychology.   The learned Henry Dodwell, a nonjuring churchman deprived of his chair at Oxford, published several works in which he laboured with great ingenuity to prove, "from the Scriptures and the first Fathers, that the soul is a principle naturally mortal; but immortalised actually by the pleasure of God to punishment; or to reward by its union with the divine baptismal Spirit. Wherein is proved that none have the power of giving this divine immortalising spirit since the apostles but only the Bishops."[2]   At a later period, Priestley, in his *Disquisitions relating to Matter and Spirit*, not only held

---

[1] Erdmann, *Geschichte der Philosophie*, ii. 650.
[2] The words of his title-page.

the sleep of the whole man till the resurrection to be the genuine Christian doctrine, but argued that the New Testament expression, "fallen on sleep," made the soul as much dead as the body, and was only another and softer name for the same thing. A peculiar position is held at present by Mr. Edward White and other defenders of what they themselves call the "conditional immortality of man."

More cautious Christian opponents of the prevailing method of identifying divine revelation as to a future life with the tenet of the soul's indestructibility, have preferred to rest the doctrine of survival on the resurrection of Jesus and the affirmations of Scripture, without insisting on the soul's natural immortality. Archbishop Whately and Bishop Hampden in our own country, with the late Dr. Rothe of Heidelberg among Continental divines, may be cited as representatives of this position. Hampden says : " This notion (*i.e.* the mediæval) of the separate existence of the soul has so incorporated itself with Christian theology, that we are apt at this day to regard our belief in it as essential to orthodox doctrine. Even in maintaining that such a belief is not essential to Christianity, I may incur the appearance of impugning a vital truth of religion. I cannot, however, help viewing this popular belief as a remnant of scholasticism. I feel assured that the truth of the resurrection does not depend on such an assumption ; that the life and immortality of man, as resting on Christ raised from the dead, is a certain fact in the course of Divine Providence, whatever may be the theories of the soul, and of its connection with the body. . . . Are we not disposed, even in these days, to rest too much on the natural or metaphysical arguments for a future state, and to imagine that the Christian faith is compromised by a denial of the immateriality of the soul?   I by no means intend to deny its immateriality. . . . But we go beyond the basis of the facts when we assume, in our abstract arguments for the natural immortality of the soul, its separate existence apart from the body. . . . What matters this to the Christian, who is fully assured that because Christ lives he shall live also; that 'as by man came death, by man came also the resurrection from the dead'?"[1]   These opinions are notes of dissatisfaction arising out of the manner in which the scriptural view of a future life has been bound up with philosophical propositions concerning the nature of the soul, some of them elaborated in other schools of thought than that of Christianity.   The real answer to these dissents should be found by connecting the Bible revelation concerning the future life with its own simple philosophy of man.

The Bible does not affirm the immortality of the soul in any abstract or general form.   Much less does it define the constitution of the soul as involving its necessary indestructibility.   So much we may freely concede. But when it is said that the notion of a separable soul or spirit in man is unscriptural, is nothing but a philosophical figment, and that the soul's separate existence is no necessary part of Christian belief, we are prepared on the strongest grounds to demur.   It is plain to demonstration that a view of the human constitution essentially

---

[1] The Bampton Lecture of 1832, pp. 310, 517.   A book which was the occasion of much controversy in its day.

bipartite is the doctrine of Scripture, and that the spirit
or soul of man is expressly affirmed to survive the body.
The personal existence of human beings after death is a
doctrine that pervades the whole system of Scripture.
The Bible sustains and illumines, in the most remarkable
and varied ways, man's instinctive belief that he was
made for an everlasting existence. Nor is at all difficult
to see how the scriptural conceptions of his origin and
nature consist with these disclosures concerning the life
to come. The immediate origination of man's life by the
breath of the Almighty, the kinship of man with His
Maker, his formation after the divine image, the possession of spiritual personality as an essential and inalienable part of the image—these are the Bible ideas with
which the doctrine of continuance after death naturally
allies itself. It would not, of course, be correct to say
that the Scripture constructs out of these propositions
any abstract argument for man's life after death. It
would be clearly incompetent to argue that man's survival is, in Scripture, based upon his possession of
" breath," or " spirit," from God,[1] even though there be
good reason to think that these expressions are so applied
to man as to imply that he specially belongs to God who
is the Father of " spirits." It would be wrong, however,
to import into these terms the metaphysical idea of an
indissoluble substance, and thus commit the Scripture to
the philosophical argument that the soul cannot die
because it cannot be dissolved or dissipated. But the
author of the Book of Wisdom seems to be fairly following the doctrine of Genesis when he says: " For God

[1] רוּחַ אֱלוֹהַּ or נִשְׁמַת, as at Job xxvii. 3.

created man to be immortal, and made him to be an image of His own peculiar nature."[1] The hinge of comparison between the Original and the copy is not abstract duration; it is spiritual personality. Man is a personal being, created after the semblance of the peculiar nature of God. And upon this ground, which may be termed at once ontological and ethical, the Bible doctrine of man's survival rests. "All souls are mine." "They all live unto Him."

It is plain, however, that everywhere belief in the life after death is bound up with some view of the nature of the soul, or, at least, of the human constitution. It is impossible to except the teaching of Scripture from this general rule. It will not avail and will not satisfy, to rest our hope of life to come upon its bare word, as some of those already referred to would have us do.[2] The Bible recognises certain grounds for that hope. But it is for us to disentangle the prevalent confusion as to what these grounds are. Our task here therefore will be to show how the Scripture doctrine of man and his future contrasts (1) with some views that are non-biblical; (2) with some that have been occasionally adopted in Christian circles; (3) to state what the Bible view really is.

1. It is of importance here to distinguish between the Bible mode of affirming man's future existence and the

---

[1] Ὅτι ὁ Θεὸς ἔκτισε τὸν ἄνθρωπον ἐπ᾽ ἀφθαρσίᾳ, καὶ εἰκόνα τῆς ἰδίας ἰδιότητος ἐποίησεν αὐτόν.—Σοφία Σαλωμών. ii. 23. Our translators have followed the less supported reading ἀϊδιότητος, "eternity." But ἰδιότητος (the Complutensian and Vatican reading) is fully as germane to the argument in hand.

[2] E.g. Bp. Hampden quoting Nemesius: "It is to us a sufficient proof of immortality, that it is taught in the Divine Oracles, which are to be trusted because they are Divinely inspired."

methods of other religions and philosophies, which
founded their doctrine of future life upon a different
idea of man's nature. This is more especially necessary
in regard to that one—the Greek—which has such close
affinities with scriptural doctrine as to have been greatly
identified with Christian eschatology, elaborated by the
schoolmen as the foundation of the faith, and often
preached from the Christian pulpit as a substitute for
the fuller light of the gospel on life and immortality.
The Greeks connected man's survival of death with his
participation of the divine essence. The scientific presuppositions of the Platonic philosophy in establishing
the immortality of man were such as these : That the
divine and therefore immortal part of man is derived
from the Supreme Creator ; [1] that the individual soul is
of the same nature and character as the universal soul,
or soul of the world ; [2] that it is a simple, uncom-
pounded, and so incorruptible principle, [3] in its own
nature indestructible even by its own evil ; [4] that it is
self-moved and the cause of motion, [5] the divine and
contemplative reason. [6] This is a doctrine of immor-

---

[1] *Timæus*, iii. 34, 35, 41, 69 (Steph.), especially in this last, παραλα-
βόντες ἀρχὴν ψυχῆς ἀθάνατον, κ.τ.λ.   [2] *Ibid.* iii. 69, 90,
[3] *Phædo*, 78, where the argument turns upon the soul being ἀξύνθετον
or μονοειδές. It has been subtly followed out by Plotinus, *Ennead.* iv. 7.
[4] *Republic*, lib. x. 609, D : Ἴθι δή, καὶ ψυχὴν κατὰ τὸν αὐτὸν τρόπον
σκόπει. ἆρα ἐνοῦσα ἐν αὐτῇ ἀδικία καὶ ἡ ἄλλη κακία τῷ ἐνεῖναι καὶ προσκα-
θῆσθαι φθείρει αὐτὴν καὶ μαραίνει ἕως ἂν εἰς θάνατον ἀγαγοῦσα τοῦ σώματος
χωρίσῃ ; Οὐδαμῶς, ἔφη, τοῦτό γε. Ἀλλὰ μέντοι ἐκεῖνό γε ἄλογον, ἦν δ' ἐγώ,
τὴν μὲν ἄλλου πονηρίαν ἀπολλύναι τι, τὴν δὲ αὐτοῦ μή; Ἄλογον.
[5] *Phædrus*, 245, C : Ψυχὴ πᾶσα ἀθάνατος· τὸ γὰρ ἀεικίνητον ἀθάνατον.
[6] *Ibid.* 249, E : Πᾶσα μὲν ἀνθρώπου ψυχὴ φύσει τεθέαται τὰ ὄντα.
This summary of citations is indicated in a paper on "The Belief in
Immortality," by Prin. Fairbairn of Mansfield College, Oxford. See his
Studies in the Philosophy of Religion and History, pp. 226, 227. 1876.

tality which deserves careful consideration from all Christian thinkers. It is well to note both wherein it differs from the scriptural doctrine, and how far it has done good service as an aid to Christian faith. It would be foolish to despise any reasoned plea for immortality, and certainly that developed in the Platonic dialogues is noble. Next to the disclosures of revelation, the reasonings of Plato have furnished the grandest confirmation in literature of man's belief that he survives death; only we must observe that the real strength of the plea does not lie in the abstract propositions above cited. Plato the poet, the thinker, is broader than his philosophy. His plea for a future life is not merely that of the metaphysician. His moral arguments from the soul's own aspirations, from the necessity of retribution, from the divine order and government of the universe, are common to him with all who have worthily treated the theme. For this instinct of life after death, "a specifically human possession," makes philosophy and religion its tributaries and servants. The nature of man demands from both what can evoke and satisfy his aspirations after immortality.

It is upon his own peculiar doctrine of knowing and ʋeing, however, that the argumentative parts of Plato's teaching on this theme chiefly depend. And the influence of even these on the current of Christian thought has been very great. Nor are its results to be regarded as only injurious. It is the custom at present very strongly to disparage them. Yet no more manifest instance of ideas preparing the way for the reception of the gospel can be cited than this great legacy of Platonic speculation, to which the Christian religion served itself lawful heir.   Nor can we doubt that, as the assimilating power of Christianity triumphs, the precious metal of this Greek amalgam will be thoroughly extracted, and the base elements rejected.   It is necessary here, in a word, to discriminate what, in the Greek view of immortality, is akin to Bible thought, and what is alien from it.   The point where they coincide is in making *personality* the ground of continuous existence.   Greek thought had too firm a grasp of the notion of personality, of freedom, of the ethical principles involved in the government of the world and in the nature of man, to allow metempsychosis to obtain a permanent foothold on Grecian soil.[1]   Still less possible was it for the Greek mind to adopt the dreamier pantheistic forms of belief in a future life which prevailed in India.   On this important common ground, then, the Bible religion and the more developed forms of Greek thinking met together, namely, that man as responsible person, as God related, must survive death.

But the divergence between the Bible thought and that of the Platonic philosophy is now very manifest. Plato analysed man's nature not only into separable, but into opposing elements.   Greek philosophy concentrated its characteristic dualism upon the nature of man.   One part of him is divine, another almost anti-divine.   One part of him is immortal, another part of him is perishable and perishes for ever,—an idea too easily confounded with that which still speaks in the Christian tongue of man's nature as made up of an immortal soul

---

[1] See Fairbairn, *Studies*, etc., p. 174.   But see Prof. Salmond's quotations from Plato, *Op. cit.* p. 146.

and a mortal body. The Hebrew, the Bible thought, has indeed its duality of man's nature, as we have shown; but it is a duality of littleness and greatness, of man's ephemeral place here on the one side, and of his kinship and friendship with the Almighty on the other. It did not, it could not, found its doctrine of future life, as Greek philosophy did, upon the elaborated distinction between the *spiritual* and the *material* in man. For that distinction, when worked out by philosophy, led to an indignant and contemptuous rejection of the resurrection of the body. Yet so grateful was Christian thought for elaborated arguments to commend belief in a future life, and to set it on a logical and scholastic basis, that the native opposition of the Greek mind to the doctrine of the resurrection was forgiven. The distinctive character of the scriptural belief was also too much forgotten. Gradually, in Christian schools, the Greek influence prevailed, and even in the Christian Church the idea of the soul's immortality for long took the place of the Scripture doctrine of a future life. During the last century almost universally,—in some philosophical sections of Christendom still,—the survival of an immortal essence of the man is substituted for that "adoption," that "complete redemption," for which the Spirit teaches Christian believers to wait and yearn. The Christian hope is too often made to appear the hope of release from the body at death, instead of the body's redemption and a perfected salvation for the whole nature of the man.

The distinctive peculiarities of the Platonic argument are the existence of ' *eternal ideas* ' and the ' *pre-existence of the soul.'* An exquisitely dramatic passage in the *Phædo* will be remembered, where Socrates brings out this crowning solution to relieve and to reassure the baffled reasoners. They had been drawn on to express the fear, that since the soul is a harmony, it must cease like music when the frame and the strings of the lyre are dissolved. " But what call we that," says Socrates, " which pre-exists the lyre ? That can be no mere harmony. What did not begin with the body cannot end with the body. The admission of the pre-existence of ideas, and therefore of the soul, settles the question. A harmony is an effect, whereas the soul is not an effect." [1] Here it must be allowed that Greek and Christian thought part company. The Bible, with its distinctive doctrine of creation, renders the pre-existence argument futile and unnecessary. Nor can we admit with Jowett,[2] that the Platonic reasoning—" eternal ideas exist, therefore the soul exists eternally "—is any true parallel to the argument from immortality, among ourselves, drawn from the existence of God. When this latter is properly based as a scriptural and Christian argument, it takes such grounds as man's formation by the one living and true God, and his moral relation to that God—grounds confirmed to us supremely in the disclosures of revelation. There is, it is true, an affinity between the Platonic reasonings and such arguments for the soul's continued existence as those employed by Bishop Butler in the famous opening chapter of his

[1] *Phædo*, 89 *et seq.* (Steph.). Consult Jowett's introduction to his translation of this dialogue. *The Dialogues of Plato*, II. 164, 165 (3rd Edition, Oxford, 1892).

[2] *Op cit.*, p. 186.

Analogy. It may be questioned how far these have been of much real service to the doctrine. To say that the soul is indissoluble is no affirmation of its immortality. That some particular element in man's constitution is incapable of annihilation, is not really to the point as regards his future personal existence. Besides, this mode of reasoning has the disadvantage of hanging too much on a mere logical concatenation of abstract propositions.

2. Let us now take some notice of those apparent oppositions that have arisen even among Christian thinkers as to the doctrine of the soul's immortality. And first (i.) of the assertion so commonly mooted, that some of the Greek Fathers held the mortality of the soul, and especially the annihilation of the wicked. The changes have been rung by Dodwell and by some subsequent writers upon a well-known passage in Justin Martyr's *Dialogue with Trypho,* to prove that this Apologist held both these positions. A famous citation from Tatian, beginning, " The soul is not immortal by itself, but mortal. It is also capable of not dying," is made to do duty to the same effect. And so with several isolated quotations from Theophilus, Irenæus, and others. Olshausen has clearly pointed out in what direction the solution of these passages is to be found.[1] All these writers held, with more or less consistency, the distinction between the *psyche* and the *pneuma*; sc that when they affirm that the soul is mortal in itself, but

---

[1] In a brief paper contained in his *Opuscula Theologica* (Berlin, 1834). For an account of Olshausen's view, with the relevant citations from the Fathers, see Note to this chapter.

can become immortal, it must be remembered that it is of the *psyche* they are speaking. According to the views of some of them, the nature of man at the first was that of a body and soul (*psyche*), upheld by the spirit (*pneuma*). Upon the fall, the *spirit* retires or is extinguished, and the *soul* dies. In redemption, the *spirit* is revived or restored, and thus again an immortality of blessedness becomes the possession of the *soul*. Now it is obvious at a glance, that unless the trichotomic character of their anthropology is kept in view, the modern reader is entirely misled when the opinions of these Fathers are cited concerning the mortality or immortality of the " soul." Of not less importance is it to observe, that in speaking of the death of the soul, these writers do not invariably, or even usually, mean cessation of existence. They use the expressions " death " and " dying " in an ethical sense. The death to which the *psyche* becomes subject upon the loss of the *pneuma* is, accordingly, ignorance of its divine origin and alienation from God in this present world, to which is added the darkness of Hades in the world to come. To these two lines of explanation, the tripartite psychology of the Greek Fathers and their tropical use of the term " death," Olshausen has called attention very pointedly. There is another consideration, which has been less adverted to, but which tends in the same direction. They were all familiar with the Platonic doctrine of the soul. Some of them had been once adherents of that philosophy. Their denial of the soul's immortality, then, it must be remarked, was not a denial of it in our sense--namely, that it survives death—but a protest against the theory of its necessary indestructibility, its essential divinity, and its pre-existence. In the passage from Justin above mentioned, this is expressly stated. "Souls are not immortal," he says, "for they were created, and their existence depends upon the will of God." [1] It is plain that this statement bears no relation to the question of the soul's continuance after death. It is simply a denial of its pre-existence, or of its absolute self-subsistence. In view of Justin's repeated and strong expressions elsewhere regarding the eternal punishment of the wicked, it is obviously unfair to quote the isolated passage from the *Dialogue with Trypho*, in the application given to it by such writers as H. Dodwell and E. White. It may be fairly enough cited to show that Justin held the annihilation of the wicked as a thing possible to the Almighty; perhaps also that in his opinion the cessation of their soul's existence was

---

[1] I subjoin the well-known paragraphs from the *Dialogue with Trypho*, in an excellent translation, *Ante-Nicene Christian Library*, vol. ii. pp. 93, 94 :—" 'Those philosophers know nothing, then, about these things ; for they cannot tell what a soul is.' 'It does not appear so.' 'Nor ought it to be called immortal ; for if it is immortal, it is plainly unbegotten.' 'It is both unbegotten and immortal, according to some who are styled Platonists.' 'Do you say that the world is also unbegotten ?' 'Some say so. I do not, however, agree with them.' . . . 'But if the world is begotten, souls also are necessarily begotten ; and perhaps at one time they were not in existence, for they were made on account of men and other living creatures, if you will say that they have been begotten wholly apart, and not along with their respective bodies.' 'This seems to be correct.' 'They are not, then, immortal ?' 'No ; since the world has appeared to us to be begotten.' 'But I do not say, indeed, that all souls die ; for that were truly a piece of good fortune to the evil. What then : The souls of the pious remain in a better place, while those of the unjust and wicked are in a worse, waiting for the time of judgment. Thus some which have appeared worthy of God never die ; but others are punished so long as God wills them to exist and to be punished.' "

a conceivable solution of the awful mystery of their
future.   But these are concessions which no one would
greatly care to dispute.

(ii.) It is not necessary now to unearth the opinions
on the soul's mortality maintained by Dr. Dodwell,
cumbered   as   these   were   by   his   extravagant   high
churchism.[1] The views of those who in our own day
hold the position of dissidents within the Christian
Church from the common belief, deserve some attention.   The chief writers among them are Mr. J. B.
Heard and Mr. Edward White, whose opinions, however,
are far from being exactly coincident.   The latter declares that " the general object of his book [2] is to show
that in the popular doctrine of the soul's immortality is
the *fons et origo* of a system of theological error ; that in
its denial we return at once to scientific truth and to
sacred Scripture ; at the same time clearing the way for
the right understanding of the object of the Incarnation,
of the nature and issue of redemption in the Life Eternal,
and of the true doctrine of divine judgment on the unsaved." [3]   He characterises the soul's immortality as " an

[1] *An epistolary discourse, proving from the Scriptures and the first
Fathers*, etc. (see this title quoted in full, *ante* p 310).   Lond., 1706.

*The natural mortality of human souls clearly demonstrated from the
Holy Scriptures and the concurrent testimonies of the primitive writers.
Being an explication of a famous passage in the dialogue of S. Justin Martyr
with Tryphon, concerning the soul's immortality*, etc. (Lond., 1708).

*A Scriptural account of the eternal rewards or punishments of all that
hear the Gospel, without an immortality necessarily resulting from the
nature of the souls themselves that are concerned in these rewards and
punishments* (Lond., 1708).

The titles of these treatises of Dodwell suffice to indicate how far his
views are the precursors of those to be immediately considered.

[2] *Life in Christ*, 3rd Edition, revised and enlarged (Lond., 1878).

[3] *Ibid.* p. 70.

inadmissible assumption." [1] He groups it among notions
which he calls "antiscriptural," and " part of the mystery
of iniquity "; [2] and declares that "the assertion of man's
natural immortality is the direct cause of the creation of
of a God-dishonouring theology." [3] On its positive side,
the theory professes to be a doctrine of future life for
man through the Incarnation. According to this writer,
Scripture teaches that the object "of redemption is to
change man's nature, not only from sin to holiness, but
from mortality to immortality ; from a constitution
whose present structure is perishable in all its parts, to
one which is eternal." This stupendous change, conveyed to mankind through the channel of the incarnation,
is realised in the individual by the indwelling of the Holy
Spirit. " He applies the remedy of redemption by communicating Godlikeness and immortality to the soul by
spiritual regeneration, and to the body by resurrection." [4]
The theory, therefore, it will be seen, exaggerates the
effects of the Fall, by assuming that man then lost the
divine image in such a sense as to come under the law
of extinction at death like the lower animals.[5] "Without
redemption, man would certainly go to nothing at death." [6]
It makes regeneration, as we have seen, a physical or
constitutional change.

Again, its view of a future life is inconsistent and
incredible. The eternal life of the saved is, quite scripturally, ascribed to their union with Christ. And this is

---

[1] *Life in Christ*, p. 104 ; in former editions, it was " an intolerable
assumption."   [2] *Ibid.* p. 117.   [3] *Ibid.* p. 190.
[4] See the quotation given in full at p. 255, Chap. XIII., *supra*.
[5] Heard's *Tripartite Nature of Man*, 5th Edition, p. 250.
[6] White's *Life in Christ*, 4th Edition, p. 96.

the strong point of its teaching. But to Christ also, upon this theory, must be ascribed the survival of the unsaved in the state of punishment. " To permit of the reconstitution of the identical transgressor, we hold that his spirit is preserved in its individuality from dissipation in the death of the man, to be conjoined again to the body at the day of judgment. This survival of the ' soul ' we attribute exclusively to the operation of redemption, with its graces and corresponding judgments." [1] Thus, " both heaven and hell, the life eternal of the one and the second death of the other, are the results of that meritorious work of Christ." [2] The statement of these consequences, as drawn by the writers themselves, is the sufficient refutation of their theory.

The whole scheme bears marks of having been elaborated under the pressure of sentiment, and with the desire of arriving at a foregone conclusion, namely, that eternal punishment is impossible. This theory of " conditional immortality," or of the ultimate annihilation of the wicked, may claim one advantage over its rival, the theory of universal restoration. In its appeal to the certainty of future punishment and to the irrevocable character of future destiny, it is certainly more in accordance than the other with the findings at once of conscience and of Scripture. But both theories are incompetent solutions of the awful problem which they attempt. It is obvious that neither of them can be made to consist with the whole doctrine of Scripture as to the future of man. The one with which we have been dealing raises far more and greater difficulties than it solves. It is im-

---

[1] White, p. 119.   [2] Heard, p. 253.

possible to make it fit in to the doctrinal scheme of the
Bible. Any moral power it may possess in the hands of
some able and earnest Christian preachers of it, is more
than nullified by its fatal concessions to scepticism and
materialism on the question of the soul. And its theory
of man's constitution is certainly not that of Scripture.
If anything further were needed to show the weakness
of the theory, it would be sufficient to point to the
exegesis on which it rests. This exegesis requires that
" life " and " death " be taken in Scripture, usually and
all but invariably, to mean " continuance of existence "
and " cessation of existence " for man. This is called
" taking Scripture language in its simplest and most
obvious sense." It is strange that men cannot perceive
how under the guise of a law of exegesis they are simply
assuming the whole point in dispute concerning the
natural immortality of man. No competent interpreter
would ever think of confining to so bald and shallow a
meaning in any other connection such deeply-charged
expressions as the Bible words for life and death. Nor
can its upholders do so consistently. According to their
own theory, the souls of the impenitent do not cease to
exist at death, but survive to await judgment, *i.e.* continue in a state of spiritual death.

3. We come, finally, to state the real relation which
the Scripture doctrine of man's constitution bears to its
discovery of a future life. We are not warranted, as we
have seen, to insist on any attribution to man's soul or
spirit of an absolute necessity of eternal continuance;
" God alone hath immortality," in the sense of necessary
and eternal existence. But when we view " the souls

which he hath made "[1] as persons, we have taken the proper scriptural position. "Personal continuance of existence has its fundamental postulate in the existence of a personal God, its final ground in the free determinate will of this God, its final reason in the counsel of redemption, for biblical psychology has to seek the solution of her eschatological problems in the revealed mystery of God's redeeming purpose." [2]

There are two leading ideas concerning man in the earlier Scripture which naturally connect with its doctrine of his future. These are, (i.) his *kinship with God* by origin and nature, and (ii.) the *unity of his being,*—an indivisible personality. Add to these, what the later Scripture only fully unfolds, that redemption is based upon (iii.) the *union of mankind with a divine-human Redeemer.* The elements of the revealed doctrine of a future state lie in these three propositions. (i.) Mark how the divine kinship of man and the unity of his being support the Old Testament belief of a life beyond the grave. The former of these, in its bearings on our theme, has been eloquently, and with some slight abatement justly, ex-

---

[1] Isa. lvii. 16. "*Neshamoth*," the only instance where it has the meaning "souls."

[2] Delitzsch, *System der bibl. Psychologie,* p. 407. This author appears to **waver** between attaching continuance of existence to personality as a necessary element, and making it ultimately rest on the divine decree. He says, in a note on p. 405, that "the Scripture teaches an eternal personal continuance of all personal beings," whereas in the context of the passage above quoted, he says, "it ultimately rests on the redemptive decree,—the self-**realisation** of which demands the eternal personal continuance of collective **humanity.**" Moreover, he draws a distinction between immortality and **mere** continuance of existence, which he says are not in Scripture equivalent ideas. "Only he who is united to the everlasting God, through the **Risen** Christ, has immortality." This distinction appears to be just ard **far-reaching.**

pressed by Bishop Perowne : " No philosophic reasoning comes to the aid of the Hebrew as he questions with himself concerning a life hereafter. He can construct no argument for the immateriality of the soul ; he can build up no plausible hypothesis. . . . He does not reason : ' I think ; therefore I am. I shall continue to think ; therefore I shall continue to be.' He does not argue with himself : ' The soul is one and indivisible ; therefore it cannot perish.' He does not draw his hopes from the constitution of man, from his memory, his affections, his intellect, his sense of law and duty. Even in face of the terrible problems of life, and in sight of all the prosperous wrong-doing which was so great a trial to his constancy, he does not escape from his perplexity by any chain of reasoning, by any analogies that nature might suggest and philosophy confirm. He does not infer, that because the world is out of joint, God's righteousness must have a larger sphere of action than this world and the short years of man, and so conclude that there is a life to come, in which the vindication of God's moral government shall be complete. His is a grander logic, for it is the logic of the heart. His conclusions are reached, not in the schools, but in the sanctuary of God. . . . There, casting himself into the everlasting arms, he knows that these shall be beneath him, though heart and flesh should fail. There, holding sweet converse with his Eternal Friend, he is sure that the God who has stooped to speak to him as a friend will not suffer him to drop into the abyss of annihilation. His life is no passing phenomenon. He is not like the tree, or the flower, or the bird, or the beast—creatures of God's hand which know Him not, and do but yield Him the homage of a reasonless praise. He knows God; he has spoken to God; he has heard the voice of God in his heart. This is no illusion, but the most blessed, as it is the most certain, of all truths. Faith and love have won their everlasting victory in those words, which will for all time remain the noblest expression of the soul pouring itself out towards God :—

> ' But as for me, I am always by Thee.
> Thou hast holden me by my right hand.
> Thou wilt guide me in Thy counsel,
> And afterwards Thou wilt take me to glory.
> Whom have I in heaven but Thee ?
> And beside Thee, there is none upon earth in whom I delight.
> My flesh and my heart may fail,
> But God is the rock of my heart and my portion for ever.' " [1]

(ii.) It is no less plain that the other idea now mentioned, namely, the unity of man's being, pervades this and all similar passages of Scripture. "Because He calls the man His friend, because He calls Himself the God of the individual, singled out by name, therefore the whole man must survive the shock of death. It is not the spirit's immortality which alone is secured. It is not a mere prolongation of existence of which the pledge is given. The body as well as the soul is God's. In the body He calls these men His children; on the body He sets the seal of His covenant. And therefore, though the flesh may turn to corruption, and the worm may feed upon it, yet from their flesh shall they see God,—see Him not only in this world, the Avenger of their cause, but see Him in the world to come, the Judge who metes

[1] "Immortality," the *Hulsean Lecture* for 1868, pp. 75–77. J. J. S. Perowne, B. D.

out to them their recompense, the Rewarder of them who diligently seek Him." [1]

Everything the Bible has to say about the life after death is strongly coloured by this fundamental pre-supposition of the oneness of the man. In that respect it entirely differs from the Greek notion that the soul of man is immortal because it is of the nature of the gods, but that his body is an encumbrance which is cast off and perishes for ever. According to the Bible, it is the man who endures, even under the temporary eclipse of disembodiment, till he be again clothed upon of God. It is to be noted that the historical instances which stand as proofs of another life in the Old Testament all take this form. It is not an abstract statement of the soul's separate existence after death. It is not the reappearance of departed spirits. It is the translation of an Enoch, " so that he should not see death." [2] It is the unseen departure of Moses " by the mouth of the Lord," [3] and the withdrawal of his mortal raiment from human ken. It is the rapture of Elijah in his chariot of fire. We have no need to suppose that the Jews drew their doctrine of bodily resurrection from Egyptian or Persian sources. For although, as may be seen in the book of Maccabees, the later Jews drew from such sources errors and exaggerations of it, the doctrine itself is obviously germane to the central idea of their own Scriptures on the subject, namely, that God claims the whole man for the inheritance of a future life.

The idea accounts for a leading feature of Old Testa-

---

[1] "Immortality," the *Hulsean Lecture* for 1868, p. 84.

[2] Heb. xi. 6.   [3] Deut. xxxiv. 5, עַל־פִּי יְהוָה.

ment eschatology.   No doubt the record affirms a divine kinship of man as such.   But the writers themselves are men who realise it.   Consequently, when they write of the future life, it is chiefly of their own hopes concerning it.   Their sentiments take the shape not of philosophical speculation, but of piety and religious faith. We have glimpses, indeed, in psalmist and prophet of ar under-world where the wicked are ruled over by death ;[1] but in the main it is the future as bound up with the hope of salvation that is presented.   And this leads to still another remark, that we are fairly entitled to distinguish in the Old Testament between the ideas of an after-life, current in the age of the writers, and the revealed hopes to which they clung.   Natural or traditional notions of Sheol as a gloomy subterranean abode, with its weak and wavering shades, its almost entire extinction of existence, may colour the thoughts of a psalmist under the cloud of spiritual depression, may lend a cold and sceptic tone to the delineations of Ecclesiastes, may be dramatically presented in the poetry of Job ; but the writers themselves teach us to distinguish these from the truth of revelation, and attach all their own hopes of a future life to the revealed doctrines of man's creation and redemption.

Following out these considerations, we may be able to account for the alleged *reticence of the earlier Scriptures* on the subject of a future life.   It has been common to represent the older revelation as excluding or disregarding the life after death.   Arguments, even, for the divine character of the Mosaic system have been built upon the assumed

---

[1] Ps. xlix. ; Isa. xiv.

fact of the absence of that doctrine from the religion of
the ancient covenant.[1]   These theories have long since
fallen out of favour.   Still the fact has to be accounted
for, that comparatively little is said in the older Scriptures of life beyond the grave.   Perowne gives well the
usual account of this fact.[2]   There is no haste in God's
teaching.   The heroism of faith needed to be strengthened.
God alone, without any direct revelation of a future
heaven, was to be enough for these ancient believers.
He cites the reason given by some of the Fathers, that
the Jewish nation was too rude and ignorant to be
capable of receiving truths so lofty.   He adds the shrewd
surmise of Bossuet, that during the times preceding our
Lord the doctrine of the soul's existence after death had
been a source of errors.   The worship of the departed
lay at the bottom of almost all idolatry.   Therefore the
most primary notion of the soul and of its blessedness
was all which the law of Moses gave.   It was reserved
for the new commencement in the coming of Messiah to
lay this foundation of religion afresh.[3]

(iii.) The chief reason for this reticence, we apprehend, is
to be found in the peculiar character of the divine revelation which the Bible records.   A false idea of revelation
underlies much of the reasoning on both sides about the
Bible doctrine of immortality.   If revelation were a
series of apothegms or oracles, of abstract utterances
even for men's need, it would be hard to understand why
the plain discovery of a future life should have been

---

[1] *E.g.* Bp. Warburton's *Divine Legation of Moses demonstrated.*
[2] At pp. 88, 89 of his *Hulsean Lecture.*
[3] Perowne, *op. cit.*, pp. 131, 132.

withheld, especially if it could have been conveyed in such simple propositions as, " The spirit in man never dies," or, " Man continues for ever." But the entire revelation is personal and historical. The foundation of all religion, the existence of God, for example, is never given in the Old Testament Scriptures as an abstract proposition. It is taken for granted. But God reveals Himself to man by entering into special relations with men. The religion of redemption becomes the possession of mankind through a series of historical transactions between God and His chosen people. It is no otherwise with the light which revelation sheds on man's future life. Man's own instinctive belief, his natural expectation of life after death, the Bible takes for granted. Abstract affirmations or confirmations in that kind would have been foreign to its whole character. The Old Testament expresses the faith of a future life, chiefly as the assurance of God's redeemed that they shall dwell with Him for ever. When it passes beyond this to more direct intimation of future glory and personal resurrection, these are almost invariably Messianic, and expressed in a form primarily applicable to the Head of redeemed humanity. Peter interprets the clearest of all the psalms on this subject, " Thou wilt not leave my soul in hell, neither wilt Thou suffer Thine Holy One to see corruption," as a direct prophecy of the resurrection of Jesus.[1] Job connects his survival of death and his return from the grave with the appearance of his kinsman-Redeemer at the latter day upon the earth.[2] Both in Isaiah and in Ezekiel the idea of resurrection

[1] Ps. xvi. 10 as quoted in Acts ii. 27.   [2] Job xix. 25, 26.

from the dead is used as a most clear and splendid figurative description of predicted deliverances which God was to work out for Israel.[1] The most distinct of all Old Testament words on the subject of return from the grave occurs in a clearly Messianic passage : " And many of them that sleep in the dust of the earth shall awake, some to everlasting life, and some to shame and everlasting contempt." [2] There is abundant evidence outside of the Old Testament canon that the ideas of future life and resurrection were making rapid advances among the Jews in the interval between the last of the prophets and the coming of our Lord.   Yet we read in Acts xxiii. 6–9 that these ideas were still subjects of discussion between Pharisees and Sadducees.   It is only when the historical revelation arrives in the fulness of time at an Incarnation, and the personal God of the ancient covenant becomes the God-man Christ Jesus, that the life beyond the grave and the resurrection of the body can be fully brought to light in the gospel.   Indeed, even the Lord Jesus brings life and immortality to light, not so much by words and sayings, though these certainly He does not withhold, as by His own Messianic experience—tasting death for every man, then, by resurrection from the dead, destroying death and him that had the power of it, that we might be delivered from the bondage of its fear.

In a memorable passage of the *Phædo*, one of the speakers says that if a man can do no better on a matter of such practical importance as faith in a future world, " he ought to choose out the best and most irrefragable

---

[1] See Isa. xxvi. 19 ; Ezek. xxxvii. 1–14.
[2] Dan. xii. 2 ; compare with John v. 28, 29.

of human opinions about it, and upon that, like a mariner on a raft, risk his way through the storms of life, unless he can proceed more easily and safely on the more sure vehicle of some divine word."[1] It is true enough to say, as Perowne does,[2] that the divine word for which Socrates was seeking, Paul had found when he wrote: "For we KNOW that if the earthly house of our tabernacle were dissolved, we have a building of God, a house not made with hands, eternal in the heavens."[3] But it is more correct to affirm that what Paul and we have is the divine word in a grander sense than these philosophers thought of, namely, the Word incarnate and now glorified, who is our new and living Way to the world unseen. We see from the whole character, therefore, of those divine transactions which the Bible records, why there is a silence and a withholding, as it were, on this theme, in the ancient Scriptures. Mere words, even divinely-given words, could not have satisfied men on the subject of the future. The revelation of blessed life for ever could only come by a Redeemer, the incarnate Hope of men,—could only be unfolded by Him as He lived and died and rose again for men, and so achieved in His own person the right to say, "I AM the Resurrection and the Life."

---

[1] Plato, *Phœdo*, 85 C (Steph). Δεῖν γὰρ περὶ αὐτὰ ἔν γέ τι τούτων διαπράξασθαι ἢ μαθεῖν ὅπῃ ἔχει ἢ εὑρεῖν· ἢ, εἰ ταῦτα ἀδύνατον, τὸν γοῦν βέλτιστον τῶν ἀνθρωπίνων λόγων λαβόντα καὶ δυσεξελεγκτότατον, ἐπὶ τούτου ὀχούμενον, ὥσπερ ἐπὶ σχεδίας, κινδυνεύοντα διαπλεῦσαι τὸν βίον· εἰ μή τις δύναιτο ἀσφαλέστερον καὶ ἀκινδυνότερον, ἐπὶ βεβαιοτέρου ὀχήματος ἢ λόγου θείου τινὸς, διαπορευθῆναι. (This sentence is put into the mouth not of Socrates, but of Simmias.)

[2] *Hulsean Lecture*, p. 94.

[3] 2 Cor. v. 1.

NOTE ON CHAPTER XV

THE GREEK FATHERS ON THE MORTALITY OF THE SOUL

THIS subject has been very succinctly and pointedly handled by Olshausen in his tractate entitled, *Antiquissimorum Ecclesiæ Græcæ Patrum de Immortalitate Animæ Sententiæ Recensentur*, which will be found in his *Opuscula Theologica*, pp. 165–184. He confines his remarks to the opinions of Justin Martyr, Tatian, and Theophilus. He considers Irenæus, though a Greek writer, to belong by his leanings to the Western Church. Clement of Alexandria he thinks should, on such subjects, be reckoned along with Origen, whose views of the soul's pre-existence, to say nothing of his many eschatological whims, put him in a totally different category from the earlier Greek Fathers. It is further very properly remarked, that the three writers named above stand in such close conjunction as to throw light on each other's opinions. Athenagoras, who for some reasons might well have been grouped with these three, is put aside because of his distinct Alexandrian tendency. So far as the doctrine of immortality is concerned, Athenagoras, following the Greek philosophers, declares once and again that souls are immortal by their very nature—a proposition which was abhorrent to Justin and the others, as belonging to a school of thought which they had renounced when they adopted Christianity.

On this topic, as on so many others, a misleading method of referring to the opinions of the Fathers has prevailed. The habit of too many writers is, when amassing citations and opinions on any subject, to dip into the Fathers for isolated quotations, as some farmers cart stones from an ancient ruin to build into a modern farm wall. The consequence is that these ancient writers are made to support opinions with which they had no sympathy, and to seem to say what they have never said.

Olshausen has exposed this mistake very thoroughly in application to the point in hand. Had the considerations he adduces been present to the minds of those writers in

our own day who have revived Dodwell's citations from
the Fathers in the support of the theory of "conditional
immortality," it is impossible that the old quotations
could have been made to figure so complacently in their
new amalgam. As Olshausen's tract is not within reach
of all, I take from it the following paragraphs:—

"It very much contributes to the understanding of
opinions concerning any doctrine, to note the opinions
entertained by the same author on kindred points. If we
are quoting the views of an ancient author about immortality, we should note whether he did or did not distinguish between soul and spirit. The Greek Fathers, for
instance, mostly adhered to that partition of human
nature which we call the trichotomy. They distinguished
the soul, not only from the body, but also from the spirit,
a circumstance which totally changes the discussion as to
the soul's mortality. Concerning the spirit, they freely
concede what we ascribe to the soul ; indeed, they allow
more to the spirit, saying that it is eternal, indestructible,
and even life-giving. But they take a very different
view of the soul. Since the fall of man, the soul separated
from spirit is mortal, and only becomes a partaker of immortality when it is, at last, re-united with spirit. Yet
this, after all, does not mean that they think that souls
will go to nothing, if they are not re-united to spirit. For
their firm persuasion was that nothing in nature could
altogether perish or pass away. Consequently, they taught
a resurrection of all men, the 'soulish' as well as the
'spiritual.' But, on the other hand, they held that the
souls of the wicked are bereft of that consciousness of
their true origin in which the souls of the good rejoice, being partakers of the spirit. Now this defect
or bereavement is what they call 'death.' It is plain,
therefore, that the opinion of the Fathers about the immortality of the soul cannot be rightly perceived unless
their views in anthropology, especially about death and
resurrection, be constantly borne in mind ; so far removed
as these are from the way of thinking to which we are
accustomed. The 'soul' and 'death' meant very different things to these Fathers from what they mean to us.

Such a proposition, as *the soul is mortal*, had a very different significance in their lips from what it would have in the modes of speech to which we are used. Nobody can wonder, therefore, that those who neglect this grave distinction between ancient and recent modes of thought and speech should land themselves in serious error."

Again, " these Fathers deny that the ' soul ' has any life in itself, until the ' spirit,' like a celestial light, vivifies and lights up the ' soul,' which is darkness. So it was in the beginning before the fall of our first parents ; and so Christ restored the state of the soul, after its conjunction with the spirit had been dissolved. In their view death, whether bodily or spiritual, was not destruction or cessation of power and motion, but want of celestial life, loss of consciousness of supernal origin. Consequently, they held that the wicked could be enduring death even in immortality itself. It is plain, therefore, that their proposition, ' *the soul is mortal,*' offensive though it sounds, had a very different sense from that which is commonly ascribed to it. Indeed, if we rightly consider, it does not greatly differ from the position of Irenæus and Origen about the *immortality* of the soul. The Bishop of Lyons protests in eloquent language that the soul is immortal, and confutes those who deny to it immortality, on the ground that it is born and has a beginning. Thereupon those who write the history of dogmas imagine that Irenæus has spoken of the immortality of the soul in a very different way from Justin, and those who hold with him. But these learned writers are gravely mistaken, These Fathers differ in their terms, but about the thing itself they agree. For Irenæus, like Justin, calls the life-giving force ' the spirit,' so that apart from ' spirit ' the ' soul ' is mortal. That is to say, he adheres to the same partition of human nature as Justin ; and upon this the hinge of the whole discussion turns. . . .

" But to bring the thing to an issue, let us compare the opinions of Justin, Theophilus, and Tatian, concerning immortality with the teaching of Scripture, in so far as this can be done. For no one would find it easy to deny that such propositions as *the soul being mortal and com-*

posite perishes, are incompatible with theology, and indeed with Scripture. Yet this we must concede to these Fathers, that nowhere in the sacred books do we read, *the soul is immortal.* Concerning God rather is it affirmed that 'He alone hath immortality' (1 Tim. vi. 16); and concerning Christ, 'I am the resurrection and the life' (John xi. 25). Christ, therefore, is the fountain of life, and imparts life to the human race, oppressed by death. As He Himself says, ' He that believeth in Me, though he were dead, yet shall he live'; in which words he seems to imply, that those who do not believe are going to really die in their death. We perceive, therefore, that the teaching of Scripture is not so very different from those patristic positions when rightly understood. Nor could it well be otherwise, since the sacred writers themselves posit that distinction between soul and spirit on which this whole way of thinking is based. For, once let this distinction be admitted, it follows that 'soul' has no life in itself, but only receives it through union with 'spirit,' —the fountain of life eternal. Nevertheless, it is badly expressed when put, ' *the soul is mortal*,' for to most minds death means destruction of substance; but the soul cannot be altogether destroyed. The more correct form of statement is this: The soul apart from 'spirit' lives in a mere animal way, without consciousness of its heavenly origin and that divine stock in which it should rejoice,— a kind of life which is properly called death. When joined to spirit it becomes conscious of its celestial origin, and lives a life worthy to be so called. Thus speaks the Scripture, and so virtually do those Fathers whose opinions we have discussed, though they do not express these in sufficiently accurate language. Doubtless, however, their position is far nearer to the truth than that vain philosophical opinion about the immortality of the soul, which is so much in vogue in our day. That ought never to be attributed to the soul which alone belongs to the spirit, for ' God alone hath immortality, and whosoever believeth in Him.' Those who live without God are in death, and are dying while they live."—*Op cit.* pp. 171–72, 180–83.

The classic passages, in the writings of the Greek

Fathers themselves, on which these discussions turn, will be found as follows :—

THEOPHILUS of Antioch, *Ad Autolycum* (his only extant work), Lib. II. cap. xxvii.

JUSTIN MARTYR, *Dialogue with Trypho*, cap. v. At the beginning occurs the famous passage quoted in our footnote on p. 322, *supra*. But one quite as often cited is the short cap. vi., which immediately follows, in the *Dialogue*.

TATIAN.—The favourite passage from this author is ¶ 13 of his *Address to the Greeks*. The *Antenicene Christian Library* (Edin., 1867–71) contains reliable English renderings of all these.

CHAPTER XVI

SCRIPTURE DOCTRINE OF THE RESURRECTION

[LITERATURE.—W. R. Alger, *A Critical History of the Doctrine of a Future Life,* with a complete Bibliography by Ezra Abbot, Harvard College (New York, 1878). Isaac Taylor, *Physical Theory of another Life* (London, 1839). Tait and Stewart, *The Unseen Universe; or, Physical Speculations on a Future State* (5th Edition, London, 1876). E. M. Goulburn, *Resurrection of the Body* (Bampton Lect. 1850). Principal Candlish, *Life in a Risen Saviour* (3rd Edition, 1863). Bishop Westcott, *The Gospel of the Resurrection* (3rd Edition, 1874). Professor Milligan, *The Resurrection of the Dead* (1894).]

IN tracing the scriptural doctrine of a future life, the revealed confirmation of man's instinctive belief that he survives death, we have been gradually led, without any marked transition, from the doctrine of *Immortality* to the doctrine of *Resurrection.* The principle of this connection is very evident. Scripture discountenances any sharp severance of the elements of human nature in regard to the future. The Old Testament especially regards God's promise of a future life as embracing the whole man, his entire deliverance, body and spirit, from the power of the grave. It is not otherwise when the fuller revelation has come. As has been already said, even our Lord's own words and deeds, on this topic, were surpassed and explained by His own personal triumph over death. In His rising again, and in His risen life, as recorded on the last pages of the gospel history, we have the real revelation of a redeemed future for man. No doubt His words and deeds during His earthly life were both clear and ample, in bringing out that the rescue of the entire human being from death's power was the goal of salvation. He argues for the resurrection of God's redeemed from their covenant position, from God's relation to them as their God. He Himself, in the exercise of His redemptive rights, broke the power of death, at least three times in the course of His ministry, by restoring to sorrowing ones their dead brought to life again. But it was when His own glorious resurrection had sealed His accomplished redemption, that it became the supreme pledge of His ultimate and universal triumph over man's last enemy. It is the Gospel of the Resurrection that forms the peculiar claim of Christianity to illuminate for man the future life. In this sense, the arguments of Whately, Hampden, and other theologians within the century just closing have real weight when they desire that Christians should make more of the Resurrection of Jesus, as the ground of their future hopes, than of those natural reasonings or philosophic theories about the indestructibility of the human spirit which were so much favoured by the thinkers of the previous century.

What it is perhaps of most importance for us to notice is that the continuance of the whole person, the redemption of the whole man, is the thing emphasised in the Bible and Christian doctrine of a future life. Hence personal resurrection, instead of being something thrown in at the end, is the very gist of the gospel discovery, and shines on its front. Doubly instructive is our Lord's argument for it drawn from the divine words to Moses, " I am the God of Abraham, and the God of Isaac, and the God of Jacob." [1] He goes for His proof, not to such special Old Testament passages as allude to the particular event of rising again from the dead, but to one of the great covenant-words which secure redemption for the entire nature and being of those on whom God has set His everlasting love. It is an instructive surprise, moreover, to find that in these words Jesus reads, not what we are so apt to think of, the survival of the spirits of the blessed. When He says, " God is not the God of the dead, but of the living," and affirms this " touching the resurrection of the dead," He evidently means more than that Abraham, Isaac, and Jacob were living a disembodied life in some unseen region. He means that the covenant-name is in pledge for their complete bodily restoration. It secures the permanence of the whole man.

Once illuminated by our Lord's teaching, and still more by His own rising again, this mode of presenting the doctrine of a future life prevails with all the apostles. When Paul went with the Glad Tidings to Athens, he did not tell the Greeks that man survives the grave, that his soul lives after death in a separate state ; this would only have been in the line of their own philosophy. He preached that which not only surmounted, but in a sense confronted their surmises. He

[1] Ex. iii. 6 as quoted in Matt. xxii. 32.

seemed to them a setter forth of strange gods when "he preached unto them Jesus and the resurrection." [1]   It is always under the influence of this new fact that the apostles celebrate the victory won for man by their Lord and Saviour. Men are "begotten again unto a lively hope by the resurrection of Jesus Christ from the dead." [2] "He hath abolished death, and hath brought life and immortality to light through the gospel"; [3] "The last enemy which shall be destroyed is death"; "O death, I will be thy plagues : O grave, I will be thy destruction." [4] "For since by man came death, by man (*i.e.* by the God-man, the Head of redemption) came also"—what ? survival of death ? No ; but "resurrection of the dead." [5] Survival of death was not first brought to light by the special revelation which the Bible contains. Man's heart and conscience have witnessed for that in all ages and among all nations. Man's intellect, whenever awakened to thought, speculates and reasons about it. Revelation clears and confirms it. Survival of death was no part of redemption. It was not a thing secured for the first time by the work of Christ. It belongs to man as man. It was "resurrection of the dead" to which our Lord bore witness in His own person, and through which He secured that all in Christ shall be made alive.

No doubt our theology cannot attain to anything like a complete view of the connection between the Person, Work, and Resurrection of Christ on the one hand, and the Future of Mankind universally on the other. We

---

[1] Acts xvii. 18.   [2] 1 Pet. i. 3.   [3] 2 Tim. i. 10.
[4] Hos. xiii. 14.   [5] 1 Cor. xv. 21, 26.

are not allowed to forget that, as regards the last things, all is not light even to the student of the latest revelation. It is under the New Testament, as it was under the older economy, mainly in the way of redemption that we have disclosures of the life to come. We are not told much by our Lord and His apostles concerning the general resurrection. The firm outline of the last judgment sets forth, no doubt, "all the dead, small and great, standing before God," before "the great white throne and Him that sits on it."[1] But how they come, and what their form of existence, are veiled from us. The fact of a bodily resurrection is affirmed plainly enough. Paul declares his "hope that there shall be a resurrection of the dead, both of the just and of the unjust."[2] He has conscience and revelation both with him when he says: "We must all appear before the judgment-seat of Christ, that every one may receive the things done in his body."[3] Our Lord's words, which seem to reduplicate on those already quoted from Daniel, are still more definite: "All that are in the graves shall hear His voice, and shall come forth; they that have done good, unto the resurrection of life; and they that have done evil, unto the resurrection of damnation."[4] The fact is distinct; but as to the mode, anything that is explicit belongs to the resurrection of the just. No doubt the principle, "to every seed his own body," is one of far-reaching application. Still it remains true that what Delitzsch has called "the night side of the general resurrection," lies buried in shadow.

[1] Rev. xx. 12.

[2] Acts xxiv. 15.

[3] 2 Cor. v. 10.

[4] John v. 28, 29.

What we are told as to the way and manner of the
re-awaking, belongs to those that are Christ's, and to
them only. When we follow the line of personal
redemption we have a clear path of light; and its course
is worthy of great attention. This "blessed hope" rests
directly on the *person* of the Saviour, and becomes ours
by reason of our oneness with Him. Jesus Himself
withdraws the sad soul of Martha from the far-off vista
of the general resurrection, to fix it upon this more
vivid and immediate ground of confidence: "I am the
Resurrection and the Life." [1] Again, it is spoken of as
the direct result of that *spiritual life* of which the
Saviour is the source: "Whoso eateth My flesh, and
drinketh My blood, hath eternal life; and I will raise
him up at the last day." [2] Further, it is expressly
attributed to the operation of the *Divine Spirit*, who is
the principle of the new life in believers: "If the Spirit
of him that raised up Jesus from the dead shall also
quicken your mortal bodies by His Spirit that dwelleth
in you." [3] Finally, Paul speaks of it as something which
lay before him as a goal of *conscious effort*, the scope of
his own strenuous, self-sacrificing faith, which counted all
things loss that he might win it, the crown of faith's
following after, apprehending, reaching forth, and press-
ing toward the mark of his high calling in Christ Jesus:
"If by any means I might attain unto the resurrection
of the dead." [4] Here, surely, is something different from
our too common view. We think and speak as if
resurrection were a bare future event, an eschatological

---

[1] John xi. 25.   [2] John vi. 54.
[3] Rom. viii. 11.   [4] Phil. iii. 11.

fact with which our present working faith had little or nothing to do, an event which must come in due time alike to all, to those in and to those out of Christ. Do not these words represent it as the crown and completion of that which union to Christ by grace secures? Here, surely, is a Scripture truth which is entitled to our living regard, and which, had it the due place, would wondrously transform the outlook of the future from a mere departure out of the body into an unbroken series of progressive glorious advances, till we be clothed upon with our house from heaven.

Of the How, the What, the When of this ultimate attainment of redemption, Scripture does not warrant us to speak with much detail, but its outlines are firm. " How are the dead raised up? " Had men observed the exact words in which the inspired reasoner allows the question, they should have had an easier path to the answer than that which divines too oft have taken. " The dead raised up." Scripture never speaks, as creeds and apologists have spoken, of " the resurrection of the flesh." It does not even place the emphasis on resurrection of the body, but on the resurrection of the dead, their manifestation, their return from the unseen into the visible glories of a ransomed universe. Had men followed the idea pervading St. Paul's exquisite analogy of the seed-corn, theology should have been preserved from scholastic quibbles about identity of matter and identity of form, when it had to state the relation between the present and the future body. " Thou sowest not that body that shall be, but bare grain, it may chance of wheat, or of some other grain; but God giveth it a body as it hath pleased Him, and to every seed his own body."[1] Had the Church followed the spiritual teaching of this fifteenth chapter of First Corinthians, instead of her own childish memories or pagan traditions our pulpits should have been long ago delivered from the charnel-house theology of the "Night Thoughts," our popular Christian belief from reproaches irreverently but not quite groundlessly cast upon it.

"When scientific thought was once more directed to the subject of immortality, it was easily seen that the doctrine of resurrection, in its vulgar acceptation, could not possibly be true, since a case might easily be imagined in which there might be a contention between rival claimants for the same body. . . . It is, indeed, both curious and instructive to note the reluctance with which various sections of the Christian Church have been driven from their old erroneous conceptions on this subject; and the expedients, always grotesque, and sometimes positively loathsome, with which they have attempted to buttress up the tottering edifice. Some deem it necessary that a single material germ or organised particle of the body at death should survive until the resurrection, forgetting that, under such a hypothesis, it would be easy to deprive a man of the somewhat doubtful benefits of such a resurrection, by sealing him up (while yet alive) in a strong iron coffin, and by appropriate means reducing his whole physical body into an inorganic mass. . . . According to the disciples of this school, the resurrection will be preceded by a gigantic manufacture of shoddy, the effete and loathsome rags of what

[1] 1 Cor. xv. 37, 38.

was once the body being worked up along with a large quantity of new material into a glorious and immortal garment, to form the clothing of a being who is to live for ever ! . . . We have only to compare this grotesquely hideous conception with the noble and beautiful language of Paul, to recognise the depth of abasement into which the Church had sunk through the materialistic conceptions of the Dark Ages." [1]

Now there is no good reason why we should ever expose apostolic teaching to try conclusions with modern chemistry. The difficulties which science raises in such subjects, riper science will solve. On this topic of the resurrection we see the answer already beginning to take shape. Science at the present day stands in a very different and more friendly attitude towards this belief of man's reappearance in the future world than did the science of one or two generations ago. We are now assured that our present bodies are the same, yet not the same, that we have had from our birth. That there is in the body some principle, law, or specific form, which remains ever the same amid the flux of particles, is now an axiom of knowledge. We may say, in an almost literal sense, that we pass through the process of resurrection constantly ; that we are always dying in the flesh, always rising anew by virtue of the law of organic identity. Behind this, again, lies the greater law of personal identity—that there is a being which thinks, feels, and wills, maintains a connected growth from infancy to age in knowledge and moral character. This being does not cease at death. The bearing of such

[1] *The Unseen Universe*, pp. 57, 58 (5th Edition, Lond., 1876).

ideas on the identity of the future body with the present is obvious. They help us to see how the undivided personality of the man in its organic unity of soul and body can be the same in a future state. It is not identity of particles, it is not resurrection of relics, that we need to render the scriptural belief truly conceivable. It is this conception in which science and faith concur, namely, that each human being shall be the same in all that constitutes the organic personality, that this unchanging life will put on its nobler form under the conditions of its nobler state.[1]

All that is necessary to establish identity is the possibility of recognition by ourselves and others. And from familiar facts we learn that this does not require identity of particles in a material body. The special point in St. Paul's illustration is that the transformation in the seed-grain does not so entirely destroy the thing planted, but that there is a sameness or continuity between the new and the old, along with an entire change of form. But we have in the New Testament something on this topic far more important than an illustration or analogy however suggestive. We have the type or instance of a Risen Life. The place which our Lord's post-resurrection appearances ought to occupy in the Christian Doctrine of the Resurrection has not been sufficiently noticed. In our Lord's case, as described in the narratives at the close of the Gospel History, we have the precise elements required—a bodily identity

---

[1] For a careful and interesting statement of this point, see Westcott's *Gospel of the Resurrection*, pp. 143–145, 155, 156 (3rd Edition, Lond., 1874).

such as to admit of recognition, yet sometimes to defy it, for it was accompanied by a stupendous change of habit and properties. "Behold My hands and My feet, that it is I Myself: handle Me and see; for a spirit hath not flesh and bones as ye see Me have."[1] In these narratives we find not only the chief ground for the fact and hope of resurrection, but also our main evidence for the nature of the resurrection-body,—"identity with difference"[2]; identity real and substantial, so that He was recognised as their own Lord Jesus; difference, as great as if the ordinary conditions of body had been abolished, as they were evidently in His case undergoing a glorifying transition.

When, however, we hear Scripture on the question, How are the dead raised up? we must rest on the great Christian propositions. It is in Christ Jesus; it is by virtue of the whole nature, corporeal and spiritual alike, being united to the Saviour; it is through the operation of that Spirit who dwells in head and members alike, and quickens both. In short, as we have said, it rests on the grand central truth of Christianity, that God, in whose image man was made at first, becomes in Christ Jesus the quickening Head of a new because a redeemed humanity. How the body which is to be, finds a connection with the body that now is—how that which is laid in the grave becomes the seed-corn of the resurrection, we must leave with Him in whom His people's life is indissolubly wrapped up for time and for eternity.

"With WHAT BODY do they come?" He who puts the question into the mouth of his reader, with a caution

---

[1] Luke xxiv. 30.   [2] Calvin, *Instit.* III. xxv. 8.

against too curious inquiry, has yet substantially supplied the answer.[1] Instead of "corruption," *i.e.* liability to decay, which is the character of our present body, the future one, he tells us, shall be incorruptible. Instead of the "dishonour" to which all that perishes is liable, it shall have glory. Instead of "weakness," there shall be power. In a word, instead of a "psychical" or "soulish" body, there shall be raised up one pneumatical or "spiritual." If Bible psychology has furnished us with a characteristic and consistent conception, it is that of spirit or *pneuma* as the distinguishing possession of man. It has traced the *pneuma* in man, and its development from the elementary idea of man's life as inbreathed by his Creator, through its use as a designation for man's free personality, up to its renewal as the law of the spirit of life—that which animates the new creature as the Spirit of Christ Jesus Himself. It has thus prepared us for the culmination of personal redemption in a spiritual body. Man was made at first a "living soul," the crown of the whole animal creation, yet capable of 'spirit.' It was natural that his frame should be a "soulish body." But the aim of redemption is that even fallen man may become spiritual. It leads by a new and more glorious way to that height of spiritual glory which he was created to attain. How fitting that its final gift should be that of a body equal to his redeemed position! In any case, man's passage out of trial into bliss would have implied some such change, for flesh and blood cannot inherit the kingdom of heaven. As it is, redemption's crown is the final

[1] 1 Cor. xv. 42-46.

triumph of the Redeemer's grace, who, according to the
energy of His all-subduing power, shall change the body
of our humiliation, that it may be fashioned like unto
the body of His own glory.[1]

The time, the WHEN of this transformation is a
question that would lead us too far afield. Scripture
clearly speaks of an interval. It allows us to conceive
of a state in which even believers shall be "absent from
the body." It describes these blessed ones as "souls"
in another state than ours,[2] "spirits of just men made
perfect."[3] But whether they are even there wholly
unclothed, devoid of all corporeal vehicle, it scarcely
enables us to determine. An opinion which seems on
the face of it contrary to Scripture, is that, no longer
confined to the followers of Swedenborg, which makes
the souls of the blessed at death put on at once the
spiritual body as they enter the unseen world, and leave
for ever that which is laid in the tomb.[4] Less apparently unscriptural, but cumbrous, is the theory of some
of the Fathers, who speak of a first and second *stola*,—
who take the "white robes" of the Apocalypse to be a
provisional body, put on for the intermediate state, worn
only till the time come for the marriage garment of the
resurrection.[5] Very beautiful, if somewhat mystical, is
that of mediæval divines, favoured by some recent

---

[1] Phil. iii. 21.   [2] Rev. vi. 9 ; xx. 4.   [3] Heb. xii. 23.

[4] The Swedenborgian position is briefly and pointedly stated by Heard,
Tripartite Nature, pp. 323–327 (5th Edition, Edin., 1882).

[5] Delitzsch refers to Augustine (*Serm.* iv., in *Solennitate Sanctorum*).
Gregory, and others, among the ancient Christian writers, for this dis-
tinction, which he quotes in the splendid form given to it by Dante.
Purg. xxv. 88–108.

theologians, which regards the bodiless spirits of the redeemed departed as having meantime a kind of borrowed corporeity, by gathering round the glorified body of their Lord,—finding there "the sanctuary and true tabernacle" of their being as well as of their worship.[1] This coincides at all events with the best thing we know about our friends fallen asleep in Jesus. They have gone to be with Him; they are now with Christ—

> "And in that cloister's stillness and seclusion,
> They live whom we call dead." [2]

It is not wise for us to attempt to say much as to when or how the spiritual body comes. We know that it shall be the fitting garb of a ransomed and glorified spirit. We know that it shall be itself a pledge and trophy that of all Christ got from the Father He has lost nothing. It shall represent the dust redeemed, the body ransomed from the grave. How it is woven in the hidden secret of the life after death, we may not venture to surmise. If we have watched how the body, even here, puts on a likeness and correspondence to the real man, to the life within, it will not be difficult to think that for the ripening Christian his future body is being prepared by the Spirit of Christ dwelling already in this mortal frame, and quickening within it that which is to live for ever.[3] It will be open to us to believe that the

---

[1] "*Interim ergo sub Christi humanitate feliciter sancti quiescunt,*" quoted from St. Bernard by Delitzsch, *Bibl. Psychol.* p. 416. Comp. Hofmann's ingenious interpretation of Heb. viii. 2 ; *Schriftbeweis,* II. i. 405.

[2] Longfellow is indebted to Dante for this use of "*cloister,*" *Purg.* xxvi. 121.

[3] "The soul which has departed in the Lord will after death be surrounded and sustained by that inner spiritual body, which it has worked out here below on the still and hidden path of faith, through the power of the Holy Spirit."—Schöberlein quoted by Delitzsch, *op. cit.* p. 434, *note.*

process is being perfected for the spirits of the just in an
unseen world, and that all these things shall be made
plain when they shall appear with Christ at His coming,
when the sons of God shall shine forth an exceeding
great army, in the day of the adoption, that is, the
redemption of their body. " Now we see through a
glass darkly, but then face to face." " Now I know in
part, but then shall I know even as also I am
known."

Thus we close this endeavour to connect the teaching
of the Bible about sin and salvation with its presuppositions as to the nature of man. We claim no novelty for
our discussion. To show in what sense Scripture is a
primary fountain for the knowledge of man's own being
and destiny, is no new or alien study in the theological
school. From the early Apologists to the Reformers, it
had always been perceived and insisted on that the Bible
gives us such knowledge of ourselves as is fitted to lead
us beyond ourselves to God ; that its teaching about man
is as unique and divine, as truly a revelation, as its
doctrine of God. But it has not been so usual in theological schools anywhere till recently, and in those in our
country scarcely at all hitherto, to fix attention on the
natural presuppositions and *principles* of the Scripture
writings *concerning man*. Our intention has been to
vindicate a place for biblical psychology in the only
sense in which it commends itself to candid inquiry. It
ought to take its place among us as throwing light on
the doctrinal statements of revelation—as, in short, a
torch-bearer to biblical theology.

There is also a collateral use which such a study may be hopefully expected to effect. The nature of man is a stronghold of modern Christian apologetic. It always has been, indeed, one of the surest defences of the Christian faith, that Christians were furnished by their religion with the most satisfactory answer the human mind and heart have ever received concerning man's own being. That religion has the supreme claim to be divine which best enables man to meet the Sphinx of nature with a solution to the most puzzling of her riddles—the one of which he is himself the subject. If the Bible can tell us whence and what we are, and whither we are going, there is nothing that will more persuasively and surely convince us that it has light from heaven. We can depend upon its revelation of God, verified and countersigned as that revelation is by its self-attesting witness concerning man. Modern thought has discerned the value of this position, and round it much of the battle between faith and unbelief is ranged. The challenge of Positivism, for example, is thoroughly pronounced. Here is one of its recent utterances: " Attention is fully fixed now on the nature and mode of development of the human being; and the key to his mental and moral organisation is found. . . . The philosophy of human nature is placed on a scientific basis, and it and all other departments of philosophy are already springing forward so as to be wholly incomparable with those of a thousand years ago. By the verification and spread of the science of human nature . . . there will be an *extinction of theology*. . . . The worst of the contest is over, . . . the last of the mythologies (that is, the Christian faith) is

about to vanish before the flood of a brighter light." [1]
The utterance would be amusing, were it not so sad. It
is so stale in its falsity, this favourite prediction of unbelief that Christianity is on the point to disappear.
But the falsity of the anticipation is equalled by the
fallacy of the ground on which it rests, namely, that
man's nature can be explained without spirit, without
God, and without the life to come. We may be very
sure that the human heart will never rest in such an
answer to its deepest inquiries. We may be as sure
that whatever tends to elucidate the Bible answer, to
concentrate attention on its sublime Anthropology, will
meet with ever-increasing assent; for it appeals to the
testimony, simple, universal, and divine, of the soul itself,
—to that which is, in the words of Tertullian, "Testi-
monium animæ naturaliter Christianæ."

A book which tells of the origin and nature of man in
a way to satisfy the soul's own witness of its Maker and
of its being; a book which solves the great riddle of
humanity, why the constitution of our nature is so excellent while its condition is so wretched; above all, a
book which reveals Jesus Christ, the Man of men, the
God-man, approves itself to be as truly human as divine
—the family-book of the human race, as it is the utterance of the God and Father of men. But, indeed, the
Person who speaks in it and through it is greater than
the book. Of Him give all its writings witness. He
shines through them all; and He knew what was in man.
His words throw light over the whole circumference of
human living and dying. His life and deeds grapple

[1] Harriet Martineau, *Autobiography*, ii. 458, *et seq.*

with their sin, and He Himself is the destroyer of their last foe.   He invites them to go forward, with their hand in His, to meet the "shadow feared of man."   "Fear not," he says, "for I am the First and the Last, and the Living One.   And I was dead, and behold I am alive for evermore, and have the keys of death and of Hades." [1] From the page of revelation to Him who is its Subject and its Author we lift our gaze and cry, "With Thee is the fountain of life ; in Thy light shall we see light!" [2]

[1] Rev. i. 17, 18 (R.V.).   [2] Ps. xxxvi. 9.

INDEX OF AUTHORS AND TOPICS

24

MORRISON AND GIBB, PRINTERS, EDINBURGH

1982-83 TITLES

0203	Dolman, Dirk H.	The Tabernacle	19.75
0603	Lang, John M.	Studies in the Book of Judges	17.75
0701	Cox, S. & Fuller, T.	The Book of Ruth	14.75
0902	Deane, W. J. & Kirk, T.	Studies in the First Book of Samuel	19.00
1301	Kirk, T. & Rawlinson, G.	Studies in the Books of Kings	20.75
2102	Wardlaw, Ralph	Exposition of Ecclesiastes	16.25
4603	Jones, John Daniel	Exposition of First Corinthians 13	9.50
4902	Pattison, R. & Moule, H.	Exposition of Ephesians: Lessons in Grace and Godliness	14.75
5104	Daille, Jean	Exposition of Colossians	24.95
5803	Edwards, Thomas C.	The Epistle to the Hebrews	13.00
5903	Stier, Rudolf E.	Commentary on the Epistle of James	10.25
6202	Morgan, J. & Cox, S.	The Epistles of John	22.95
7000	Tatford, Frederick Albert	The Minor Prophets(3 vol.)	44.95
7107	Cox, S. & Drysdale, A. H.	The Epistle to Philemon	9.25
8403	Jones, John Daniel	The Apostles of Christ	10.00
8404	Krummacher, Frederick W.	David, King of Israel	20.50
8405	MacDuff, John Ross	Elijah, the Prophet of Fire	13.75
8406	MacDuff, John Ross	The Footsteps of St. Peter	24.25
8801	Lidgett, John Scott	The Biblical Doctrine of the Atonement	19.50
8802	Laidlaw, John	The Biblical Doctrine of Man	14.00
9513	Innes, A. T. & Powell, F. J.	The Trial of Christ	10.75
9514	Gloag, P. J. & Delitzsch, F.	The Messiahship of Christ	23.50
9515	Blaikie, W. G. & Law, R.	The Inner Life of Christ	17.25
9806	Ironside, H. A. & Ottman, F.	Studies in Biblical Eschatology	16.00

TITLES CURRENTLY AVAILABLE

0101	Delitzsch, Franz	A New Commentary on Genesis (2 vol.)	30.50
0102	Blaikie, W. G.	Heroes of Israel	19.50
0103	Bush, George	Genesis (2 vol.)	29.95
0201	Murphy, James G.	Commentary on the Book of Exodus	12.75
0202	Bush, George	Exodus	22.50
0301	Kellogg, Samuel H.	The Book of Leviticus	21.00
0302	Bush, George	Leviticus	10.50
0401	Bush, George	Numbers	17.75
0501	Cumming, John	The Book of Deuteronomy	16.00
0602	Bush, George	Joshua & Judges (2 vol. in 1)	17.95
1101	Farrar, F. W.	The First Book of Kings	19.00
1201	Farrar, F. W.	The Second Book of Kings	19.00
1701	Raleigh, Alexander	The Book of Esther	9.75
1802	Green, William H.	The Argument of the Book of Job Unfolded	13.50
1901	Dickson, David	A Commentary on the Psalms (2 vol.)	32.50
1902	MacLaren, Alexander	The Psalms (3 vol.)	45.00
2001	Wardlaw, Ralph	Book of Proverbs (3 vol.)	45.00
2101	MacDonald, James M.	The Book of Ecclesiastes	15.50
2201	Durham, James	An Exposition on the Song of Solomon	17.25
2301	Kelly, William	An Exposition of the Book of Isaiah	15.25
2302	Alexander, Joseph	Isaiah (2 vol.)	29.95
2401	Orelli, Hans C. von	The Prophecies of Jeremiah	15.25
2601	Fairbairn, Patrick	An Exposition of Ezekiel	18.50
2701	Pusey, Edward B.	Daniel the Prophet	19.50
2702	Tatford, Frederick Albert	Daniel and His Prophecy	9.25
3001	Cripps, Richard S.	A Commentary on the Book of Amos	13.50
3201	Burn, Samuel C.	The Prophet Jonah	11.25
3801	Wright, Charles H. H.	Zechariah and His Prophecies	24.95
4001	Morison, James	The Gospel According to Matthew	24.95
4101	Alexander, Joseph	Commentary on the Gospel of Mark	16.75